I'm Rubber, You're Glue

by Shannon Shea

ISBN: 978-1-943201-01-3

Library of Congress Control Number: 2015944935

First Published by Dark Ink, 10/15/2015

www.AuthorDarkMikeInk.com

Dark Ink and its logo are trademarked by AuthorMike Ink Publishing.

For Tracy – the industry tested our relationship and we beat it.

CHAPTERS

PROLOGUE

I was sitting in a small conference room in a Woodland Hills, California, production company. Fearing being late in Los Angeles traffic, I had arrived early for the 4:00 pm meeting and had been shown into the room where I had taken a seat, to wait for all of the other department heads.

As I sat trying to plan the best route home after this meeting concluded, the other department heads began filing into the room and taking seats around the table. I was genuinely surprised to recognize Mark Dippe, who was acting as the Visual Effects Supervisor on the film. I had worked with Mark on *Jurassic Park* when he was employed by George Lucas' Industrial Light and Magic company in Marin County. I also knew that Mark had directed the film version of comic book mogul Todd McFarland's *Spawn*. I didn't work on the film, but the company I was representing at that meeting had. I couldn't help wonder what the heck was he was doing there.

I introduced myself and he seemed very friendly and affable, and we started talking about the practical vs. the digital creature needs of the film. Just then, another man I recognized sat down across the table from me. It was director of photography Dean Cundey.

Now, Dean couldn't pick me out of a lineup even though I had worked with him on *Jurassic Park*, *Looney Tunes: Back in Action* and Ivan Reitman's film *Evolution*. We acknowledged each other with a simple nod, but it was unmistakable. I could see it in Dean's eyes. He presented himself professionally and was quiet and attentive as people continued to file into the room, but *that look*. It was the "I can't believe this is what I have to do for work now" look. It was surprising enough to see Mark Dippe, but seeing Dean Cundey made me feel both better and worse simultaneously.

The film we were about to discuss was *Scooby Doo! Curse of the Lake Monster* a direct-to-dvd sequel to the reboot of the live-action franchise. What the heck were Mark and Dean doing there?

Then it hit me.

What was I doing there?

I was no slouch. I, too, had worked, not just on *Jurassic Park,* but *Dances with Wolves*, *Terminator 2*, *Predator*, and *Pulp Fiction,* and that was just the tip of the iceberg. Deep down I knew what I was doing there. I was a motion picture professional and I was there to do one more job. But unlike previous jobs, this time I was there to discuss lighting stand-ins for the Computer Generated Image (CGI) of 'Scooby Doo' as well as practical creature parts (specifically hands and feet) of the titular Lake Monster himself. I knew going into the meeting that the effects would be leaning heavily into the CGI world but we, at KNB EFX had managed to land the contract for the few practical effects that would be in the film.

The meeting commenced as director Brian Levant sat at the head of the table, but I confess my mind had begun to wander. How the heck did *I* get *here*? If I could trace my steps could I find a time I might have done something differently? Might I be on the crew of *Harry Potter and the Deathly Hollows*? Or *The Wolfman*? Or even *Attack the Block*?

I decided that once I got out of the meeting, I would look back. See how it all began. Re-visit the experiences I had collected over my thirty years in the industry.

After years of reflection, organizing a bunch of old photographs, digging out home video I had shot in different shops and different locations, I started a blog about my career. Six years later, thousands of people had visited the site, looked at the photos and video, made comments and asked questions. It was obvious the time had come. It was time to tell my story...from the beginning.

CHAPTER 1

A Season of Monsters

And then there we were all in one place, a generation lost in space.
"American Pie", Don McLean

Where to begin? Or more accurately, who is to blame?

It seems silly to begin with the cliche "I was born..." but I suppose that is how everyone begins on their individual adventures, and so - I was born in New Orleans, Louisiana, in 1962 on St. Patrick's Day. My

At 9 years-old in the back yard with our dog, Barbara. Awkward to say the least.

childhood was a steady parade of green birthday cakes. Oh yes, I was a fat kid. I was a fat kid when obesity was not the national norm and if that wasn't enough, I was pigeon-toed and sported a Moe Howard (of the Three Stooges) bowl-style haircut furnished by my dad who would cut my brother's and my hair to save money. You have my permission to laugh uncomfortably.

My mother, Janet Shea, was a public school English/ speech teacher with a penchant for acting. My father, Al Shea, was an on-camera, entertainment journalist for the NBC affiliate in New Orleans, WDSU-TV. My older brother,

My father, Al Shea, interviews Clint Eastwood on the set of "Paint Your Wagon."

Scott, was heading for his third birthday in September when I arrived that late winter/ early spring of '62, and it would be nearly two years before our sister, Jennifer, was born. Okay, so that is the cast of characters: Janet, Al, Scott, Shannon, Jenny. The scene

My mother, Janet Shea, at a cocktail party. She is still an accomplished actress of stage and screen.

is set: New Orleans, Louisiana, and the clock moves forward to 1965.

Few people believe this, but I have a *very* strong memory from that year. We lived in a small house on Loyola Street in New Orleans. I can still remember the sidewalks cracked and raised by the roots of Oak trees that fought like old Southerners attempting to push out the Yankees of urban development. I was a normal kid with cap guns, skinned knees, and a little tricycle that I'd ride carefully, trying not to get the front wheel caught in one of those aforementioned sidewalk cracks, resulting in yet another injury.

However, the end of my normalcy came quite unexpectedly.

Our living room was dark. The light fell from lamps in amber pools, illuminating furniture that was skinned in artificial leather and stood on dainty wooden legs. The silver-blue glow of our television set gave a throbbing, defining outline to everything in the room, including my brother's head. He and my father were watching a movie when I toddled in. And as I

Our Terrytown, Louisiana back yard. I had a G.I. Joe on the picnic table prior to the "life-like hair and beard" stage of his existence.

stood there, foot turned in, I became mesmerized. What I saw transformed me almost instantaneously into what is now referred to as a "Monster Kid."

On our grainy black-and-white television, I saw a dinosaur moving through a lush primordial jungle. Not just *any* dinosaur, it was a Stegosaurus! A group of men began shooting it with rifles and the giant reptile turned and thrashed its spiked tail before collapsing to the ground. The movie was RKO's 1933 classic *King Kong*, and that was my introduction to the fantasy world of motion picture creatures.

Good-bye, normal childhood.

From that moment on, I had dinosaurs on the brain. My parents were patiently supportive. My father took me to any dinosaur film that opened in the local theaters, and the "Monster Kid" gods smiled, so one of the first films that I saw in a theater was *One Million Years B.C.*

I was four. With the recent addition of my sister, the family had moved from the East Bank of New Orleans, across the Mississippi River, and into the brand-new suburban sprawl called Terrytown. There were two small theaters on the West Bank each with two screens. There were also at least two drive-in theaters in the area. Since it was my father's job to review movies, he was aware of and saw most movies that were released in the New Orleans area. I can still see the halftone ad for *One Million Years B.C.* in the newspaper that my father cut out to show me. Cavemen! Cavemen fighting dinosaurs behind that annoying girl standing in front of them! I was agog. At night my obsessed brain would imagine being in dense green jungles surrounded by immense dinosaurs. My dreams would be interrupted, however, by an urge to pee, which meant I'd need help to get to the bathroom.

Doctors tried to correct my "pigeon-toes" by having me sleep in brown leather shoes attached at the heels by a flat, chrome bar that forced my feet out so that I had the posture of Mary Poppins. In retrospect, I was attached to a base like a plastic army man. This meant I couldn't just climb out of bed and go to the bathroom. Instead, I would just call out, "Daddy, I have to go to the bathroom" until my father would appear, half-asleep and irritated. He'd grab me under the armpits and carry me to the bathroom, holding me over the toilet until I finished; he'd then carry me back to the room I shared with my brother, and drop me back into bed. Eventually, my father succumbed to his weariness and ended up doing what I would have done: He took the braces off my feet, let them turn in, and we all slept through the night.

On Saturday mornings, having no understanding of the value of adult sleep (since most experience so little during the work week), I would get up and, fearing my father's wrath, would create a fantasy world of dinosaurs transforming my sheets and blankets into mountains and caves. I would sit for hours playing with my Marx-toys plastic dinosaur figures while my brother read a book in his bed across the room. Years later my father would commend his sons, saying that we could "quietly entertain" ourselves, something he patted himself on the back for instilling in us.

My dino-fascination wasn't corralled by the confines of my home or the theater. I could be taken to the local mall, and while my parents shopped I would hypnotize myself for long periods of time staring at the giant palm trees that were planted in the mall gardens. I would imagine the long neck of a giant *Brontosaurus* as it grazed the fronds standing twenty feet above my head. In the back seat of the car, on the way home, I would look out of the window to the horizon and in my imagination, see the leathery wings of a *Pteranodon* flapping as it soared above the tree line.

It didn't take much of a shove to broaden my horizon to include stop-motion creatures made by Willis O'Brien and Ray Harryhausen or even modest efforts like *The Lost Continent,* starring Caesar Romero. However, the result was not a dream of making movies about dinosaurs, it was of studying dinosaurs. I wanted to be a paleontologist. Eventually, thanks to birthdays and Christmases, I had dinosaur books, toys, banks, anything I could get my pudgy little fingers on, which, at the time, wasn't much.

This seems like a good time to drag my rocking chair out onto the porch, throw a shawl over my shoulders and pour myself a cup of tea with a Geritol chaser. In them-there days, we were offered three television stations: NBC, CBS, and ABC. We listened primarily to AM radio, had one console stereo in the house that played vinyl records. I was VERY lucky that my father worked in media, because at his office in the French Quarter he had cabinets that held press kits and movie magazines, including a couple of issues of "Monster World" that I can remember.

True, the Beatles had come to America, Sean Connery was James Bond, and Walt Disney was still alive, but going to the movies for most was an event. Something you saved up for (unless you were a horny teenager). Television was king, and up until that time it was black and white. In the Shea household, however, one day color television arrived - and another paradigm shift happened.

The rare genre television we enjoyed, like the Super-marionation show *Fireball XL-5* as well as *The Munsters* and *The Addams Family*, that were broadcast in black and white, were suddenly joined by television shows like *Voyage to the Bottom of the Sea*, *Batman*, *Lost in Space*, *Land of the Giants* and *Star Trek*. Week after week, super-heroes, aliens and MONSTERS invaded our living room and fueled my fertile imagination.

Every now and then, my brother and I would catch an evening bus in Terrytown and ride to the New Orleans business district and walk into the French Quarter to my father's office. He'd take us to dinner then to movies (always with a press pass; he'd never pay). He knew we would enjoy *Thunderball, Danger: Diabolik,* or *Tales from the Crypt.* Sitting between us, he would pass out just after the opening credits, then wake up at the end of the picture, exclaiming that it was "awful." That was a huge lesson for me about media critics even then.

However, more often than not, my father would go out during the week accompanied by my mother. He had movies and plays he needed to review generally starting on Wednesday, and we children were often left with sitters. To quell our restlessness, Dad would give us coloring books, comic books, and every now and then, *Famous Monsters of Filmland* magazine.

Seeing those old Basil Gogos covers brought new life and depth to the old Universal Horror movies we'd see at the Coliseum revival movie theater downtown and on television on Sunday mornings (I always thought it was weird that you could watch *Tomb of Ligeia* as you were supposed to be getting ready for church, but such was the pageant of life). Every now and then, I'd see photos of dinosaur movies that I had never heard of: *The Lost World, Beast from Hollow Mountain,* and *The Animal World* (which only "existed" on View Master slides). But all of the comics, magazines, stickers, model kits, etc. never seemed to be enough; I started drawing monsters.

In books, notebooks, on construction paper pads, I began drawing dinosaurs and monsters, often creating my own monsters with their own origins and stories that I shared with my family. I don't think anyone thought anything of it when I was a kid. Again, in retrospect, I think about what a typical family of today would think about taking their six year-old children to James Bond movies, giving them not only *Creepy* and *Eerie* magazines, but also the infamous Eerie Publications that nearly always featured decapitations, enucleations and dismemberment. We owned the infamous "Monster Scenes" model kits that not only came with tiny, plastic machines of torture, but offered for purchase a female "Victim" kit to, well, victimize.

Mind you, this was in the wake of the "Helter Skelter" years and it wasn't long before the kits were yanked off the shelf after pressure from parent groups. My point is that I've met so many filmmakers and effects people who have shared similar stories and none of them have ever turned their ghoulish fascination into a real-world pursuit. No one I knew ever brought a gun to school (not even in the rougher public schools), much less shoot anyone. I'm not saying that my generation was devoid of men and women who grew up to become criminals; that would be ridiculous. What I'm suggesting is that there was a generation of boys and girls brought up on genre material (prior to it being so popular, accepted and mass-marketed), who grew up with imagination and the drive to make movie monsters.

And I was walking the road, without knowing it.

CHAPTER 2

In Defense of the 1970s

These are the good old days...
"Anticipation," Carly Simon

I think that it is a general misconception that when the decade changes on New Year's Day, that everyone just runs to a giant incinerator and throws all of their clothes, their books, and their philosophies into it. Change is much slower. Like evolution, it happens gradually so that those of us living it don't realize until it is past and recalled in hindsight. The 70s began and looked suspiciously like the late 1960s. Hippies were still around, fashions were still a bit psychedelic, civil unrest and the Viet Nam war hung around like guests too drunk to leave a party long since over.

However, these were problems for the giants, the adults. I was still a kid living in the relative safety of suburban Louisiana. Every now and then, we were "touched" by what was going on in the world when someone would show up selling P.O.W. Bracelets (my mother bought one and wore it until the soldier named on it was found). And to a pre-teen, nothing was worse than having a television show interrupted for a "Special Newscast." And there were plenty during the 1970s.

For we monster/creature fans, the decade came in like

a lamb and left like a lion. In the wake of movies like *Planet of the Apes*, and *2001: A Space Odyssey* we enjoyed films like *The Abominable Dr. Phibes, The Valley of Gwangi,* and *The Omega Man. Batman, Star Trek,* and their contemporaries left the screen and with the moon landing of 1969, I think the public was more intrigued by space fact than space fiction; at least during the beginning of the 1970s.

During the early 70s, I was convinced I was going to grow up and become a great paleontologist. My sketchbooks were full of dinosaur drawings, my bedroom was littered with dinosaur toys and my beloved "Prehistoric Scenes" model kits. And, being a kid, I was not of the collector's mindset. We PLAYED with our toys, never realizing that one day they would be valuable items. We abused our G.I. Joe figures (which no longer sported the clean-cut armed services look and instead became adventurers complete with "life-like" hair and beards), tearing their heads and limbs off, losing critical pieces, etc. As the neighborhood expanded, we would frequent the construction sites after school and on weekends using the enormous piles of sand used in pouring cement foundations as playgrounds. Somewhere in Terrytown, I'm sure that there are houses that have bits of toys and models in their foundations, because we'd return home at dinner time and take a quick inventory realizing that we no longer had G.I. Joe's flare gun, or a Neanderthal Man model kit was shy one club.

But, these prolonged hours of play were just fertilizer for my imagination.

Meanwhile, my father lost his job at the television station, which had become the victim of a hostile corporate take-over. My mother switched from teaching public grammar school to teaching public high school, and my brother became a teenager three years before I would. No longer would we take our toys outside and destroy them together; he discovered his love of music and spent hours reading books and listening to the hi-fi that separated our little twin beds. Don't misunderstand. He was primarily reading the recent paperback adaptations of Kenneth Robson's *Doc Savage* series, most of which had incredible cover paintings by James Bama.

He still loved comic books and although I was primarily reading Gold Key publishing's *Turok: Son of Stone* series, while he read popular titles from Marvel and DC comics, we both joined "F.O.O.M." - the Marvel Comics Fan club. We both joined *Star Trek* fan clubs and began going to the local *Star Trek* convention "Vul-Con" annually. Yes, we were nerds, geeks, outcasts, whatever you might call it. Not that our lives would have been better had we lived in Los Angeles, New York, or Chicago. Genre interests were specialized and not mainstream at the time. You could be a "fan" but you had to be careful with whom you would share that information. I was lucky to meet two friends in grammar school with similar interests (we're still friends to this day). And we discovered that we could have conversations about the things we loved while avoiding being persecuted by the rest of the people our age.

Which leads me to something really important: bullying. Bullies have been around since the beginning of time and they have consistently picked on those who were different or challenged their narrow (and ignorant) worldview. And yes, while bullying continues today, many of us who were genre fans would have the comic books or magazines we had stashed in the stacks of our school books snatched by a bully and destroyed before our eyes while the rest of the schoolyard populace cheered. Our faces hot and flushed, we would be escorted to the principal's office attempting to stifle the tears of humiliation only to be told, "You shouldn't be bringing your comic books to school, anyway."

I can't imagine what any of my grammar school bullies would have done if they had known the truth.

My father had found a job working for the United Way as a press agent while keeping his "critic-status" alive writing for a couple of smaller, local newspapers. Every now and then he would do a radio interview or be asked to host a local television show. He rarely seemed happy at home and the rest of us referred to him as "King Kong" behind his back because of his hair-trigger temper. However, his critic status kept him and my mother, not just going out during week nights and weekends, but also traveling the world on press junkets.

Again, before the days of EPK's (Electronic Press Kits), distribution companies used to fly critics out to sets or to press conferences to interview the filmmakers, actors and actresses. Although he had been flown to New York and Los Angeles on numerous occasions, his press travels flew him and my mother to Italy to meet Peter O'Toole and Sophia Loren for *The Man of LaMancha* and to Hawaii to meet Blake Edwards and Peter Sellers for *The Pink Panther Strikes Back*.

In his suitcase, my father had packed an acrylic painting I had done of "The Pink Panther" and had Blake Edwards and Peter Sellers sign it; however it got better.

Legendary animator Richard Williams not only signed it, but drew a "Pink Panther" in pink, by the way, and sent it back to me with his regards. Although my father did things like this, and seemed encouraging, he was very acerbic and was quick with his hand, belting my brother and me (but more often, me) any time we disobeyed him or had done something he thought was stupid or below par. "Second rate!" was one of his nasty outbursts if we had done something that was not up to muster.

One summer, the Vul-Con (I can't remember the number or year) was happening at a hotel in downtown New Orleans. Knowing that neither of our parents would dare make the drive across the Mississippi River Bridge and through traffic to drop us off with a bunch of *Star Trek* fanatics, my brother and I got on a bus (as we had done so many times previously when we met our father at his office) and rode to the convention. The weather, as it is down South started getting bad and soon heavy rain began to fall.

Inside the hotel, warm and dry, my brother and I ran to the "Huckster's Room," where merchants from all over the region would gather to sell things that we had limited or no access to in our area. Magazines like "The Monster Times" was a favorite of mine, while my brother purchased movie stills, movie posters, and one year we both bought little furry "Tribbles" featured in the *Star Trek* episode "The Trouble with Tribbles." As we ignored the thunder outside, the convention rooms began to close, and finally, looking outside we could see that the weather had taken a very bad turn.

My brother called home from a pay phone and roused King Kong and asked if he would drive downtown and pick us up. Ho boy. I think we would have done better calling him and telling him we were going to sleep in the lobby and we'd see both of our parents for lunch the next day, because dad said he was coming and there was no turning back.

After about 40 minutes, my father's familiar beige Ford Pinto appeared in front of the hotel. Protecting our goodies from the pelting rain, we ran to his car and jumped inside. One of my father's most incredible talents was yelling. Dear lord, I don't think I have known someone since who could scream at such a decibel level, uninterrupted, for the amount of time he could. I'll be honest, I couldn't repeat one thing he said that evening because it was like being beaten up for 20 minutes solid; eventually, I couldn't hear or feel anything anymore. Everything shut down and all I was aware of was an angry din in the car that was only reduced by the sound of heavy rain on the roof.

As he maneuvered the Pinto down one of the newer thoroughfares on the West Bank, we could see a familiar sight in New Orleans – rising water. My father began driving down the center of the road while water was rising fast in the gutters. The rain fell like welding sparks illuminated by the street lights, as the sky exploded with dramatic lightning and thunder. Soon, plumes of water were cascading from the Pinto's wheels as the waters surrounded the little car. We were about three miles from home when the water had risen high enough to kill my father's engine. What a happy, happy day!

My father was not going to ditch his car by the side of the road and call a tow truck. No way. That would cost money, and he was incredibly cheap. Instead, with Dad screaming at us above the cacophony of the storm, we pushed the dead car through knee-high water until we got home, where a beating was waiting. I don't think I was even dry before my dad belted me. Whenever things like this happened, he would chalk it up to "The Shea Luck." Most times when this "luck" kicked in, we could all laugh at it months or years later. We never laughed about that stormy night. Ever.

You might think that beating would alter my mindset, that it might be like a figurative bucket of water thrown on the fire of my interests. Nope. I can still recall hearing my brother, muttering in his bed, about how stupid dad was and how ridiculous it was for him to get angry at us because it stormed and it stalled his car. He reassured me that we truly had done nothing wrong and to just avoid Dad for the next day or so. We did and the 70s pressed on.

CHAPTER 3

The 70s Bring Change

You've just taken your first step into a larger world.
Obi-Wan Kenobi, Star Wars

It was during this decade that certain genre films were being redefined by bold filmmakers. Francis Ford Coppola re-defined the gangster picture with *The Godfather*, William Friedken re-defined the horror genre with *The Exorcist* as well as his cop-drama *The French Connection*. There was no doubt film was getting grittier, with some exceptions.

The *Planet of the Apes* franchise, which had debuted in 1968, had been followed by inexpensive sequels, but honestly we kid-fans didn't care. I loved *The Apes* movies and would cut out and collect any articles I could about John Chambers and the makeups he created. He was truly *the* first makeup artist whose name I knew. But with *The Godfather* and *The Exorcist*, I had become aware of the work of Dick Smith as well. At a time when there wasn't even a regular category for makeup artists in the Motion Picture Academy, a few magazines would publish feature articles about the work of these artists (including, of course, "Famous Monsters of Filmland" to whom most of us in the industry owe a huge debt of thanks).

Having been drawing dinosaurs, I began stretching

my subjects to include movie monsters, most of which I copied from the pages of my Pictorial History of Horror Movies, written by Denis Gifford. My mother, recognizing my passion for art, decided to enroll me in painting classes taught by an artist friend of hers, Bettina Johnson. It was an education. No creatures, no monsters, no dinosaurs in sight. Instead: still lifes. My subjects included bowls of fruit, candles, and rumpled fabric. I bitched a little. No, I bitched a lot. However, thanks to Bettina Johnson, and then my next art teacher, Jackie Juge, I learned a lot about the basic lessons which serve me to this day.

However, drawing and painting were beginning to frustrate me. I wanted to *make* monsters not just draw them. With absolutely *no* knowledge of what to do, my brother and I had made papier mâché masks of a couple of our favorite *Star Trek* aliens and wore them to a less volatile Vul-Con convention than the one during the storm. I had won a "Special Recognition" award for being one of the youngest contestants at the time. I had heard terms like latex, and foam-latex, but had no idea what they meant. I had read about "ball-and-socket" stop-motion animation model armatures, but didn't have the faintest idea where to start thinking about designing and building one.

All of my information was theoretical, so I made things with whatever I could. I made a horrible *Planet of the Apes* prosthetic mask using clay covered in papier mâché. It was so heavy that the spirit gum I lifted from my father's theatrical makeup kit (yes, oddly he owned one) wouldn't hold it on my face, so I had to augment it with a piece of elastic. Not having any access to anything that would function as one of the ape costumes from the film,

I did what I could with a green sweatshirt and tights. Oh brother. Imagine a plump 12 year old kid, wearing one of his mother's old wigs, a papier mache ape mask, and a sweatshirt and black tights running around the New Orleans Garden District on Mardi Gras day. Thank god for the naked people who would run around and attract more attention than I ever did.

By this time, my father again had lost his job at the United Way and was working for an advertising agency

writing copy. Still pounding out reviews on his manual Underwood typewriter, he would receive the weekly editions of the Hollywood industry newspapers: *The Hollywood Reporter*,

Mardi Gras (I'd say 1975). Dad, Jenny, Mom, and me in my horrible "Planet of the Apes" makeup attempt.

and *Variety*. I had learned from my brother to check them out prior to my father's return from work. Even as a preteen, the "trades" (as they are called) were very interesting, although we tended not to read the articles beyond headlines that revealed Roger Moore was replacing Sean Connery as 'James Bond' or that Ray Harryhausen's latest film was being distributed. But one day, something very strange caught my eye.

It was a full-page, black and white ad announcing the filming of a new motion picture entitled "The Star Wars." I can still recall the image of the characters portrayed, one of whom was wearing a Flash Gordon-esque head-

dress. I had been a fan of the reprinted Alex Raymond illustrated *Flash Gordon* in comic book form for years, and
this looked *a lot* like Flash Gordon. But I was distracted.
There were other movie ads announcing soon-to-be released genre films that were equally enticing including
the big-budget remake of my favorite film, *King Kong*.

Actually, *two* had been announced and only one
filmed. Universal Studios *The Legend of King Kong* never
got past some preliminary production work, so only producer Dino De Laurentiis' version was made. I can't be
sure how and when I heard the news (my guess is that it
was, again, in the pages of *Famous Monsters* magazine)
that Kong was not going to be stop-motion animation
like it had been accomplished forty some-odd years earlier, but this time would be a full-sized robot, with some
of the performance augmented by a man in a gorilla suit.
On top of that, there would be no dinosaurs in the film!

This all made me very dubious, but in the article was
mention of the man who not only would be building the
suit, but playing Kong, a young man named Rick Baker.
Now, to be perfectly honest, my interest in motion picture special effects was still very rooted in stop-motion,
so I "cataloged" Rick's name and went on my merry way.

Since Kong was being released by Paramount Studios,
my father began receiving all sorts of press material about
the film. Posters painted by artist, John Berkey, began
surfacing (including his iconic shot of Kong straddling
the World Trade Center buildings) and I started getting
hooked. My father handed me a book entitled *The Creation of Dino De Laurentiis' King Kong*, and I scoured the
pages for information and saw plenty of photos of the
mechanical hands as well as one photo of the giant gorilla

robot's head, but very little was shown of the Kong suit.

Okay, admittedly I didn't read the book, but I was smart enough to find the answer to a *King Kong* trivia contest held by a local movie host. First prize was a Kong statuette. No, I didn't win. I got second place and won a movie poster and a key chain that held "actual hair from King Kong" in it.

I fared better when my father returned home from a junket in Dallas, Texas for the sci-fi film *Logan's Run*. My father had a dear friend, Addie Addison, who was the local MGM representative who made sure my father was given first-class treatment. Dad returned from Texas with a windfall of *Logan's Run* swag including temporary tattoos of the famous "life crystals" that the citizens of the 23rd century all had in the palms of their hands.

Both films came out in 1976, the same year most of the country was going crazy for the story of a down-on-his-luck, southpaw boxer from Philadelphia, *Rocky*. That summer of 1976, I picked up a paperback book at the Vul-Con (and yes, a friend and I were both dressed as Sandmen from *Logan's Run*) entitled *Star Wars*. If you don't know the story, then do yourself a favor and look it up. There was a handful of color photos in the middle of it, but with the exception of a couple of shots of Imperial Storm Troopers, there was not a lot that would herald what would become a world-wide phenomenon.

But it would be a year before it was to happen. 1976 was not just America's bicentennial, it was the proverbial calm before the storm.

I was fortunate enough to pick up a copy of the "American Cinematographer" magazine that featured the latest

King Kong film that featured a lot of behind the scenes shots of Rick Baker and the gorilla suit that had created such as stir. I got a bit ahead of myself there, because when *King Kong* opened, I had read some interviews with Rick Baker in which he had voiced his dissatisfaction with the gorilla suit. However, being raised on 'Three Stooges' shorts and *Gilligan's Island*, I had seen many gorilla suits, but never anything like what had been featured in *King Kong*. Rick Baker had re-defined the gorilla suit and what he made was a marvel.

A year or so before, while perusing a copy of *Cinefantastique* magazine, I saw an add for a new publication, *Close Up*, "devoted to the world of stop-motion animation." I had found one tattered back issue of the Ernie Farino published *FXRH* (focusing on the effects of Ray Harryhausen) at a convention, so I was excited at the announcement of this new magazine. I gave my father some of my saved cash and he sent a check to *Close Up* to begin my subscription with issue number 1.

Unfortunately, the magazine only ran three issues in spite of the fact that it was printed on high quality paper and had good photo reproductions (some of which I hadn't seen reproduced in the pages of *Famous Monsters*). However, the third issue was completely devoted to *King Kong*. A lengthy interview with Rick Baker appeared in it, and I was a bit shocked to hear how dissatisfied he had been with the entire experience of the *King Kong* remake. He even dropped a few "f-bombs" which I had never read in a printed interview before. I was instantly intrigued.

There were more reasons 1976 was an outstanding year to be a genre fan. *Starlog* magazine began showing up at the local Walden's book store. I've mentioned *Fa-*

mous Monsters and *Cinefantastique,* both of which were available, but from my youthful point-of-view, *Famous Monsters* was a silly magazine, full of goofy puns that published as many reprinted articles from earlier issues as it did new features, while *Cinefantastique* was *deadly* serious if not pessimistic. *Starlog* was situated perfectly in the middle: not too silly, but not so pessimistic that it trashed every genre television show and movie to come out of Hollywood. *Starlog* was for fans and ran *new* stories about television's *Space:1999* and *Star Trek* from an appreciative perspective. And it didn't take long before Rick Baker's name began popping up in the pages of *Starlog* in stories about *King Kong* and a horror film called *Squirm* about bloodthirsty worms.

And then...the world exploded. And it didn't explode with one big concussion. It was like a chain-reaction of blasts, each building upon the one before it. For me it started with *Time* magazine.

I'll never forget the cover. It featured Israel's Prime Minister at the time, Menachem Begin and in the corner was a yellow banner cutting diagonally across that read: "Inside: The Year's Best Movie." Honestly, I expected to find photos of Sylvester Stallone as "Rocky" since *Rocky* had won the Best Picture Oscar a couple of months before. I opened the magazine to an image that has been forever burned on my brain (as it has millions of people all over the globe). There were two spaceships, one pursuing the other firing bright green energy rays. I don't recall the title of the story, but I think it read: "Get ready for *Star Wars.*"

I didn't stand a chance. I was fifteen years old and although I was getting ready to complete my freshman year of high school, I still had maintained my love of the genre, my imagination, and my love for art. Yes, my piles of sketchbooks still contained drawings of dinosaurs and monsters, but now images from *Logan's Run* and the *King Kong* remake had crept into it. But what I was looking at in *Time* was blowing my mind at a level I had never before experienced. There were clear photos of Imperial Storm Troopers and a "Wookie?" what the hell was *that*? Darth Vader? Robots? All of the concepts I had read about in the paperback book had now been illustrated and it exceeded my expectations.

That doesn't happen that often. Maybe that is why everything changed the way it did.

CHAPTER 4

A Brave New World

I just want to know that this is really happening.
Roy Neary, Close Encounters

It was as though the top of my head had been opened, my brain had been doused with lighter fluid, and someone had put a match to it. Thoughts raced through my head so fast that it was difficult to control them. Apparently, I was not alone. The collective consciousness of America had *Star Wars* fever as the publicity machine raced across the United States and then the world and evidence began piling up like a mid-January Chicago snow. Television shows, news reports, newspapers, magazines, all seemed to use any excuse to use the words "*Star Wars*" to increase sales and circulation.

Problem was, I hadn't seen the film yet.

One Saturday morning, my brother, who had just graduated from high school burst into our bedroom, ranting a bit. "I just saw a movie that I know you're going to *love*!" he said. I sat up in bed, woozy but hooked. "It was called *Star Wars* and I've never seen *anything* like it!" he continued, "You're going to love it! Love it!" My guess is that this was May 26, 1977, the day after *Star Wars* opened, but I can't be sure. What was for sure is that from that moment I had to see this movie! I had never seen my reserved brother so worked up over a movie before. He had been a rabid *James Bond* fan, but this reaction from him was new.

I believe it took a week. One very tortuous week before my brother could drive me to see the film. Why? Because *Star Wars* started with a limited release in New Orleans only playing at one theater, the Lakeside Cinema and, as the name suggests, it was close to Lake Pontchartrain as opposed to where my family was: south and across the Mississippi River. As far as my parents were concerned, neither of them was interested in driving the twenty-five minutes or so it would take to get from our door to the theater.

So it was June before my brother loaded my thirteen year-old sister (against my protestings – Dad insisted) and me into the oxidized silver Chevy Nova he had inherited from my mother when she traded up and drove us to the Lakeside Shopping Center where the theater was located.

It was a Saturday evening and the lot was full. Driving through the parking lot, a car shot out of a space and smashed into the front right of my brother's car. BLAM! A middle-aged woman jumped out of the car and started fussing at my brother, but I have to give him credit. He kept his cool, stood his ground, and told her that she hadn't bothered looking behind her when she pulled out.

Back in those days, the cops came out for a splinter, so we waited, and waited for the police to show up and make a report. Meanwhile, I saw the sun dipping below the horizon and I knew...I knew...I would not see *Star Wars* this week. I know it sounds like I didn't care about my brother and his car; nothing could be further from the truth. I did care. I could just tell that something *really* wanted me to wait before seeing this film. Anticipation. For a fifteen year-old it was intolerable.

As for Dad, well, wouldn't you know it? He had been "cut off" from receiving any press passes, or material from 20th Century Fox because he had panned too many of their films. That meant he hadn't been invited to any press junkets or received any preview materials whatsoever. And he didn't like paying for movies. However, with my brother out of commission, dealing with insurance companies, he was resigned to taking my sister and me to the theater to see *Star Wars*.

Two additional weeks went by before my father drove me and my sister back out Lakeside Theater to see the film. The ticket line was still around the block and with my father's impatient complaining, we finally took our seats in the theater to witness the phenomenon.

From the opening 20th Century Fox logo, I knew I was in for something spectacular, but I had no idea *how* spectacular it would be. As the opening crawl stretched out into the infinity of space accompanied by John Williams' bombastic score, I was transfixed; however when the rebel blockade runner ship appeared overhead pursued by the enormous Imperial star destroyer that was the moment of metamorphosis. I changed. All of the molecules in my body shifted and I was not the person who had walked into the theater.

The best approximation of what I felt was the realization of the potential of motion pictures not just to entertain, but to transport an audience to a world of imagination that seemed real. Authentic. Not that I felt any less about movies like *Logan's Run*, but after *Star Wars* an imaginary line had been drawn: "Before *Star Wars*, After *Star Wars*" and I had no idea how correct I was. *Star Wars* redefined so much about getting back to the roots of storytelling as well as kicking the door open for special effects (and I'll refer to them as 'special' until 1992). Moreover, it wasn't just "nerds" or "geeks" or "fan-boys and-girls" that seemed to love the movie. Just about *everybody* loved the movie. Everybody, that is, except my dad who summed it up thus: "It was too loud!" No wonder 20th Century Fox dropped him.

Unlike any other film I had attended before, *Star Wars* seemed to create an industry of fan magazines and books about the film that sprouted up like mushrooms and, of course, I had to own them all. Most of them ran the same fifty production stills augmented with illustrations and fleshed out with hastily reported news on other genre films. However, I had been lucky, because three months earlier, I had asked for a subscription to *Cinefantastique* magazine for my birthday and the very next issue was a double issue featuring the making of *Star Wars*.

I loved Ray Harryhausen and his films and had it not been for the *Sinbad* and *Eye of the Tiger* issue featuring Ray with his animation models for the film, I might not have subscribed. As it was, a large white envelope appeared at my house in July stuffed with *pages* of photos and stories about *Star Wars* that none of the other periodicals seemed to have. It was astounding.

In the pages of that special double issue, I learned new names. Not just George Lucas (because, hey, I had been a huge fan of George's since *American Graffiti*; I owned the vinyl soundtrack album that I listened to repeatedly), but names like Dennis Muren, Phil Tippett, Adam Beckett,

Robert Blaylock, Joe Viskocil, and of course, John Dykstra who became a new hero for me.

However, there was a name I was familiar with: Rick Baker. Rick had been responsible for helping British special effects makeup man, Stuart Freeborn, populate the famous Cantina with additional aliens. I suppose that is what truly made *Star Wars* special. Unlike *Star Trek*, or *2001: A Space Odyssey*, *Star Wars* had elements of miniature (model) work, matte paintings, rotoscope animation, stop-motion animation, as well as practical mechanical effects and creature work. There was a little bit of everything and it all worked.

It would be easy for me to either stop here or continue writing about *Star Wars* but 1977 was a banner year for another film that was to debut that winter. Director Steven Spielberg's *Close Encounters of the Third Kind.* Where I had seen some early concept art for *Star Wars, Close Encounters* (or *CE3K* as it became known to fans) had been shrouded in secrecy.

The advanced movie posters featured very little information save for a desolate road, stretching out to a horizon lost in a bright bluish glow. The advertisement copy described what "Close Encounters" were, so it was easy to discern that UFOs would be involved. But as to the plot or aliens, it was a complete mystery.

A few years earlier, in neighboring Pascagoula, Mississippi, two men claimed they had been abducted by aliens. Their story of their alien encounter had fired the imaginations of everyone in the South and it started a rash of UFO sightings. Years later, I would discover that across town my future wife and her father would be launching fake UFOs, one of which was covered with aluminum foil, appeared on military radar and scrambled jets from the local Alvin Calendar Field Naval Reserve. So UFOs in the Deep South were a hot topic in the 1970s and now the director of the smash-hit film *Jaws* had tackled the subject, so I knew it would be more than the run-of-the-mill UFO movies I had seen earlier.

If my father had been *persona non grata* at 20th Century Fox, he was "in like Flynn" at Columbia Pictures. He was flown to a *CE3K* press junket in Texas where he received all sorts of swag including a hand-sized full cassette recorder, a book with color-coded cassettes, a satchel, movie posters, press kits all emblazoned with the "CE3K" logo (I wish I had all of that stuff today – it would be worth a fortune). Strange though that the critics interviewed the director, the producers, actors, and Doug Trumbull, the special effects supervisor and designer without having seen the movie!

When my father returned, he gave me a poster and the book of cassettes and then summed up meeting Doug Trumbull by complaining that he had refused to sign an autograph for me. "Who the hell does he think he is?!" barked my father, "He should be flattered that *anybody* would want his autograph!"

That seemed to bother him more than it bothered me. I had been a fan of Trumbull's since *2001: A Space Odyssey* and *Silent Running*. Trumbull seemed to have vanished since the latter film, but now that he was back working on another event picture, I was agog with anticipation.

My father also had told me that Shawn Bishop, who played Brad Neary, son of actor Richard Dreyfuss' character 'Roy Neary' was the son of his friend's and our family would be accompanying theirs to the New Orleans preview of the film. Now that was more like it! Unlike seeing *Star Wars* a month after everyone else, I'd see *Close Encounters* before anybody else! But, truth be known, I had NO idea what the film was about or what was in it?

For the rest of the summer of '77, I had haunted movie theaters on the West Bank (after *Star Wars* had been released to more theaters) and sat through the film twenty-two times. That is not a misprint. I sat through *Star Wars* twenty-two times, which is still more than I've seen any film with the exception of the 1933 version of *King Kong*. I still had *Star Wars* on the brain when I sat next to Shawn at the screening. I would describe him, but just watch *Close Encounters*, take note of the older son, and there he was, sitting next to me in the movie pointing out moving points of light in the Indiana skies in the film.

Time magazine, once again, ran a feature on *Close Encounters* that revealed a shot of the alien mother ship, but to be honest, I didn't quite understand what I was looking at. You have to understand that prior to *Close Encounters* UFOs were saucer-shaped, generally silver, and had 'chaser lights' that circled around a smaller dome on the bottom of the craft. Until *Close Encounters* about the best 'flying saucer' I had seen in a movie (not counting *Forbidden Planet* or *Earth vs. Flying Saucers*) was probably Disney's *Escape to Witch Mountain*.

That was the zeitgeist I had experienced prior to *Close Encounters,* which explains my reaction to Doug Trumbull's UFOs.

The best way I can summarize it is this: When the mother ship rose up behind Devil's Tower, I giggled. I nervously giggled because I could hardly believe my eyes. I was seeing something, experiencing something I never had before and it was flabbergasting.

Where *Star Wars* had transported me to a 'galaxy far, far away' *Close Encounters* brought the fantastic down into our backyards. I recall Trumbull talking in an interview saying that *Close Encounters* was a more difficult film to achieve because no one had ever seen a 'Death Star' but everyone knew what a country road looks like and how light reacts in our atmosphere, whether they are conscious of it or not. The public *knows* and reacts negatively when they are unconvinced.

By Christmas, I had changed again. *Star Wars* made me want to do special effects. *Close Encounters* made me want to *direct*!

CHAPTER 5

The Parade

Another rock group down the street is trying hard to learn this song.
"Pleasant Valley Sunday", Carole King and Gerry Goffin

The die was cast. I asked for a Super 8mm film camera for Christmas, I took over the family ping pong table which became my area for building miniature sets. I had met a new friend at a Vul Con convention, Jeff McKay, who was a year older than me and attending the high school where my mother taught. He, my grammar school/high school friends, Tim Guillory and Peter Donnes, joined with me, to become a group that went to, discussed, and sometimes made genre films. True, my simple "brownie" camera (fixed focus – automatic exposure) was about as far from the computer-controlled "motion-control" camera that had shot effects for both *Star Wars* and *Close Encounters* as possible but that didn't stop me from trying to make films featuring stop-motion animation, rotoscoped laser blasts, and miniature sets.

They were crap.

I suffered from a deplorable excess of imagination and ambition with absolutely no resourcefulness. At least Jeff made films that had some sort of story to them.

It was about this time that my mother asked if I was interested in working at a local theater in the French Quarter where she was starring in a production of the play "My Fat Friend." I was to work in the prop/scenic department. I agreed and it was during one of the rehearsals of that show that I spoke with the theater production designer, Don Hood, who told me that I was only about two blocks from a store that sold liquid latex.

By the way, Don Hood went on to be a fairly successful character actor in Hollywood, appearing in films like *The Toy* with Richard Pryor. But I digress.

The only information I had about liquid latex I had read in an issue of *Close Up* magazine that described animation model skins being made of "self-vulcanizing" latex. What the hell did *that* mean? I had seen a film of Goodyear tires being vulcanized, which is a process that heats the rubber, setting it, and making it more durable. I mentioned all of this to Don and he looked at me like I had grown a third eye on my forehead.

"Kid, you just put it on your skin and it dries." Don said to me.

I was perplexed and excited at the same time. Where was this magical place? I was instructed to walk a few blocks from Le Petit Theatre du Vieux Carré, the theater where my mother was acting to Royal Street and St. Ann Street where I would find The Vieux Carré Hair Shop and the liquid latex!

I don't know why, but I put my sketchbook under my arm and set out into the French Quarter. It was late afternoon and violet shadows bisected the west-facing buildings as I walked past tourists in Jackson Square. I reached my destination and found a little grocery store, but just past it, on Royal Street, hung a little black and white sign that read "The Vieux Carré Hair Shop." Initially I expected to see some sort of barber or beauty shop but as I drew closer, I realized I couldn't be more wrong.

The store had high, narrow windows, with open, black shutters on either side. Staring out onto Royal Street were stacks of eyeless faces, rubber monster masks! There they all were: Frankenstein's monster, Dracula, The Phantom of the Opera, The Mummy, The Creature from the Black Lagoon all beckoning tourists into the store. I had spent years looking at the advertisements in the back of *Famous Monsters of Filmland* magazine: I knew they were from the famous Don Post studio in Hollywood, California! What I had only seen in black and white on newsprint pages was now real, in stark color. I entered the store and met the first truly influential mentor I would have in my life – Herb Saussaye.

If you've seen *Pee Wee's Big Adventure* then you will be able to picture what it was like for me to step inside Herb's shop. The Vieux Carré Hair Shop was a theatrical makeup and hair store, so named because they would actually make custom wigs for any theatrical venture or Mardi Gras ball. The store was made up of two big rooms that sat side by side. The main room was subdivided into three smaller rooms: The showroom floor, the work room, and Herb's office in the back. The neighboring room had a smaller mask/wig showroom and a stock room, and it was packed to the rafters with theatrical makeup, wigs, and masks (both traditional and contemporary). I reference *Pee Wee* because of the scene where he enters the novelty store to "buy supplies." My first experience was not unlike that.

Fate must have stepped in, because Herb's son, Bob, usually ran the makeup counter, but when I walked in I was greeted by Herb himself, a fairly tall man with a warm smile, wearing a shirt and tie. He asked if I could help, but I think he could see that I was far beyond any reasonable help. I told him that Don Hood had sent me. This must have struck a chord with him because he asked who I was. I introduced myself and he smiled broadly. He knew my parents quite well. From that moment on, I was treated like a member of the family.

Herb took me on a tour of the shop, introduced me to everyone there and let me try masks on. This Pied Piper played and I was helpless. Finally, I showed him my sketch book of monsters and mentioned the latex. Herb disappeared in the back and then returned with a bottle of "flesh tone" liquid latex that he *gave to me*!

"Go on, take it home and try it out," Herb offered. He then showed me some exquisite latex rubber noses and explained how they were made from a plaster mold of a clay sculpture. I thanked him and returned to the theater, eager to experiment with my first bottle of latex and happy to know that Wonderland was just a few blocks away from the theater.

I went home and began playing with the latex, stippling it on my hands and rubbing it off to form torn up, dead skin. I painted my hand with red paint, stippled the latex on top of it, powdered it, then tore the surface revealing the red flesh below. I was hypnotized.

Meanwhile, Hollywood began the parade. In the wake of the successes of *Star Wars* and *Close Encounters* more genre films were being produced including a big-budget version of *Superman* as well as a very enigmatic science fiction film entitled *Alien*. In addition, Italy had offered *Stella Star* a cheap, colorful space opera starring Caroline Munro, while Japan had offered *Message from Space,* a science-fiction fantasy with glowing walnuts, tons of miniature spaceships, an R2-D2 rip off, and actor Vic Morrow. The popularity of *Star Wars* had kicked open the door and dragged what appeared to be a substantial population of genre fans into the light. And if Hollywood loves anything, it loves to market to those who are willing to pay for entertainment.

In Terrytown, Louisiana, I had bought plastilina clay from the hobby store and tried to fashion a rudimentary nose on a piece of wood. I covered it with plaster of paris and made a mold, then tried to pour latex into it. After many botched attempts, I finally learned, the hard way, that latex casting was about patience. I pulled a successful nose out and returned to Herb Saussaye to show him my result. Now, of course, a nose sculpted by a fifteen year-old looked like a nose sculpted by a fifteen year-old, but Herb, being a monument of patience and encouragement, praised it, and then disappeared into his office and re-emerged holding something wrapped in plastic. It was a prosthetic of a wolf brow and nose that resembled the prosthetics used in *Planet of the Apes*, made of *foamed* latex, just like they did in Hollywood-land. A young local artist named Eddie Henriquez had made it and given it to Herb as a thank you gift. Henriquez now worked for makeup legend John Chambers in Los Angeles, but he had started his career working with Herb in New Orleans.

As the story went, my father was interviewing John Chambers who was in town doing publicity for one of the *Planet of the Apes* sequels. My dad called Herb and asked him to send Eddie down to meet Chambers. He did and the rest was history; Henriquez had gone on to assist Chambers on an *Island of Dr. Moreau* remake. And there I stood, holding a real foam latex werewolf prosthetic. The introduction of air into the liquid latex, made the prosthetic soft and flexible like a marshmallow rather than like the sole of a tennis shoe. Somehow, I felt "connected" to the industry in a way I had never known before.

Through Herb, I learned of a place called Paramount Theatrical Supply. He had shown me a catalog that had everything from theater lights and stanchions to *foam latex* kits! I contacted the company (it was called Alcone/Paramount Theatrical Supply then – now it is just Alcone) and ordered a catalog. Within a few weeks I had saved enough money from my supermarket job to purchase a foam latex kit.

When it arrived at the house, the box contained four glass bottles – latex base, foaming agent, curing agent, gelling agent. There were instructions, of course, but knowing nothing about how the material worked and what was needed to make a prosthetic, I began mixing foam latex in the kitchen with the family electric mixer and baking it in open molds in the oven.

The house began smelling of cooking rubber and the resulting pieces could not even be described as prosthetics. Shriveled and dense, they were more like vulcanized tires than they were like Henriquez's marshmallow-soft prosthetic. The piece that I sculpted was my take on something that had really frightened me as a child, the creatures from the 1972 TV movie *Gargoyles* that had been credited to Ellis Burman and Stan Winston. No matter what the inspiration was, the result I produced was a dismal failure; however, it wasn't enough to dissuade me from my film and effects pursuits.

Eventually, Herb offered me a job at the Vieux Carré Hair Shop; I'm not sure whether he was being encouraging or I was hanging around so much it just made sense to put me to work. Working with Herb's wife and grown kids: Barry, Bob, and Lynn, I started doing small jobs, like decanting spirit gum into small glass containers and cleaning up the shop, but eventually the family trained me to make and apply crepe wool beards and craft Mardi Gras masks for the folks who rode on the floats. It wasn't Hollywood, but I was being paid to do something creative.

CHAPTER 6

Growing Up

Good morning yesterday, you wake up and time has slipped away
"Times of Your Life", Paul Anka

By the end of winter and beginning of spring of 1979, a lot had changed. First and foremost, I had lost fifty pounds after seeing a school dance photo where I resembled a chubby young girl. I had my driver's license and my father's car. Since the year before, my mother had had enough of his abusive behavior (all of it emotional – I don't recall my father ever hitting my mother; he reserved that for his kids) and had thrown him out and was seeking a divorce. Dad lived in the French Quarter now, and having a car was and expensive inconvenience so it was out of necessity that I was driving his small economy station wagon. My brother, having graduated from high school in 1977, had moved on campus at Louisiana State University in Baton Rouge, but rumor was that he was unhappy and would soon be dropping out of school to come back to New Orleans. I was in my second semester of my junior year of high school and had begun dating.

Magazines were full of rumors about the new *Star Wars* film, but now the public psyche was focused on a film entitled *Alien* that was due to open that summer.

I had made a full descent into fandom, buying *Famous Monsters, Starlog,* and *Cinefantastique* and now *Super 8 filmmaker* and *American Cinematographer* magazines and read incessantly about Rick Baker, who had become one of my new heroes. My awareness of the effects industry had grown exponentially and while most of the guys I went to high school with were following the careers of sports figures, I had no idea nor interest in any sports, instead choosing to focus on news regarding Doug Trumbull, Dick Smith, Stan Winston, John Dykstra, Dennis Muren, Phil Tippett, and of course, my childhood hero Ray Harryhausen who was still making stop-motion animation films.

I had seen pre-production art and a few publicity stills for *Alien;* however, since it was being released by 20th Century Fox, my father suffered from the press embargo. I cannot express how lucky I feel having grown up in a time when the public could still be 'surprised' by a motion picture.

Pardon this mini-rant but it is necessary to explain that during this time, which is now referred to as "the photo-chemical age of motion picture effects," there was no digital solution for motion picture visual effects. True, there were some very crude computer displays for *Star Wars* that had more in common with the video game Pong than it did the digital graphics that would define three new *Star Wars* sequels two decades later.

The public was still innocent. There were primarily four commercial television stations, and only the wealthy could afford home video equipment or cable television. So whenever an event film like *Superman* or *Alien* rolled into town, it was greeted with wide-eyed enthusiasm.

The public *wanted* to be transported to another reality; they wanted to believe a man could fly. And so it was with *Alien*. The advertising campaign for the film was ingenious. Television spots that featured a strangely-textured egg floating over an alien, smokey environment accompanied by creepy sound effects and eerie music. The egg cracked a bit and piercing light emitted from within. What any of this had to do with the resulting movie was beyond me? However, it made the public so curious that, once again, there were lines around the block.

I have said that *Alien* saved my life, and in a way, it is completely true. If it hadn't been for my then-girlfriend's stupid reaction to the alien chest burster I might have hung around longer, but I didn't. That moment defined her for me, and I knew that if I stayed with her, my life would take a very different path. *Alien* had scared the crap out of me. Not just me, but millions of people all over the world. Swiss artist H.R. Giger's alien design was so unique that it was difficult to perceive it on the screen because very few had ever seen Giger's work, much less having it integrated into a film.

So I left my ex-girlfriend's house feeling a bit guilty about dumping her, but knowing deep down that it had to be done. And time proved me right. A few weeks later I met a girl I had known about but had never spoken to, at an end-of-the-year Speech Club party. I was attending an all-boy Catholic school, she was attending our "sister" all-girl school. Her name was Tracy Fletcher, we met that night on June 30th, and have remained together ever since. Thanks *Alien*!

Having a steady girlfriend changed everything about my life. Not that I was 'out playing the field,' because nothing could be further from the truth. I was more interested in making things – films, paintings, sculptures, whatever I could. And, after the 1979 Mardi Gras season, Herb had to lay me off, so I went to work in a local grocery store.

The summer of 1979 was the year of *Rocky 2*, the sequel to the last "Best Picture of the Year" in a pre-*Star Wars* Hollywood. By this time, many houses had clunky video tape machines and I had seen *The Buddy Holly Story* when visiting Tracy's neighbor, who subscribed to HBO. Because I was three years ahead of Tracy in high school, her parents were very strict with her. I only saw her a few hours once a week and could only talk to her on the phone for three minutes! This meant that I'd see her on Friday night, leave her house (get kicked out) at 10:00 pm., then rendezvous with my friends and go to the midnight movie, which had risen in popularity over the past five or six years in New Orleans.

Midnight movies were truly magical. Many are familiar with the midnight showings of *Rocky Horror Picture Show* and the resulting cult audience shows; however, what we were seeing was very rare, strange films that ran the gamut between *2001:A Space Odyssey* (a favorite of pot heads), to animator Ralph Bakshi's *Wizards*. My friends, Pete, Tim, Jeff and I would *speed* through New Orleans to get to a theater that would be showing *A Clockwork Orange* either drinking on the way, or sneaking Miller "pony" bottles in our socks and drinking in the theater. Eventually, we invited my brother along and the 5 of us would sit (and often fall asleep) in films like *The Last House on the Left* and Eerie Midnight Horror Show.

Speaking of horror, while I was working at the supermarket, I happened to pick up a copy of *Famous Monsters* magazine. I had stopped buying them when they dropped the painted covers by aritst Basil Gogos, in favor of photographed covers and when the child-like puns and goofy comments no longer served my teenage sensibilities. However, this particular issue ran a story about a new film entitled *Friday the 13th* and showed something I had never seen before: a woman having her throat slit.

It was horrible. The effect was credited to a makeup artist I had recently heard of, Tom Savini, but the picture was so 'real' that it upset me down to my core. The year before, my friends and I snuck into an X rated screening of *Dawn of the Dead*. We had seen a review of it on *Sneak Previews* critics, Gene Siskel and Roger Ebert's show before they went on to *At the Movies*. They touted it as an artistic success, but also revealed that it was gory and very shocking. That was the understatement of the year.

I never saw the "gore" films of filmmaker Herschel Gordon Lewis, such as *Blood Feast*, although I had seen black and white photos in my book "Movie Magic", nor the infamous 1970 film *Soldier Blue* that had graphically depicted the slaughter and rape of Native Americans. So nothing prepared me for what we saw in director George E. Romero's *Dawn of the Dead*.

From frame one, the film is filled with such dread that by the time we saw the first graphic makeup effect, a man getting his head blown off with a shotgun, we realized we were on a violent, bloody adventure where anything could happen. By the time the last zombie had been shot in the head with a juicy "bullet hit" known in the industry as a "squib", everyone's adrenaline was running high. I nearly wrecked the car driving home that night because I had been so emotionally affected by the movie.

I should also note something else: my friends and I saw *Last House on the Left* in 1980 just before we graduated and went our separate ways. I didn't see director John Carpenter's *Halloween* until I got to college; however, I did see *Assault on Precinct 13* on cable TV. We did go to the theater to see *Friday the 13th* after we had experienced *Dawn of the Dead*. However, what is important to note is that now Tom Savini was the name on fans' lips, having been touted as the "King of Gore."

Being a senior in high school meant the choice of a college career and I was still convinced that I would go to film school and be a director. So much was publicized about USC Film School that I decided I would apply there as well as UCLA, having heard that they, too, had a good film program. However, my father would indirectly affect my college choice.

He was interviewing legendary Disney animator, Eric Larson, who was on a press tour for the theatrical re-release of *Sleeping Beauty*. My father invited me down and advised me to bring samples of my work, which I did. Larson was a sweet man, who, after the interview, patiently looked through my pencil color drawings and acrylic paintings and suggested I look into California Institute of the Arts as a college choice. I had never heard of CalArts (as it was known). Larson explained that it was the school that Disney built; I'll admit that I had my doubts.

Since *Star Wars*, Disney had become kind of passé. The studio was in its slump prior to the re-invigoration it would experience at the end of the 1980s. I spoke to my Guidance Counselor at the high school, and he had never heard of CalArts. Most of my classmates were either going to school locally, or regionally. Very few of them were interested in venturing out of the

Meeting with legendary Disney animator, Eric Larson.

state. I found the address to CalArts at a local library and wrote them for a catalog.

A few weeks later the catalog arrived and unlike the "collegiate" look of the USC and UCLA materials, CalArts' catalog was colorful, full of photos of students doing creative, artistic things. It was very intriguing but what sold me was the Alumni section.

Mentioned among the Film School alumni were Peter Kuran and Adam Beckett, both of whom had worked on *Star Wars*. Those recognizable names, and the fact that the freshman curriculum required access to film cameras and equipment during the *first* semester of school were instantly attractive. Ding, ding, ding, ding, ding, ding, ding! We had a winner! USC Film School required two years of general studies then putting in an application to be accepted into the film school and the expensive tuition was the same price as CalArts. There was truly no other choice for me.

When it came time to take my SAT exams and enter the three schools that would automatically receive my grades, I indicated them in this order: CalArts, USC, and UNO (the University of New Orleans that had a "me-

My first commission: A painting for my High School Socio-Economics teacher.

dia" program). In my heart, I was convinced that if I would not be accepted into CalArts, that my college experience would be disappointing.

I stayed in touch with one of the admissions counselors at CalArts and when he came to New Orleans, I had an appointment and portfolio review. I put all of my art together, along with my plans to make an animated version of *Beowulf* which was among my favorite stories of those I was exposed to in high school. Weeks went by before I received my acceptance letter. My mother spoke with me about it and said she'd pay for one year; after that I was on my own. I was going to CalArts.

This was horrible news for Tracy. We had been going together for a year, seeing each other briefly because of her restrictions, and now I was going to put half a continent between us. It wasn't going to be an easy separation, but I knew then (I really did) that she was "the one" and I was willing to try the long-distance relationship.

Sculpting a design maquette of "Grendl" for my CalArts portfolio. I never did make the movie.

Believe it or

not, it hit my father the hardest. He was in denial about my leaving for college until the day I left. He told me that I was unsuited for Hollywood and imagined I would do better working in personnel for some corporation. He hugged me good bye and wished me "God speed."

CHAPTER 7

California, the First Attempt Begins

When an irresistible force such as you, Meets an old immovable object like me... "Something's Gotta Give", Johnny Mercer

I was eighteen years old. My brother was twenty-one. I think I had about $2000 on me and I drove a red 1974 Pontiac GTO. I had hand painted "The Lizard King" on the trunk in honor of Jim Morrison of 'The Doors'. It was August of 1980, and there was roughly 2000 miles between my house in Gretna, and my school in Valencia, California. I don't think either my brother or I had been further west than Dallas, Texas, and we were about to take the first major road trip of my life.

After thirteen years of Catholic school from kindergarten to senior year of high school, I decided to grow my hair, my sideburns and to attempt a beard and mustache. I looked like a teenaged mess. My brother, a bit more conservative, grew his hair over his ears, and just to the back of his shirt collar. With a selection of eight track tapes ready to go, we said good-bye to our mother and hit the road.

I'm not Jack Kerouac and this isn't *"On the Road"* so I'll spare most of the details of our trip. I will say that the highlights included hitting a deer very early one morning in Texas. It dented the crap out of the front left side of my car and then hobbled off of the road (probably to die, unfortunately). But for two "flat-landers" like my brother, Scott, and I, one of the big highlights was driving through the mountains of Arizona with the *Star Wars* soundtrack playing. It was inspiring!

When we arrived in Los Angeles, the first thing that struck me was the smog. After decades of hearing *The Tonight Show* host, Johnny Carson, joking about Los Angeles smog, to experience it in person left much to be desired. However, CalArts was located north of the San Fernando Valley in the Santa Clarita Valley, so we continued along the Golden State 5 Freeway and out of the brown smog belt.

The plan was to stop by the school, drop my stuff off, and then drive another forty-five miles north to Palmdale, California where a friend of our parents, Marilyn Porter, lived with her boyfriend. Once there, my brother would stay a week or so before flying back to New Orleans. I would return to my dorm room prior to that.

While we were driving, Scott admitted that he would be returning to college right away. He said that it didn't feel right that I might graduate before him, so he registered at the University of New Orleans when he returned to Louisiana.

When we arrived on the campus of CalArts, we drove past huge trucks in the parking lot; I gawked at film equipment being handled by the crew. My initial thought was, "Wow! This Film School is serious!" We found our way to the one-and-only dormitory, parked and went inside to find my room. Dragging some of my crap to the elevator, we were joined by two fellow students, a young man and a young woman.

My first glimpse of the CalArts campus, complete with the CalArts van parked in front of the main building.

The young man had curly blonde hair and addressed my brother and me.

"You new?" he asked.

I replied that it was my first year as the elevator reached the next floor. The elevator door opened, the woman he was with took her shirt off (wearing nothing underneath). He said, "Welcome to CalArts" and they walked down the corridor as the woman laughed.

What the hell was *that* all about?

The young man turned out to be Merritt Buttrick who graduated that year and became a working actor. He started out on television on a show called *Square Pegs* and then went onto motion pictures where he played David Marcus in *Star Trek 2: The Wrath of Khan* – Captain Kirk's illegitimate son! How was that for strange? But it got stranger still!

After we had unloaded the GTO and put my junk in the dorm room, Scott and I went to look in on the filming that was being done across the street in the main building. We walked around the front of the school where the trucks were parked and started looking inside the trucks when a man with long hair and a walkie talkie stopped us. "Can I help you?" he asked. We explained that we had just gotten into town and were starting school, and then asked what was going on.

He told us they were shooting John Carpenter's next

film, *Escape from New York*, and were using the main hall as the lobby of the World Trade Center.

What? John Carpenter? Here? Now? Shooting his new film? At that moment, Adrienne Barbeau appeared and told the man speaking to us that she was going to her trailer for lunch. We had only been in California for a few hours and we had seen our first celebrity. Since the crew was at lunch we asked if we could go in and check out the set. I wish I could remember the name of the man who spoke with us that day, but I do remember what he said: "Yeah, go ahead, it's your school, now."

That was a very strange feeling. We walked up the stairs and into the Roy O. Disney Hall of CalArts. The walls were all covered in white paper scrawled with spray painted graffiti. At least two wrecked cars sat on the floor, as well as a Native American tipi. The floor was strewn with debris and smoke was rising from what looked like a recently extinguished campfire. There was so much to take in with the entire experience that I was a bit over-whelmed.

However, when I examine my time at CalArts, the most important aspect was meeting my roommate, Stephen Burg. Steve, a New Jersey native, came to the school already a genius. Inspired by *2001: A Space Odyssey*, further fueled by *Star Wars, The Empire Strikes Back* (the 1980 sequel), *Alien*, and *Star Trek: The Motion Picture*, Steve excelled at drawing futuristic "hardware" (space-craft, vehicles, environments, etc). His style showed influences from Joe "*Star Wars*" Johnston, and Ron "*Alien*" Cobb, but he had tooled it into a look all of his own. We were both eighteen years old and unprepared for the Cal

Arts experience.

Steve and I were polar opposites: I was brunet, under six feet tall and outgoing; Steve was tall, thin, and a bit shy. He told me, years later, that when he first came into the dorm room and saw how I had decorated my side of the room and met me in person, he was frightened. Like any first-time meeting, Steve and I were socially awkward, but then found that we had much in common and could spend hours, countless hours, talking about motion picture special effects. However, not all was good in paradise.

My roommate, Steve Burg, and me with groceries in front of the dormitory.

In retrospect, I'm convinced that it was a combination of envy and immaturity that put Steve and me on a rocky course that first year. Unlike me, Steve's parents could afford CalArts with no financial strain; I, on the other hand, had to take a work-study job at the school to make ends meet.

Honestly, I could probably write an entire book just about my experiences at CalArts; however, for the sake of brevity, I'll try to give a general overview of what the school was like in the autumn of 1980.

California Institute of the Arts was divided into five schools: Fine Art, Music, Drama, Dance, and Film. At the time I was accepted there were less than 800 students on campus in all of the different disciplines. I was one out of under 200 students who had been accepted into the school that year, again, in all of the programs. Today, CalArts is a sprawling place with multiple buildings and dormitories. Then it was two buildings: the school facility and the dormitory. Historically, CalArts started out as Chionard, an art school established by the Disney family; because of this, the "Disney School" existed as a department within the Film School.

I didn't understand a few concepts when I applied to CalArts. My high school art teacher, Marlene Harris had tried to transform what was an "Easy-A" class designed to help elevate football players' grade point average into a real class that studied art. She not only taught art technique, but art history, insisting on giving written tests about artists and the evolution of expression through history. Needless to say, I was one of only a few students who cared.

However, what we didn't discuss much was "avant-garde"and the Dada movement. I didn't know what it meant when I read it in the CalArts catalog. I probably thought it meant "cutting edge." I had *a lot* to learn when I started class.

Both Steve and I had been placed in the "Experimental Film Graphics" program at CalArts. My interpretation is that this was the program where students were dumped that were unclassifiable. Not necessarily animators, not necessarily live-action film students, the Film

A rare, damaged photo of some of the work I did my freshman year: A foam latex dinosaur hand puppet, and a latex mask of "Grendl" (I hadn't lost enthusiasm by then). If you look closely you can see my copy of The Land that Time Forgot comic book on the floor.

Graphic students ran the gamut of focus and abilities.

CalArts was self-described as an avant-garde school, and from what I could tell, the history of art began with Picasso and he didn't get it right. The history of music began with Schoenberg; the history of dance – Isadora Duncan, and so on. There was no appreciation or attention given to anything prior to the 20th Century (well certainly not more than a passing glance) and it became very clear, very quickly that the few of us at CalArts not in the Disney program that were interested in pursuing a commercial career, were not at the right place.

This was a school for self-expression; it wasn't a trade school. Film was not taught in the conventional way, but was instead encouraged as a medium for artistic expression. What that meant was every Monday morning I would have to sit in a class conducted by my mentor, Jules Engel, and suffer through three hours of short films that were a combination of experimental music paired with abstract images. I'll give an example.

One film that I had to sit through multiple times was titled "Trapunto." At the time, I didn't know that a trapunto was a type of quilt. The film was just a slowly building series of filmed strips of fabric that had been run through an Optical Printer until the illusion of a trapunto appeared on the screen. A folk guitar player accompanied all of this. The film was at least 5 minutes long (it felt like an eternity) and I didn't see the point of it. The filmmaker made a trapunto. On film. Using traditional film equipment. It was an abstract representation of a different art form.

There was a lot at CalArts that was like that. I was an immature eighteen year-old young man with ambitions of having a successful, professional career, and CalArts was designed for existential artistic pursuits. It wasn't a good mix.

Jules was a retired animator who had worked at UA anima- tion studios when they were producing short cartoon subjects like

A semi-successful life cast done for me by James Belohovek. In order to lubricate my eye- lashes and eyebrows, he used mentholated pe- troleum jelly. My eyes swelled up and for about fifteen minutes, I thought I was blind.

Mr. Magoo and *Gerald McBoing-Boing*. He was a very, very nice man who had no idea what to make of me. He gave me a few animation assignments (traditional ani- mation assignments with paper and pencil rather than computers) and I tried them but didn't like them. I ex- plained that I was interested in stop-motion animation and creature effects, but not only did he not understand contemporary practical special effects, he was having difficulty understanding how I would translate it into a form of artistic expression. He was a sweet, wonderful man who recognized my growing frustration with the school, but had nothing much to offer beyond his advice: "The skull," he said, "keep drawing the *skull!*"

CHAPTER 8

The Phantom of CalArts

Be careful how you wish, for wishes do come true
"The Incredible Mr. Limpet", Sammy Fain

At first, it might seem that going to CalArts was one of the biggest mistakes of my life and although I would complain (and boy, would I complain) about the classes, the lack of instruction, and the avant-garde narrow mindedness of the students and faculty, I was at the right place and at the right time.

Valencia, California was not the suburban sprawl it is today. In fact there were only little pockets of civilization connected by miles of lonely highways. CalArts, like a feudal castle, sat on top of a hill overlooking a small neighborhood attached to a golf course. It was clear to me that the few local merchants down the hill tolerated the students, but did not condone or understand what happened behind the security gates that kept visitors at bay.

My side of the dorm room at CalArts.

One of the conveniences I had discovered was that the Theater School shop sold liquid latex by the gallon. Through new friends I had met who were a class or two ahead of me, I learned that I was not the first "creature maker" to grace the halls of CalArts.

The first was James Cummins, but unlike me, he had been accepted into the Disney animation program based on his illustration skills. However, once at the school, he abandoned his animation dreams and concentrated more on the design and manufacture of creature masks and puppets. He left the school along with a friend he had made in the live-action film department , Henry Go-las, and they were out in search of work in Hollywood. It is interesting now, that no one ever mentioned director Tim Burton while I was there, but like I said, the students and faculty were more interested in esoteric artists and experiences.

My first experience with James happened when he wasn't around. I had gone to buy latex at the Theater School shop and the shop foreman told me he was sold out. The remainder of the contents of a fifty-five gallon drum of latex had been purchased by an ex-student for a project. Yep, James Cummins bought it. The foreman went on to tell me that a new barrel had been ordered and should be there in a matter of weeks.

I had moved out of the animation cubicle I had been assigned and onto a table in the large classroom and it was common for someone to pass by, see the work I was doing and ask if I knew James Cummins. Artist, legend, or ghost, his name always came up whenever anyone saw the creatures I was attempting to make. Meanwhile, Steve Burg had figured out pretty quickly that aside from the technical classes like learning the Oxbury Animation

Camera or the Optical Printer, most of the courses were jokes. He spent most of his time in our room churning out incredible oil paintings of spaceships and alien vistas.

The Oxbury Animation camera was an enormous, heavy stand that held a camera that pointed lens-down at a glass table. Lining the table on top and bottom were "animation pegs" that held specially punched animation paper or clear acetate cells for producing traditional 'cell animation' (known popularly as cartoon animation). Animation was shot one frame at a time. To ensure the most flexibility in shooting each frame, the stand had very precise workings that could move the camera along at least three axes of movement. The glass table could rotate 360 degrees and be panned up and down, left or right. Learning to use this monstrosity happened during

the first week of classes for Steve and me.

Also during the first week, we learned how to load and use the Optical Printer. The Optical Printer was a machine that allowed already pro-

One of my first, crude, plaster molds made for casting latex.

cessed film to be "re-photographed." It was essentially a camera and a projector facing each other. This was handy for producing what is known as a "matte" where part of a frame of film is replaced with either another piece of artwork or a moving image. It was a very tedious process, but between the animation stand and the printer, it was how most visual effects were accomplished prior to the computer. Needless to say, any attempt at doing anything that could be construed as mainstream or commercial was strictly frowned upon.

Not that I could afford it. We were required to shoot 16mm film if we were going to make any type of film. Home video was not available and the few video cameras that the school had were bulky and shot on 3/4" tape. Film stock cost money and what little money I had from my work-study job paid for food, gas, and *my phone bill*! I tried to call my parents and Tracy when I could, but the phone rates were so outrageous that I could only afford to talk to them for 10 minutes at a time, and I'd still end up with a $100 bill at the end of the month. Purchasing and developing film stock was a luxury that I simply could not afford.

In a film school without being able to make a movie - It was not a good position.

During my time at CalArts, I was required to make one thirty second film. That's correct – thirty seconds. The assignment required that it be exactly, to-the-frame, thirty seconds and when dealing with twenty-four frames per second that meant a LOT of counting. My film, like most of them, was absolute crap but it did force me to shoot, edit, and sound mix an actual film and for that I am grateful.

One evening, someone appeared at the door to our dorm room. He was tall, had thick brown hair over thick expressive eyebrows. He scanned the room looking at all the movie posters we had on our walls and he said, "I must be in the right place." From behind him, across the hall, another friend of ours who had similar interests, James (Jim) Belohovek appeared saying, "That's them!" I could hear Jim say. The stranger reached out his hand to shake mine, "James Cummins," he said. I shook his hand

and then he introduced himself to Steve. I had finally met the Phantom of CalArts, the "other" monster-maker who had preceded me and left the school.

Our initial friendship was as easy as falling off of a log. Although we shared the same influences and the same interests, we had different ambitions. James, from the very moment I met him, fancied himself primarily a writer. He loved good story-telling and introduced me to the supernatural works of Algernon Blackwood. Another thing that separated James and me was that he had already developed a very strong visual style. His sculptures and illustrations had an appealing "ropey" look to the features and musculature that were distinctly his own. My work, on the other hand, could only be described as crude. At this point I was still much more comfortable with drawing than with sculpture.

James apologized for purchasing the latex but told me that he (and Henry) needed it for a creature suit they had built for an ABC Movie of the Week entitled *The Intruder Within* (aka *The Lucifer Rig*) which was basically a television version of *Alien* but instead of it taking place in outer space, the setting was an off-shore oil rig. I was impressed. He was twenty years-old and already working on his own projects professionally.

Even though James lived in Los Angeles , which was easily a thirty-five to forty minute drive, he would often drive up to CalArts and hang out with Steve and me. We went to movies, discussed effects and future projects, but most of all, James was very encouraging where it came to my art. He began working for makeup artist Tom Burman on movies like the remake of *The Cat People* and later, *The Beast Within*.

The previous winter (because this was the beginning of our second semester), Steve Burg and I had gone to Westwood (a small city outside of Los Angeles that is the home of UCLA) to go to the movies. Westwood, at the time, had all of the best theaters and a college crowd that appealed to us (strange, now that I think of it). We went to see *Altered States,* which had been receiving critical acclaim. My father had sent me an article

My first set of fangs! They were made under the guidance of James Cummins.

about makeup artist Dick Smith's "air bladder" accomplishments for the effects in the film and I was eager to check them out. So many new effects developments were happening and so few people had seen (or remembered) Dick's similar effect in *The Exorcist* when he made Linda Blair's throat swell, or makeup artist Joe Blacoe's swelling abdomen effect in Canadian filmmaker David Cronenberg's *They Came from Within.* The result was that audiences were freaked out when it appeared that William Hurt's, arm began to swell and pulse like something was alive under his skin.

It actually started a trend in film that was referred to as "Change-O" effects.

For those of us who were buying all of the genre magazines and frequenting genre films, we knew the name, Rob Bottin. Young protege of Rick Baker, Bottin had ventured off on his own to work on films like *Piranha* and John Carpenter's *The Fog.* Bottin and Baker had fallen out over competing werewolf films, both of which had elaborate transformation effects planned. Bottin's was *The Howling* directed by Joe Dante, while Baker's was director John Landis' *An American Werewolf in London*.

What was so strange was that Baker had started *The Howling* then, had to bow out due to a previous obligation to his friend, John Landis, and turned the show over to Bottin. As luck would have it, *The Howling* hit theaters first and the great werewolf rivalry began.

I'm not going to compare/contrast the effects of either film. They are both fantastic in their unique ways. What is much, much more important was that, like the opening shot in *Star Wars,* these werewolf films were the heralds of what became the beginning of the great age of special makeup effects.

James, Steve, and I went to see *The Howling* at a tiny theater in Newhall, just outside of Valencia. As we exited, all of us were so inspired that we all went our separate ways and worked on our art. In the weeks to come, the special makeup effects fever built with the release of *Scanners,* which featured new, state-of-the-art, fluid-filled bladder prosthetics that made actor Steven Lack's arm veins seem to expand and burst with blood. However the effect that caught all of us off guard, was a decapitation effect in a B movie entitled *The Exterminator.*

During a flashback to the Viet Nam war, the protagonist witnesses a friend's execution. Tied to a post, the victim has the side of his neck slashed with a machete so severely that the head is partially decapitated, hanging by a small piece of flesh. The effect was the work of Stan Winston, a makeup artist I was aware of primarily because of his character makeup work. Winston and his artists (including, I came to find out, James Cummins) had built a sophisticated dummy featuring a puppet head with cable-controlled features.

Unlike what Tom Savini had done with his gore effects, Stan's work had a "high-polish" about it and was photographed in a way that didn't telegraph that a gore effect was about to happen. Savini's incredible work was accomplished much more like a magician using cinematic cuts as misdirection to convince the audience that what they were seeing was a real injury. What Winston had accomplished was in one, long take, showing something that could not have been an actor just wearing a bleeding prosthetic. It would become one of Winston's calling cards for the rest of his career.

As my first year of college rolled to an end just before the summer of 1981, I received an excited phone call from James on his birthday. Drunk somewhere with Henry Golas in Hollywood, James called with news that had heightened his twenty-first birthday celebration: "I just got a call from Rob Bottin!" he said slurring into the phone, " I'm working on *The Thing*!"

CHAPTER 9

The Sad Summer of 1981

You Can't Go Home Again
Thomas Wolf

"You have a California accent," my seventeen year-old sister said, accusingly. I ignored her. I had just returned to Terrytown, Louisiana, from CalArts after driving, by myself, across country for three straight days. On the second day, a partially-filled, plastic five gallon water container had overheated in the Texas desert firing the lid like a champagne cork and sprayed hot liquid latex inside my car. I had pulled over and cleaned what I could, but my GTO was definitely on a decline.

My old friend, Tim, had arranged for me to apply for work at the Winn-Dixie Supermarket for the summer. "Hey, just don't tell them you're going back to California in the fall." he suggested. I was however, very happy to see Tracy again having only seen her briefly during the Christmas break.

Things were weird. They were. I mean, how can you return to your little New Orleans suburb, unaffected after spending a year at CalArts? The things I had seen. The stuff I had experienced. Home felt very alien and the people in my immediate circles seemed a little like strangers. Most of my high school friends had gone to college in New Orleans, including my brother, who was running into these friends on the campus of the University of New Orleans and hanging around with them. Things were weird.

I showed up and Winn-Dixie and met one of the Assistant Managers who hired me and put me to work in the produce department. Shoveling rotten peaches gave me a lot of time to reflect on everything that had happened toward the end of my freshman year of college.

Things had not ended too well. First of all, CalArts decided to increase its enrollment the same year they decided to break ground on a new dormitory building. Any student wishing to return to the dormitory the next year would have to put their name into a lottery, and if your name wasn't drawn, you would have to find housing off-campus next Fall. I got lucky. A Disney animation student, James Fujii had asked if I was interested in renting a room in his house next semester and I jumped at the chance. I preferred to have my housing settled rather than leaving it to a lottery.

Then there was Steve. I had been a dick. There is no kind way of describing how I treated him toward the end of the second semester. Unkind is far too kind a word to use. I had been an asshole and the truth behind my feelings was that I had been jealous.

Steve, completely funded by his parents, incredibly talented, focused, and churning out at least (at *least*) one painting a day, not to mention the mountains of cool sketches he did, was leaving for the summer having completed a substantial body of exquisite work. I, in comparison, had to put in about twenty hours a week in the Life Support Office at CalArts, would return to our dormitory to find Steve, sitting on the floor with at least one new masterpiece, and at the mere suggestion, would chose not to do any artwork in favor of food or entertainment. Immaturity plain and simple. I was returning home with a few drawings, some fake arms I had made, an incomplete dinosaur puppet, and a latex face-mask. Hardly anything to be excited about.

Toward the end of the semester, I was not just excluding Steve whenever possible, I was often short, difficult, and rude to him. It is one of many things I've done in this life that I'm not proud or happy about and it haunts me to this day. That we remained friends in spite of this is why his friendship is one I will always treasure.

At the time, I was curious if I would see him much the following year, because he had put his name into the dormitory lottery and been chosen to return. Prior to our separating, Steve had purchased a paperback book from Hollywood Book and Poster, a store we frequented to buy magazines, movie stills and books, including a relatively new publication *Cinefex* which was committed to the reporting solely on the effects for movies (Steve started his *Cinefex* collection with Number 1 which was all about Douglas Trumbull and the effects for *Star Trek: The Motion Picture*, I had started my collection with Number 2 which was about the effects for the *Star Wars* sequel, *The Empire Strikes Back*).

The book he had purchased and read was the novelization of a new film by Stephen Spielberg, entitled *Raiders of the Lost Ark*. I had asked Steve if he could tell me what the story was about; whether he was irritated with me by that point and just didn't feel like talking to me, or if he truly wanted me to be surprised, he told me that "it was too complicated to just sum up" or some dismissive statement like that.

I'm glad he didn't tell me anything. Summer started off with a huge *bang* that year with the release of *Raiders of the Lost Ark*. The stylish homage to the pulp adventures and motion picture serials of the early 1930s captured the imagination (and let's face it, the pocket money) of the population. Believe it or not, this was a "come back" movie for Spielberg after his disastrous attempt at cashing in on the success of John Landis' *Animal House*, a period World War II comedy, *1941*.

The exploits of adventurer/archeologist, 'Indiana Jones' culminated with the melting of two Nazi villains' heads and the exploding of a third. These were credited to a relatively new makeup effects artist named Chris Walas. With his studio in the San Francisco area, Walas was definitely a new contender in the special makeup effects Renaissance.

Speaking of John Landis, that summer also saw the release of his film, *An American Werewolf in London*. Finally, we would see the result of Rick Baker's efforts and the latest entry in the 'Change-O' effects category.

I took Tracy, and we met a group of friends at a theater in Algiers, Louisiana. The film began and just before the lead character, 'David,' played by actor David Naughton, transforms into a werewolf, the power in the theater went out and the emergency lights came on. The audience began groaning and yelling until an usher appeared and told us that if we went to the lobby, we would all get complimentary tickets for our next visit to the theater. We all began filing out of the seats and we received our passes at the door. We had almost made it to the lobby doors when all the electricity in the building came on, and everyone ran back into the theater to watch the rest of the film in its entirety.

The transformation in *American Werewolf* was not just a scene in the film, it was an announcement that not only was Rick Baker the king of makeup effects but that there seemed to be very little that he and his group of dedicated artists could not do. His company, from the point-of-view of a fan-boy like me, was the zenith. To have the opportunity to work for him would be the recognition of my talent. I had to work for Rick.

So, with all of this going on, why was the summer of 1981 so sad?

That summer, alongside *Raiders of the Lost Ark*, and *An American Werewolf in London*, was the year that my longtime inspiration, Ray Harryhausen's film *Clash of the Titans* premiered. Now before you get all crazy, thinking that I'm going to diss one of the greatest visual effects artists if not the best stop-motion animators, I want to be clear. I love Ray. I love his work. His films, although many criticize them for being boring unless one of his creatures is on screen, are like tonics for me. They are chiropractic adjustments for my soul and they have withstood the test of time for me. I can watch The *Valley of Gwangi* nearly any day of the week. Twice.

But *Clash of the Titans* revealed that Ray's movies had become anachronistic. The artists and technicians at George Lucas' Industrial Light and Magic had been pushing the state-of-the-art consistently since *Star Wars,* and this included creatures. The quality of the stop-motion animation of the taun-tauns (if you don't know what that is, you might be reading the wrong book) in *The Empire Strikes Back*, not to mention the battle with the Imperial Walkers, set a new level of realism for that discipline.

Me? I still love the kraken in *Clash of the Titans* and I think that Harryhausen went out in complete style. He finally had a fantastic cast of A-list actors including Lawrence Olivier and Maggie Smith, a solid script, and a big bally-hooed release. The Medusa sequence is one of the finest examples of a stop-motion creature in a motion picture. The film performed well and managed to inspire yet another generation of Harryhausen fans who could look back at his incredible library of work and appreciate it. However, when it came to stop-motion creatures, *Clash* paled when compared to a new film from Disney studios entitled *Dragonslayer*.

There have been very few times I have been absolutely stumped by the effects in a motion picture. *Dragonslayer* has the distinction of being one of those times. Forget about plot, characters, whatever...that film is about the dragon and what a heck of a dragon it was. *Years* before the digital dragons we've all seen in *Reign of Fire, Harry Potter,* and *Game of Thrones*, the dragon of *Dragonslayer* named 'Vermithrax Pejorative' was a clever combination of full-sized animatronics, miniature hand puppetry, and a new advancement in stop-motion animation known as "go motion."

But when I watched the film, I truly did not know what I was looking at. It was like some sort of nightmare ripped from someone's subconscious and recorded onto film! I was completely flummoxed. It was at that moment, I wanted to discuss it with Steve Burg. If anyone knew how the dragon was done, it would be him; however, my guilt prevented me from calling. It would have to wait until fall.

I had taken Tim's advice and now told the Assistant Manager of Winn-Dixie that I was going back to California to college after all, and I thanked him. He didn't seem that torn up about it. I had painted a *huge* advertisement sign for the store featuring King Kong holding a Chiquita banana. Tim, of course, suggested the double entendre copy: "Grab a Banana!"

As summer began to wind down, I knew that I would have to move my furniture to James Fujii's house in Newhall. Fujii's parents had bought the house specifically for James to live in and with two additional students renting, we probably paid the house note. I spoke with my brother and my mother about renting a small U-Haul trailer and packing it; it seemed like the best option. I gave myself an extra day's driving to compensate for towing a trailer and decided to leave early.

I started packing up my bedroom at my mother's house, disassembling the bed I had slept in for thirteen years. I took just about everything I could including my books, my records, my desk and loaded them into the back of the U-Haul trailer. I borrowed my mother's car to drive to Tracy's house to say goodbye. She was starting her senior year of high school and I was going to miss all of it. I told her that if I could come home early, I would try, but I would definitely see her at Christmas time.

The next morning a tropical depression (not quite a hurricane) bore down on Louisiana. Stubbornly, I said goodbye to my mother and got into the car and began the drive to California. It was frightening for the first four hours as high winds knocked around the trailer behind me; however, by the time I had passed Lafayette, Louisiana, the skies lightened and soon I was back in Texas heat.

I had no idea that was the last time I would ever set foot in our house in Terrytown again. It was probably for the best. Had I known, I might have hung around a few days and made everyone, including myself, more emotional. This felt right and in the long run it was. Roughly three and a half days later, I found myself pulling up to James Fujii's house. I was home.

CHAPTER 10

California, The Second Attempt Begins

Pick yourself up, dust yourself off, start all over again.
"Start All Over Again" Dorothy Fields and Jerome Kern

James Fujii's one-story house was on a cul-de-sac just off of the I-5 in Newhall, California. It had three bedrooms and two baths. The third tenant was another Disney animation student named Alan Wright who was a few years older than James who I believe was a little older than me. I unloaded the trailer and returned it to the U-Haul center then spent some time unpacking and setting up my room.

James was extremely generous and encouraged me to use the garage as a studio for sculpting and making my

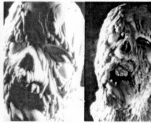

The first sculpture I did when I returned to CalArts in the Fall of 1981. This demon became an over-the-head latex mask.

"Wax-Man" - a project that I mistakenly labeled "My first successful latex mask." I had forgotten about the demon until I discovered the missing slide recently.

Posing with the finished "Jenifer" head in James Fuji's Newhall, California garage.

Proudly holding "Wax-Man." I think I took these photos to mail to my parents in Louisiana to prove that I was actually getting some work done.

creatures. Who was I to argue? I claimed a little work bench that had some shelves above it and established my work space.

Even before the semester began, I could already feel that this year was going to be different. CalArts had been demystified and at the end of this year, I would be submitting my work for review to the faculty. I knew I had my job in the Life Support Office, which was a fancy name for student services. There were four student advisers: Susan Harris and Dick Jenney, who were psychologists, Nancy Wolfe who was in charge of international student affairs, and Henry Scott who was the student advocate. The office was run by Alexandra Florimonte and I assisted them all in some capacity or other.

I drove onto campus, parked and made my way to the Main Hall to sign up for the first semester of classes. As I pushed through the crowd, I saw Steve Burg standing in line. I don't remember exactly what I said, but I ran up to him and asked "Did you see *Dragonslayer*?!"

He looked genuinely surprised. "Yes!"

"How did they do the dragon?"

He smiled and replied, "I don't know!"

And just like that, we became friends again.

By the way, *Dragaonslayer*'s dragon was accomplished by a new development in stop-motion animation called "go-motion" that involved moving the animation model slightly during the exposure of a frame of film. This created the illusion of movement by giving the model a natural blur that occurs when filming any real-time action. Genius!

In time, James Cummins began showing up at the house after his work day on *The Thing*. During a time when studio secrecy about the project was a mandate, James would roll up to the house with a stack of Polaroid photos of the sculptures and finished puppets and specialty prop pieces. I can tell you now that a few of the photos were of effects that were cut from the finished film or difficult to see because of the way the final effect was "dressed" and photographed on set.

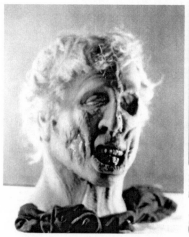

An early latex zombie mask.

A Neanderthal sculpture for a mask. I had run out of cream-colored oil-clay and switched to rust-brown-colored clay to finish the piece. Photo by Steve Burg

The finished Neanderthal Mask. Photo by Steve Burg

Sitting at my work bench in the garage. I believe this photo was meant for my girl-friend, Tracy. Note the Flash Gordon T-shirt.

For example, for the scene where the character 'Bennings' is revealed as 'The Thing' and is chased out onto the snow, we can see that his hands have been altered some way. James' photo of the sculpture revealed that the character's skeletal hands had grown and burst through the skin. The sculpture, he told me, was the work of James Kagel, a sculptor that had worked with Stan Winston previously.

Casa del Fujii had become animator central. Now that I lived with two Disney students, my social circle had grown and was now almost exclusively animators and learning about Disney's animated films, and watching my friends work increased my respect and wonder for that art form. Meanwhile, unlike my freshman year, I began working on things in the garage, making monster masks, molds and latex casts.

Because I was no longer living in the dormitory, my introduction to different students in different schools had dropped. However, one of my friends visiting me at work in the Life Support Office asked if I had seen a recent production of the CalArts Theater Department (I have no idea what the play was). They said that in the show there was a creature called a "Pooka," which was represented as a goat-like demon with horns. I was intrigued. Where did *that* come from? I asked around and was told that a new student had enrolled in the Theater Arts program and was interested in creatures and makeup effects.

His name was James (Jim) Beinke.

My introduction to Jim is a fog. I think someone gave me his dorm room number and I just knocked on the door and introduced myself. In stark contrast to me, Jim had already trashed his dorm room in the scant few months he and his roommate Andrew Kenworthy had shared the space. He had projects in different stages of completion all over the room. One of the most amusing remnants of one of his projects was a hard, dark red, oval on the carpet in the kitchen area. Seems Jim attempted to cast up some gelatin and it spilled all over the floor - where he left it. Now weeks later it was like hard plastic fused into the carpet. Jim just laughed it off and part of me admired him for it.

A huge beast I sculpted for a CalArts theater PSA that was never filmed. I never finished this because it was so big that I couldn't afford the plaster and latex to finish it at the time. Photo by Steve Burg

"Fetoid" sculpture. This was a design for an alien-fetus creature that was fairly disgusting. Photo by Steve Burg

Picture 029 – The finished "Fetoid" mask. The yellow sections were meant to look like veiny-sacks of mucus.

One of the things Jim introduced me to was a very peculiar clay he was using. I had been buying large five pound sticks of rust-red plastilina to sculpt in,

"Chisel-Face" alien sculpture. This sculpt was based on a photo of a rodent skull that Steve Burg gave me as inspiration. Photo by Steve Burg

"IChisel-Face" latex mask in all of his glory. Photo by Steve Burg

even though James Cummins and Mark Shostrom had both suggested I "graduate" to Roma plastilina brand which was then the industry standard. Jim had been given a big box of used clay that was dark charcoal gray, soft, and very easy to manipulate and tool. The problem was that being used clay, there were small chips of old plaster and debris in it that Jim would have to sift through before he sculpted in it.

He gave me a little to experiment with, and when I returned home, James Fujii told me that he thought it was 'Disney clay' which was used by animators to sculpt 3D character models to assist with their drawing. I asked James where I could get more clay like it, but he said that no one in the school had used it for some time. Frustrated, I went back to my rusty plastilina.

I decided I would attempt my first over-the-head latex

mask. Not having a life-cast of a person, I just built up a form out of wood, newspaper, and masking tape. On top of this, I began sculpting in cream-colored plastilina. Rick Baker's work on *The Incredible Melting Man* was so inspirational that I attempted to do my own interpretation of his concept. I dubbed it the "Wax Man." I rolled hundreds of little pieces of clay to simulate dripping candle wax and applied it over a rudimentary skull I had sculpted.

James had already taught me how to make fangs out of dental acrylic and I owned some loose acrylic teeth to put into the clay. However, what I didn't count on was how much the latex would shrink and I knew nothing of how to make a two piece mold. I ended up making a one piece plaster mold, then I pulled the wood, newspaper, tape and clay out of the opening at the neck and then painstakingly cleaned all of the residual clay out of the mold. It took hours!

One of the great things about being good friends with a visual effects artist is that Steve Burg knew how to photograph things. He came to James Fujii's garage and it and photographed my sculpture making it appear to be much better than it actually was. Then when the piece was cast in latex and painted, he photographed it again (shooting everything on slide film which was the portfolio standard at the time). I learned how important presentation of the work was from Steve's fastidious lighting and photography.

Of course, with the latex shrinking as much as it did, there was no way I could pull the mask over my head, so I never attempted it. But the bug had bitten and I began sculpting bigger and bigger masks, building large arma-

A predatory alien design I did that was part of my early portfolio

tures and covering them with inexpensive plastilina. Before I knew it, the garage began filling up with plaster molds and rubber masks.

When I had about six different masks cast and painted, Cummins suggested I visit one of his past employers, Tom Burman of The Burman Studio, and show him my work. I called the number James gave me and spoke with Sandy Burman, who was not just Tom's wife, but running the office there. She was so sweet and encouraging and set up a portfolio review with Tom at their studio in Van Nuys.

I felt sick.

I really didn't have a portfolio as much as I had a collection of slides Steve Burg took for me and a few drawings, but I worked up my nerve and drove to the studio.

At the time, The Burman Studio was housed in a one-story, brick industrial complex. I found parking on the

A copy of the letter I sent to makeup legend, Tom Burman. It worked!

street and was surprised to see a sign that identified the company. I had thought that most of the makeup effects studios were shrouded in secrecy and would be surrounded by curious fans, fighting to get in to see what was happening inside.

I rang the bell and Sandy appeared with a big smile. She invited me in and took me to her office. It was exciting to see posters (many of which I had copies of myself) hanging on the walls along with photos of Tom applying makeups on different actors for various shows. She asked me to wait a second because Tom was working with an actor at the moment. She appeared a moment later and showed me the way into the back workshop/studio.

From my perspective, the workshop was huge. There were work tables set up in the shop with some fake heads in various stages of completion, rubber masks, shelves full of stone molds. While an actor sat in a tall director's chair, Tom Burman stood holding a piece of glass and a palette knife, mixing cream makeup. Tom stopped a moment, shook my hand, introduced me to the actor and explained that he was mixing a custom base to be used for the performer's regular, daily makeup on a movie set (known as "straight" makeup). He asked me to excuse him for a minute and suggested I go to a table at the far end of the shop where two people were sitting working on projects.

The two young men at the table were Tom's son, Rob Burman, and Dale Brady who had been working at the studio for some years. Both of them were very friendly; Rob even went so far to invite me to a beach party that weekend. They asked about my connection to the studio and I mentioned James Cummins. They both had nothing but good things to say about James and his work, especially James' unique sculpting style.

By then, Tom had finished mixing the makeup and he had called me back over. He looked through my slides and drawings, thoughtfully questioning me about each one, asking how I had accomplished the sculpture, the mold

When challenged to design a creature with no recognizable human/animal features, this is what I came up with. Don't ask, I couldn't explain it if I tried.

making material, etc. One of the more obscure drawings caught his eye. It was a creature I attempted to design that had the least amount of identifiable Earth-creature physical attributes. When I explained what it was he smiled and commended me for my imagination.

Then came the treat; he took me on a tour of the studio. At that moment, The Burman Studios was working on special makeup effects for the film *Halloween III: The Season of the Witch*, and the fake heads on the tables were being finished for that film.

Again, to my nineteen year-old mind, this was thrilling. Tom demonstrated how each head worked – one gruesome one in particular was made so that a performer (playing a murderer) could shove his thumb and index fingers into the victim's eye sockets, grab around the bridge of the nose and pull it outward, effectively breaking the nose. As was the case in those developmental days of makeup effects, exotic materials would become the rage and spread through the different studios (each attempting to discover another application for that material). One in particular was a urethane elastomer (a polymer with a great elasticity) known informally as "Smooth-On" named after the company that manufactured it. This material had been a favorite ever since Dick Smith had used it to make the custom air-bladders for Altered States.

I had heard of Smooth-On, I had even seen one of the Smooth-On air bladders made by Rob Bottin from *The Howling* that had come into James Cummins' possession (don't ask me how). But Tom Burman had cast an entire head out of the material for a scene where a man was to have his head torn off. Running down the side of the head and neck, I could see where the seam line (the material that invariably leaked in between the two pieces of the mold) had been cut with a blade. I asked Tom how he planned on getting rid of the seam to make it invisible, and he offered this advice:

"Shannon, one of the things you are going to learn in this business is to never get caught up in the effect. We make illusions for movies and they are shot very carefully so that no one will ever see how they are accomplished," Tom said. I think that was his way of saying that he wasn't going to get rid of the seam; I don't think anyone could have fixed those seams. In years to follow, I concluded it was impossible.

Finally, Tom took me to a table and showed me a couple of custom masks that the Burman Studio was creating for retail sale. One was the final creature from the film *The Beast Within* and the other was the 'Boar Man' that Tom had designed for *The Island of Dr. Moreau (1977)*. It was a treat to see cleaned castings of the masks in raw latex without the paint job distracting my eye; I could study the sculpture, the form and the detail, and that in itself was an education.

Finally, Tom said good bye, assuring me of my future success in the business. He invited me to come back after I graduated and show him my portfolio again. I left the studio and drove back to the Santa Clarita Valley instilled with a new sense of confidence.

CHAPTER 11

All Phoenixes Must Burn Before They Rise

I don't care what you say anymore, this is my life.
"My Life" Billy Joel

Most of my classes at CalArts were nothing if not ineffectual. One class in particular was Sculpture Seminar. Not only did I never meet the teacher of the class (it was taught by a teacher's assistant), but there was no syllabus. Each student was required to do a one hour presentation of a sculptor or sculpture type and that was that. Attendance assured that you would receive a "pass." Do a good presentation and you would receive a "high pass." I was the third student to give a presentation and then just sat in class and listened to the other presentations for the rest of the semester. No tests, quizzes, or reports. Nada. I also took a beginning piano class where we didn't learn to play the piano. All we did the entire semester was transcribe different key signatures and then play the scales on the piano. I didn't even learn to play "Mary had a Little Lamb." I began to get disillusioned with CalArts.

If that wasn't enough to begin to sink my spirits, I received a one-two punch from James Cummins. He had quit his work on *The Thing* saying that, in his opinion, Rob Bottin was insane and it was too difficult to continue working with him. Then, he confessed that he and his friend, Henry Golas, had managed to get the contract to do the Special Makeup Effects for a new film *Strange Invaders*. It was then I got my first lesson in "the biz."

Who was one of James' best friends? Me. Who had been taking James' advice, working hard, learning, trying to put into practice everything James taught? Me. Who would *not* be asked to be a part of the crew? Me.

James corrected my assumption that I would be joining the crew that was scheduled to travel to Canada for shooting (I didn't even have a passport at the time). He stated that since it was a professional project, he was only in the position to hire professionals and I was still a student. He would be happy to work with me when I had gained some professional experience. Of course this perceived slight was being interpreted by my nineteen year-old brain. At the time, I didn't understand International labor laws that protected local talent by limiting the size of a crew coming in from a foreign country.

My immaturity won over and I allowed James' decision to affect my self-confidence.

Little did I know that a series of events would occur that would lead to some professional experience, but it wouldn't be an easy road.

When I first applied for my work-study job at CalArts in the autumn of 1980, I had been hired as the athletic assistant. To be clear there were no athletics offered at CalArts while I was there. At the start, I was responsible for distributing, collecting and caring for what little sports equipment CalArts owned. However, this job hardly required the hours I was available to do the work, so eventually Alexandra Florimonte had worked me into the office staff. Soon I was handling the athletic duties intermittently. But one day the phone rang and it was forwarded to me because no one knew who else was qualified to deal with it.

On the phone was a representative from the Pasadena Art Center, a prestigious art college whose primary focus seemed to be on commercial art and product design. The representative wanted to challenge CalArts to a friendly game of basketball and since I was the closest thing to an athletic coordinator, the task fell to me.

I spoke with some students who played basketball and they were interested in a game. I found a local gym that agreed to give us access to play one evening and the game was afoot!

The Art Center team arrived in beautiful, professionally made uniforms and brought uniformed cheerleaders with them. Our team looked like they just came off of a municipal basketball court; half of them weren't wearing shirts. Needless to say, they may have looked better, but we won.

After the game, it fell to me to give them the grand tour of the facility. I was taking them through the Film Graphics room, past my table when one of the cheerleaders mentioned that her boyfriend was a makeup effects artist. She wrote his name and phone number on a piece of paper and suggested that I call him. It was Mark Shostrom. At the time, I had never heard of him. But who was I to be arrogant?

I'd had my sophomore year review and the faculty didn't get what I was doing. They tried to explain what I could do to make my work more avant-garde but in the end, it was Myron Emery, the assistant dean of the Film School, who said, "Shannon, if you want to do commercial work, then leave school and get a job." So why not call this Mark Shostrom?

When I initially contacted Mark, I was unprepared for how calmly and thoughtfully he spoke. A year or two before, at the suggestion of Herb Saussaye, I had called Eddie Henriques to introduce myself. He was pleasant enough, but I could tell he was just being polite and really wanted to get off of the phone. Mark on the other hand was patient, answered questions and finally invited me to his studio in Pasadena.

The trek from Santa Clarita to Pasadena took roughly an hour and required a lot of "map research" to figure out what freeways and roads to take. It was afternoon when I arrived at Mark's studio, which was on California Avenue, just east of Lake Boulevard. Don't bother looking it up, it has since been demolished. Mark invited me in and my first reaction was that I had walked into Dick Smith's West Coast facility.

Shelves of appliance molds were just inside of the door, each one painstakingly labeled and stacked. There were beautiful Roma plastilina sculptures of human heads that had been done freehand without the use of life casting.

By that time, I had invested in a small portfolio. Mark looked through my masks and drawings and was very complimentary and supportive. He then handed me his portfolio and my mind was blown. Mark had expertly replicated nearly every important makeup of Dick Smith's and somehow managed to put his own personal spin on it. As it turned out, Mark was another West Coast protege and regular correspondent of Mr. Smith's.

We spoke for a few hours, and at the end of our time, Mark offered me a stone life cast of his friend (future production designer) Phillip Duffin to work off of rather than building up armatures out of wood and newspaper. I thanked him, loaded it in my car, and drove back to Santa Clarita.

On the way back, I started to reflect on what had just happened. This total stranger gave me a gift, to encourage me in my work, and one of my best friends just kicked me to the curb. My nineteen year-old mind tried to come to grips with it, but the bottom line was that by the end of the school year, I had to make some decisions about what I was going to do one way or the other.

Should I go home? Should I stay at CalArts and try to graduate? Why? I was already in debt with a new student loan for my second year and my review hadn't gone that well. The assistant Dean had been transparent about my interests being opposed to the school's core philosophy. My friend, James Belohovek, from the Experimental Animation Program, had managed to land a job on *The Thing* assisting Sue Turner with building the miniature flying saucer featured in the film. Many of my traditional animation friends were being hired, with Disney taking them out of school and putting them to work before graduation.

Then there was my girlfriend, Tracy. I was going to miss her senior prom, which for me was so alien, but I could understand how important it was going to be for her. Both of us had been loyal to one another. For me it was easy, because I had spent the majority of my time developing my art and making business connections. My refusal to cheat on her, though, was based as much in practicality as it was in fidelity.

I went back to the garage and set to work. By the spring of 1982, I had all but taken over James Fujii's garage. I had at least eight full-head plaster molds and a double oven I had purchased from the want ads and used for baking foam latex, I didn't want to have to pack up everything and go back to New Orleans, so I decided to stay in Santa Clarita, but had no idea what I would do for work.

One of the services provided by the Life Support Office at CalArts was job placement. I went out on a couple of odd jobs that asked for sculptors. One was to replace the head of a cowboy dummy in the middle of the enormous lobby of a dentist's office. I sculpted, molded, cast, and did the hair work on the replacement head, then installed it to the delight of the dentist and the staff.

I also drove down to Santa Monica to a place called Crownsmiths. They, too, had advertised for a sculptor and when I arrived they took me into the back to take a dexterity test. The company made crowns for dentists to replace patients' teeth. I didn't do too well on the test, but either they were desperate or I was cheap enough because they wanted me to hang around and be trained.

In that moment, my entire life flashed in front of my eyes. I would be trained, get proficient, and spend the rest of my life sculpting other people's teeth. I couldn't do it. I thanked them and left. Besides, there was no way I could support myself driving from Santa Clarita to Santa Monica daily. I returned to the job board.

I could feel the walls pressing in and I knew I had better get some kind of job, any job immediately. James Fujii and some other animators had taken to caricaturing at the local amusement park. He offered to teach me the system (they all had to learn a specific style in creating the drawings). I think I tried for a day or two at the house but didn't have a knack for it. With my money running out, I got desperate and applied for work at a new ice cream parlor that was about to open.

I got the job.

At first, I was happy to have a job. I let my family (and Tracy) know that I wasn't returning home that summer and that I wasn't sure if I would be returning to CalArts. After my semi-disastrous review I had been put on academic probation. I began my training at the ice cream parlor when reality began to sink in like sharp talons. I was twenty and in college while all of the other employees were teenagers and going to the local high school. Ouch. The management was nice enough and it wasn't difficult work. True, it was physically demanding but at least I wasn't digging ditches.

The parlor opened to throngs of people. I wish I were exaggerating. I had never seen lines for ice cream that ran out of the door. And there I was, hustling back and forth, in my white jeans, scooping ice cream and occasionally dipping cones into warm liquid chocolate. I must have been doing well because the manager informed me that he wanted to begin training me in the preparation of ice cream cakes and novelties.

One of those nights, when the line was out of the door, I was scooping like mad when I heard a familiar voice call my name. I looked up and there was Jim Beinke and one of his friends from CalArts. I was instantly humiliated but what could I do? He asked what I was doing there and I explained that I was just trying to stay in California for the summer. He asked if I wanted to continue scooping ice cream, because he might be able to offer me a job. The pay wasn't great, but it was creative.

I asked what the job was and he told me it was making props and specialty wardrobe for a stage show entitled *Celestial Lords*. There were even going to be a couple of fabricated dinosaur skeletons. When I asked what the heck *Celestial Lords* was, Jim just laughed and said that it was scheduled to be the official entertainment show for the Gay Olympics held in San Francisco.

CHAPTER 12

There's No Business Like Show Business

"Walking has been described as 'controlled falling.'
Every time you take a step, you lean forward and fall slightly."
George Maestri

What could I do? I put in my notice at the ice cream parlor and returned to CalArts where *Celestial Lords* was being constructed in the Theater Department's "Wondershop" (the scenery and props shop for the college's productions). I need to give you an idea of what the shop is like now so that you will understand a story I'll tell you later.

The shop was huge. The main building area was (I'm guessing) about 200 feet or so wide by roughly 100 feet deep. One side of it was fairly open, used for assembling large pieces where the other side was occupied by work tables and bench tools. Through a large passage way was a smaller room that housed an office and a "tool cage" where Jim had set up the clay sculpting area. On the far end of the shop was a corridor that led to dressing rooms, a theater green room, and restrooms; across the hall from this was the CalArts modular theater.

I met with Jim and he introduced me to the producer, who was a former student named Roz (I can't recall her last name), and the construction supervisor, Marcia

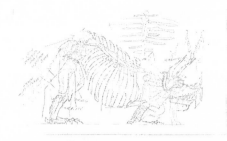

One of the designs for "Celestial Lords." This Triceratops creature was made of foam pieces that were carried by dancers, when they stood/posed in a specific way, the pieces they carried formed this skeleton. I never saw how it turned out.

Hinds, who was on the CalArts faculty. Where it would fall to Jim and me to produce clay sculptures, mold them and cast them, Marcia would handle all of the large set pieces and make sure everything was being completed on time. Roz handed us designs. Again, this was 1981 and I've forgotten the name of the man who had designed the show. I know he was the production designer for the *Ice Capades*.

The show was defined by "ages", stone age, iron age, post apocalypse, etc. and we were to make pieces for both male and female dancers. The pay was $100 a week which was less than I was making at the ice cream parlor, but hey...show business, right? The hours were un-specified. Jim had already begun blocking out a male headpiece for an aquatic couple. We looked through the designs and Jim suggested I begin sculpting one of the modified gasmasks for the post-apocalyptic age. The male gas masks had long hoses hanging off of the front of them that would fit into openings on the front of the female gas masks. I would also have to sculpt the codpiece which looked like a

The female counterpart to the "Age of Armageddon" mask I sculpted. This mask was sculpted by Jim Beinke.

scrotum made up of two hand grenades.

This is a good time to let you in on the secret I mentioned in passing before. When I was working at the theater in the French Quarter, one of the actors there asked why Al Shea's homosexuality was the best kept secret in New Orleans. Well, if this actor knew then it couldn't have been much of a secret, but I hadn't known. I asked my mother and she confirmed it. In that moment, my entire childhood had made sense. The theme parties, the theatrical friends, the crazy clothes my Dad wore including purple socks and clogs. Most of my friends' fathers didn't dress like Dad. That there were no sports in the house, the Broadway show tunes that played on the stereo, the love of Liza Minelli and Barbara Streisand, it was all part of my childhood under my father's roof. After learning about his orientation, I comprehended so much more about my father including his constant frustration and anger. It must have been very difficult for him to deny his true nature and pretend to be a heterosexual husband and father to three children which was not the norm at that time.

After my parents' divorce, I discovered one of my father's hand-written journals that described his feeling trapped by a traditional family. He later confessed to me, once I had a child of my own, that he found it much easier to appreciate his children as adults more than he had when we were younger. Ironically, he also confessed that whenever he dreamed about me, I was perpetually an eight year-old.

I saw myself as some sort of strange 'Tarzan' but instead of being a human raised by apes, I was a heterosexual man raised by a gay father. The result was that being in the company of gay men seemed somewhat normal to me and was never a source for discomfort. As a result, working on *Celestial Lords* for me was like working on any theatrical production I had been a part of in New Orleans and I set out sculpting the grenade scrotum without a second thought.

I learned quite a bit about exotic materials working on the show. Not only was it my first introduction to expanding polyurethane, which was used to decorate large wings that had been cut out of Styrofoam by Marcia and her crew, but we also used or tried to use a material that I had never used before or would encounter after. It was described to me a liquid neoprene or doll head plastic.

It would be poured into plaster molds filled to the top and left to sit. The longer it sat, the thicker the plastic skin would be (much like latex). Once it dried, it was semi-rigid and could be cut with a craft knife.

Production designer, Marcia Hinds, led a crew that was cutting out huge styrofoam shapes and covering them with soft-expanding polyfoam to produce set pieces.

We tried to pour the gas masks out of the doll head plastic, but it shrank so much that we couldn't get our heads into them. Casting latex was decided upon for ease. In order to dry the latex faster, Jim converted one of the bathrooms on the far side of the shop into a mold oven. We covered one of the walls and part of the floor with thick aluminum foil, and then set up heat lamps. We would pour latex into the molds, let them dwell in the oven, pour them out and in about half of the time it would take if we let them sit at room temperature, a casting would be ready to de-mold.

Jim and I kept strange hours. I'd show up for work around ten in the morning and we'd work all day into the late hours, not just because we had deadlines, but because we loved what we were doing. I was 20 years old and I was being paid to make latex masks. As we began moving into finishing some of the pieces, Roz showed up, looked at what we were doing and was convinced we were on drugs. She couldn't believe that two artists could be so creative and *not* be on drugs. She set out two lines of cocaine for Jim and I and left.

Now, I had smoked a little pot when I was younger, but it had never left me wanting more. I preferred a drink over a smoke and still do. James Cummins had come by James Fujii's house during my sophomore school year and given Steve Burg and I mushrooms and it was a weird trip, but again, not enough for me to want to repeat it. I've never taken cocaine in any form. Seeing the lines on the table was a bit insulting to both of us. It insinuated that we weren't creative enough on our own and needed coke to accomplish what we were doing.

I told Jim I didn't want it. He told me he was going to

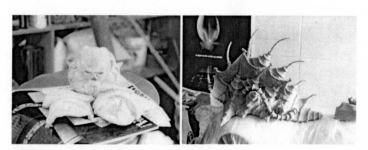

Some latex costume pieces ready to be finished.

An impressive shell back-pack sculpted by Jim Beinke.

sell it. I have no idea who ended up taking it. It was the first and last time I had seen cocaine that close up in my life. *Celestial Lords* was also the first and only time I experienced something I would categorize as a "haunting."

Toward the end of our build schedule, the work load became more demanding and Jim and I would work twelve to sixteen hours a day with no real break. With the bathroom-oven running nearly non-stop, we would try to get latex pulls out of molds twice a day (which is a difficult thing to do since latex has to dry completely before it is de-molded; otherwise it can be damaged).

One of these late nights, I found myself weary and decided to go home early at around two o'clock in the morning. I told Jim that I would check on some molds we had poured around midnight before I left. Jim was sculpting in the tool cage. I had walked through the small shop and into the big main shop when I felt like I was being followed. I remember wondering why Jim was walking behind me and I was going to turn but then thought he might just be going out for a cigarette break.

I crossed the large shop, went down the corridor to the bathroom-oven and stepped inside to check the molds. I put my hand into one of the helmet molds and discovered that the latex was nearly cured after only a couple of hours. What happened next was not imagined. I heard a human whistle. Not a faint "did-I-hear-that-or-not-whistle" but more like someone with a strong whistle exclaiming surprise at how quickly the latex had set. I thought it was Jim. Without looking behind me, I said something like, "Yeah, I can't believe how quickly this dried. We'll be able to pull these out in an hour or so." I turned around and no one was there.

I now know the feel of that chill people describe when encountering a ghost because there was no mistaking it. I was standing in an oven, hot enough to set liquid latex in an hour and suddenly I was freezing. I ran to the door, thinking that Jim was messing with me. He wasn't there. I ran to the main shop and it was still. With all of the papers and drawings lying around, I don't think he could have run through without making some noise or upsetting something on one of the tables. Everything was deathly still. My heart began racing and I ran across the main shop, into the small shop and to the tool cage where Jim was still seated, sculpting.

"Were you just behind me?" I asked him . He looked at me and reacting to my expression said, "You *saw* it!"

My blood drained from my face, I could literally feel myself going pale and faint. Jim went on to tell me that the CalArts Modular Theater was rumored to be haunted. Many reports from multiple witnesses described a figure that would appear in the light booths, would disturb things on the catwalks. It was well known in the Theater Department that the dean's ever-present dog would never step foot inside of the theater, but would stop and sit at the threshold rather than enter.

I don't think Jim was joking with me and if he was, then it has been a joke he has kept up for thirty plus years. No, I think he *truly* wanted to experience the ghost himself. He built a simple Ouija board and cut his finger, dripped blood on the planchette and on each letter of the alphabet and then we crept into the catwalk of the modular theater and set it up taking note of the exact position of the planchette. Every night until the end of the show we would check to see if it had moved. It never did.

In retrospect, I can't remember whether we removed the board or not. I can only imagine the reinforcement of the ghost legend that occurred the first time a lighting technician walked the catwalk and discovered a crude Ouija board lying there.

As pieces were finished, they were collected and sent up north for final assembly. To be honest, I never saw what the completed costumes looked like; however, for two kids under twenty, I think we did okay. Whether the show was a hit or not, I have no clue. As the project shut down, both Jim and I had to figure out our next moves. He cleaned out the bathroom oven and moved into it. And by moved into it, I mean he started living in it for the remainder of the summer. At one point, he built an art installation and converted the bathroom into a verdant forest. It was quite impressive.

Celestial Lords would haunt me a few years later during a visit home in New Orleans. For some reason MTV was

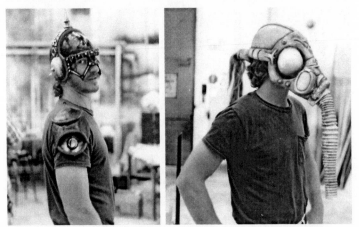

Wish I could remember this guy's name. He was part of Marcia's crew and he's modeling one of Beinke's helmets.

The latex-cast helmet I sculpted that ended up in the Quiet Riot video "Metal Health."

on, though I wasn't a frequent watcher. The rock band Quiet Riot's "Metal Health" video was playing. During a purposefully disturbing dance club scene, I saw the gas mask I had sculpted for *Celestial Lords* swinging his nose-hose around. I asked Jim the next time I saw him and he confirmed that not only had he constructed the featured mask for the album and video, but he had lent them the left over masks from *Celestial Lords*. And that, folks, is how one mask ended up giving me two credits on my early resume.

The meager money I had earned on *Celestial Lords* was barely paying my rent. I had been in contact with Mark Shostrom since our initial meeting and had been by his studio/apartment a few times. When Mark discovered that *Celestial Lords* had wrapped and that I was unemployed and having trouble making my rent, he suggested I consider rooming with him. I asked him how much rent was and he said I wouldn't have to pay rent, because he wasn't paying rent. This confused me, but I decided that the remoteness of Santa Clarita, the lack of local work, and the opportunity to be living and working with someone I understood to be a working professional made sense. I packed up my room, thanked James Fujii and drove my GTO to Mark's apartment. While driving through the Tujunga pass, my car lurched and stuttered a couple of times. This wasn't a good start to a new chapter in my life. I had no clue at the time that it was an omen of things to come.

CHAPTER 13

Life with Mark

Living is easy with eyes closed...
"Strawberry Fields Forever" John Lennon

How apropos that this is the thirteenth chapter of this tale. Unfortunately it is a tale of woe. Not that it started that way. Oh no, *far* from it! My initial experiences with Mark were amongst the most entertaining of my education, because in retrospect I was in my makeup effects "apprenticeship."

When I arrived at Mark's place in Pasadena, he explained why there was no rent being paid. He was in a legal battle with his landlord over the condition of the building. To illustrate, he went to the kitchen, knelt down by the sink and put his hand through a six-inch round hole in the wall that was opened to the outside. That was just one of the many slum-like problems with the building and Mark flat-out refused to pay rent until the landlord fixed the problems. The next thing I discovered was that there wasn't much room for what little I had brought with me. Mark was an incredible pack rat and there were all sorts of things stacked and stuffed in places. I recall that my possessions never left the boxes they were packed in and were stacked in a back room. The last thing I learned was that Mark had no work either.

I moved in with Mark shortly after he had completed work on a low-budget film *Android* for which he built a pretty spectacular head of actor Klaus Kinsky. He had done some work for Rick Baker on *Videodrome* but, like me, was in search of a paying gig. He had a lead for a film entitled *The Last Resort,* which was another low-budget, independent film that could best be described as a Country/Western *Beauty and the Beast fable.* Mark asked if I was interested in doing some illustrations that would help secure the job and assist the filmmakers in attracting financing. Using a small clay sculpture (a maquette) Mark had done, I produced a few drawings of the crea-

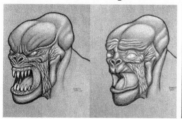 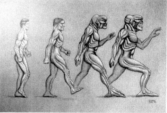

A color pencil sketch I did for "The Last Resort." I was asked by Mark Shostrom to come up with two "states" of the lead creature: Anger and Sympathy.

Another color pencil sketch I did showing the transition from man to creature which was very popular in the 1980s.

In "The Last Resort" the creature sucked the DNA out of its victims and the lead female character finds herself in a room full of human husks. Another color pencil sketch.

What does it look like when you have the DNA sucked out of you? I sculpted this model as a proof-of-concept for "The Last Resort" while living with Mark Shostrom.

ture that demonstrated some of its behavioral features. The project went nowhere.

In the meantime, Mark took me step by step through lab techniques, many of which he had learned through his correspondence with makeup artist Dick Smith. I learned how to make molds using Ultracal 30, which was the industry standard gypsum cement and the much harder and denser dental stones. The dental stones were more expensive but made much more substantial molds. At that time, most of the West Coast foam rubber used for motion picture prosthetics was being supplied by makeup veteran Charlie Schram, and Mark taught me how to run this very challenging foam system. I'll confess that I learned more working with Mark Shostrom those months than I had from James Cummins or any book I had read. But it wasn't just work. Mark Shostrom was one of the funniest people I had ever met.

Mark had a 'joke board' that was made up of articles he had cut out of newspapers and magazines that he had juxtaposed with non-related photos. The results were hilarious. There were nights that I laughed so hard that I thought I was going to die, and that isn't an exaggeration. But all the while the money was going away. My car would not operate past third gear; it would just stutter and die. I took it to a garage that boasted a 'We'll get it right or you won't pay' policy but after its third visit to their garage, they asked me to stop bringing it.

To distract ourselves, Mark would do fairly elaborate disguise makeups on me. I was twenty years-old and had a baby face. Mark wanted to see if he could put me in a subtle age makeup that would fool the clerk at the convenience store into believing I was old enough to buy beer without checking my I.D. The weird thing was that in Louisiana, I had been old enough to buy liquor for two years and had done so on numerous occasions. Reducing the rosiness of my face, adding beard stubble, a scar, lightening my hair, dirtying my fingernails and putting hair treatment to accentuate my hairline, I was sent to the corner liquor store and within minutes would return with a six pack of beer. That is, we'd buy beer when we had money. No, wait, we bought beer even when we were low on money.

Dinner would be, literally, a shared package of Bratwurst (two each), mustard, and 32 oz soft drinks we bought at the corner gas station. We would rinse out the cups and keep them for our expendable supplies. At one point, things got so desperate that I called Tracy in New Orleans and asked her to lend me money. Tracy, who had just graduated High School, whose prom I missed, whom I had not seen since Christmas and whom I probably wouldn't see until the following Christmas, went into her savings, money carefully accrued since she was twelve years old, and sent me a check for $2500. I would never and will never forget that supreme act of generosity and kindness. Truthfully, I felt like a shit accepting money from her. She wasn't even eighteen, yet! Shameful.

But it wasn't just me borrowing money from my girlfriend. Mark, too, would borrow money from his girlfriend, Shan, whom I had met at CalArts. This and other frustrations revealed something I hadn't known about Mark Shostrom: he had one hell of an explosive temper. As our financial situation became more and more strained, Mark got angrier and angrier. He would scream obscenities at the top of his lungs in machine gun rapidity while his pale, nearly translucent skin would get bright red. He told me that it was "healthy" that he released all of the anger in his system so quickly and completely, and that may be true, but it certainly didn't make it any easier to live with him.

One early summer morning before the sun rose, we heard a banging at the front door. Mark tried to ignore it, but eventually woke up, cursing and stomping to the door. He opened it and a summons server was there and put legal papers in his hand; the eviction process had started. Mark threw the papers across the room and slammed the door in the server's face.

When he woke up in the early afternoon, Mark was determined to fight his landlord. He ran around the apartment taking photos of the disrepair of the building. After living with Mark for 6 weeks or so, I wasn't sure if he hadn't been the cause of much of the destruction himself. Eventually, armed with Polaroid photos mounted to black matte board, Mark went to court to defend himself and bring his slumlord to justice.

We were given thirty days to vacate the premises.

With the days of summer getting shorter, Mark and I found a rental house in East Pasadena, about 30 minutes away from where we were living. Anthony Showe, a friend and collaborator of Mark's helped us move to our new place. But there was no way we were going to make our rent every month. During our move, I had spoken with Tracy, and whether it was the money, or my absence, she had had enough and didn't want to see me any more. I wasn't sure whether or not things could get much worse.

To cheer ourselves up, Mark suggested a drive to the studio where Anthony was working. It turned out to be

John Beuchler's studio at Roger Corman's Santa Monica complex, a place known affectionately as "The Lumber Yard." On the way there, Mark coached me. He told me to notice that every puppet in John's studio had three movements: Eyes roll upward, jaw open, lip sneer. That was it. And if I asked, not only would John demonstrate every head in the studio, he would show me his portfolio!

We arrived at around eight that evening. John and Anthony had just opened Ultracal life castings they had completed earlier of actress, Jamie Lee Curtis' legs from the knees down. I have no clue what had happened but what Mark and I saw on the workbench were two nearly perfect cylinders of gray stone, with what appeared to be a toe or two sticking out of the bottom. To this day, I couldn't tell you what they had done to ruin these casts and have them turn out like that. Adding to the disaster, John and Anthony insisted that the actress had come on to them both. I was standing in delusion land.

Taking Mark's advice, I asked John for a tour of the shop, which was about fifty feet by thirty-five feet or so. As predicted, John demonstrated heads that all had the same three identical mechanisms in them. As they moved, Mark stood behind John, out of his sight, imitating the heads. John broke out his portfolio, which was an extra-large photo album (not an artist's portfolio). To add show titles to the sections of the album, John had used red vinyl press-on letters, and at one point had run out of vowels, because toward the end of the book, more black vinyl As and Os appeared amongst the predominately red words. Yet somehow, John was able to work.

Not that my work was anything stellar, but at least I knew a *little* about presentation. We left shortly after, leaving the two of them to their fantasy. It was a distraction, but hardly made me feel better. A few weeks later, Mark was approached by a producer he had previously worked for, Sandy Howard, about doing a few effects for the sequel to the cult classic *Vice Squad* entitled *Deadly Force*. I drove with Mark down to the production office and sat in a reception area while Mark spoke with the producers and director.

When Mark emerged, he told me that he was going to make *some* money, but not enough to pay me, but I could assist him with a few things. A few days later, we returned to the production office and Mark did an out-of-the-kit casualty makeup on me. The art director carefully twisted a wire coat hanger around my neck and they took me to an alley behind the building and shot crime scene photos of me. As requested by production, I also provided them with a portrait-style photo. If you ever see *Deadly Force*, if you look carefully, you can see my face directly between actors, Joyce Ingalls and Wings Hauser, on the police evidence board (toward the end of the film). And speaking of Wings...

Mark had talked production into letting him make custom bruise makeups for Wings who was now playing the policeman rather than the psycho-killer he'd played in *Vice Squad*. We drove to his house in the Hollywood Hills to cast his face, which is never the best situation for either actor or makeup artist. We put a vinyl bald cap on Wings and got him all prepared for the alginate, a flexible, seaweed- based molding material. Mark made sure to ask if Wings could breathe through his nose because during the casting process, we wouldn't use straws, though many assume that is standard. Instead, the alginate is applied around the nostrils, leaving openings for the subject to breathe. This prevents distortion that occurs when using straws. Wings said he was ready. We mixed the alginate into the cold water and began applying to his face.

Everything was going fine, until we began the second part of the process, which involved applying a few layers of plaster bandage (to support the flexible alginate) to the cast. Wings began to wave his hands, then flap his arms. He stood up waving his arms wildly and he was a tall man, over six feet! Mark quickly grabbed the plaster bandage and alginate and ripped it off of Wings' red face. The actor had thought he would be able to hold his breath during the entire process since he had trouble breathing through his nose due to a deviated septum. We cleaned him up, and re-cast him with his mouth open so he could breathe.

By this time, I had been forced to get a job. I had no more money and even though I had made arrangements for Steve Burg to come to the house and share the burden of the rent the following January, I was too broke to hang on that long. I got a job at Bank of America reviewing ATM requests through a temporary service agency. I was miserable.

Remarkably, I had managed to somehow patch things up with Tracy, who had started college, but going to work in an office and supporting Mark financially while he sculpted and made molds for a show was killing me. I could work in a bank in New Orleans and be just as close to getting a break in motion pictures.

Then one night, a miracle happened. My mother called me out of the blue and said that she had the feeling

I was in trouble. I explained my situation and she asked, "Do you want to come back home?"

CHAPTER 14

A Brief List of Facts and Incidents

Dear Reader: This is supposed to be the story of my life in motion pictures and of the twisted events that led me there. At the risk of sounding dismissive, the rest of 1982 until the autumn of 1984, I had returned back home to New Orleans. So I'll try to list events that took me from Mark Shostrom's in 1982 back to Mark Shostrom's in 1984:

I sold my GTO to two Hispanic men for $400. They brought a battery with them (since mine had long-since died from trying to figure out what was wrong with the car), started it and while revving the engine, discovered tiny pin-holes in the fuel line. The repair probably cost $50.

An ink and pencil color design I did of a "Shovel Tusker" creature for my portfolio. Drawing was infinitely easier and more affordable to pad my portfolio than investing in clay and sculpting.

I left nearly everything I owned to Mark. My books, my records... though to be honest, I packed a few and sent them home. I told him that he could sell whatever I left to make ends meet.

I flew home with nothing. I was greeted at the airport by Tracy and my mother and they both informed me I had a job interview at the New Orleans Hilton Hotel the next morning.

I got a job as a cashier and went to work at the Hilton.

By the following spring, I had decided to enroll in the University of New Orleans, and to forsake special effects and become a geologist.

The Hilton wouldn't adjust my schedule so that I could return to school, so I got a job along with Tracy at Fox Photo. These were little photo booths set up around the city that would develop film overnight, which was a big thing in those days.

The University of New Orleans taught me quickly that I wasn't going to be able to hack it as a geologist. I failed chemistry *horribly*.

Steve Burg flew to Los Angeles and moved in with Mark Shostrom. James Cummins returned to Los Angeles from Canada with stories, photos, and new friends he had made. During the spring of '83, James and Steve came to New Orleans for the Vul Con convention. I had talked the organizers into bringing James down as a guest and to do a panel on *Strange Invaders*. It became a three day drinking binge that ended up with the convention officers angry with all of us.

By the end of my fall semester at the University of New Orleans, I had decided to change my major from geology to Fine Art. My classes there were less avant-garde than CalArts; however, it felt like the department was

James Cummins and I at VulCon 10 in New Orleans, clowning around.

I made a foam latex mask for a pumpkin for a national pumpkin-carving contest I won a Polaroid camera.

My first foam latex mask of a Yeti. I didn't understand the concept of "coring" so he was slushed like a regular latex mask.

Stealing a kiss while casting Tracy Fletcher's head on her back porch in Louisiana. A guy's gotta do what a guy's gotta do.

attempting to be something more than it was. I was told by most of my teachers that I had no talent for anything from drawing to sculpture. I was told my work was too "representational" and that I was not truly an artist capable of expression. In an act of desperation, I put a package of photos together and sent them to Dick Smith, asking him for a critique.

About three weeks later, my mother knocked on my bedroom door and told me that Dick Smith was on the phone and wanted to talk with me.

I won't be the first to have said this, but it bears repeating: Dick Smith was one of the nicest, most helpful, and certainly the most inspirational individual at this crossroad in my life. I asked him, directly, if I should stop my pursuit and he calmly explained the difference between university-level art school and commercial art and how little they had in common. He then assured me that I had a promising career ahead if I just stuck with my practice and kept pushing myself to improve technically as well as artistically.

A few days later, a package arrived in the mail from Dick. It was a set of xerox-duplicated notes that he was in the habit of sending to promising young makeup artists. Within the pages were tips on everything from making prosthetic breakdown molds to fabricating Smooth-On elastomer air bladders. Thus inspired, I set to work immediately.

Now that the principles of Foam Latex had been explained to me, I tried my hand at overlapping appliances, and over-the-head masks. Of course, the biggest challenge was where was I going to get the materials that Dick described in his pages. He was kind enough to furnish the names of companies who would offer free samples of a small amount of their products, but when it came to mold making supplies, there was nothing local.

I finally called the toll-free number for United States Gypsum and discovered that the closest distributor for Ultracal 30 was in Houston, Texas. I took the number, called and ordered two hundred pounds. Each bag of the gypsum cement only cost $7 at the time, but the shipping was going to cost $150! Luckily I had a job and was living with my mother, so this purchasing/shipping arrangement became a necessary investment.

About six weeks later a huge big rig truck arrived at my mother's house, its trailer scraping the low-lying oak tree branches that lined the street on either side. The confused driver rang the door bell and I accompanied him to the truck where all that was left from his cargo were two 100 pound bags of Ultracal 30 on a wooden palette. I signed the papers, thanked him then muscled the bags into the garage one at a time.

My plan was to take a cue from Mark Shostrom and try my hand at a "Dick Smith tribute" makeup. I chose the Mr. Hyde makeup he had done for actor Jason Robards

My first successful foam latex face-mask. A stylized zombie based on art I had seen in Warren publications like Creepy and Eerie.

Tim Guillory, a long-time friend, in the zombie makeup. I did a Klingon prosthetic makeup on him later. He was always a good subject and had a great time.

After speaking with Dick Smith I attempted an overlapping prosthetic makeup on my brother, Scott. Here he is in mid-transformation.

The disastrous result! He was supposed to be Mr. Hyde but turned out looking more like a witch or a goblin. Back to the drawing board!

The last sculpture I did while I lived in Louisiana – A Dog-Demon puppet that was abandoned and thrown away when I moved to Los Angeles.

which, although it was unused, still had many of the physical traits that Dick would use for his Reagan makeup for *The Exorcist*.

I made so many technical mistakes along the way that by the time I was gluing all of the foam rubber pieces onto my brother, he looked like the goblin, *Blix,* from the film *Legend* and not at all like Mr. Hyde and this was a year or two BEFORE *Legend*! I was mortified.

By this time, Tracy's father, John Fletcher, had talked me out of leaving my cushy job at Fox Photo -seriously, the best job I ever had-to work for his company, Driller's Electric of Harvey. He said he needed an artistic eye to help with their new catalog, so I went to work drawing receptacles and bug-blowers as well as advertising art that was silk-screened onto plastic "geaux cups." These were plastic cups given to bar patrons so they could legally drink on the street. Hey, it was New Orleans in the 1980s!

Everything was moving along fine until one day I received a call from Mark Shostrom. It was late August of 1984. He had just been awarded a job working on *Ghost Soldiers* for which he needed a real "crew." He mailed me a photo of the test makeup he had done on his friend, Phillip Duffin, and then asked if I would be interested in coming out to work. What did he really think I was going to say?

CHAPTER 15

The Supernaturals aka Ghost Soldiers

Who is more a fool? The fool or the fool that follows?
Obi-Wan Kenobi, Star Wars

I think I can say, without hesitation, that I *could* blame Mark Shostrom for everything. After all, it was he who encouraged me to leave CalArts and pursue a career apprenticing with him. It was he who convinced me that neither of us had to pay rent which, eventually got us kicked out of the apartment. He refused to get a job, which forced me to find one so we could pay bills and eat. And now it was he who called and opened the door to a real job working on a motion picture, luring me back out to the West Coast.

I *could* blame him, but it was me. I knew what I was getting myself into, and yet I marched along - young, immature, inexperienced as well as thrilled, enthusiastic, and full of youthful strength and stamina. Casting my mature vision backward, I can see now how foolhardy it all was; however,

I wanted it.

There were some logistics that had to be worked out. Mark wasn't going to pay for my transportation or living arrangements. If I could figure that out, I had a job. By then, my old friend/ex-roommate, Steve Burg, had forsaken living with Mark and was in his own small apartment in Alhambra, California. He said that if I could figure out how to sleep on the floor without getting in the way, I could stay with him, rent free. I would have no car, but only a mile and a half separated Steve's apartment from Mark's studio in South Pasadena. I could walk that.

So all that was left was to say goodbye to Tracy and my family, again, and fly out to Los Angeles.

I was greeted at the airport by Mark Shostrom and Bart Mixon. Bart was a burgeoning makeup effects artist out of Houston, Texas who had moved out to Los Angeles. The three of us went to a diner on Fair Oaks Avenue in South Pasadena (I can't recall the name but it is where Shakers restaurant stands today).

We had dinner and although I cannot repeat one thing that was said at the table, I do remember this: I hadn't laughed that hard in my life. Mark was nothing if not entertaining and disrespectful which, for a twenty-two year-old like myself was hilarious. Sometime during dinner, Mark discussed the broad strokes of the job with us. The project was titled *Ghost Soldiers* and was being produced by Sandy Howard productions (the same folks who had produced *Deadly Force*).

The film dealt with a small battalion of army recruits who have to defend themselves against reanimated Civil War soldiers - Confederate Rebels, to be accurate. Without concerning myself with the logistics of the story, what was intriguing was that not only would we be designing and executing the various deaths of the recruits, but we'd be making the Ghost Soldiers themselves. However, we would be joined by one more person, Ed Ferrell, who had worked on location with Mark in North Carolina on a film called *The Mutilator*.

Mark hadn't changed his strategy at all. He looked to Dick Smith's effects on *The Hunger* as an aesthetic guide-

The core crew of The Supernaturals: Bart Mixon, Ed Ferrell, Shannon Shea, and our leader, Mark Shostrom

line for what we were attempting to accomplish. After dinner, we drove around the block, down Mission Street to Mark's studio. Located on the second floor, above a series of retail shops, Mark's studio consisted of two "rooms" that were connected by a door. It was obvious that at one time in the past, this had been some sort of hotel. There was only one bathroom on the floor and it served everyone who rented space there. On one side of Mark was a commercial illustrator (I wish I could remember his name) and on the other side was a counselor (a marriage/family counselor, I believe). Then there were a couple of units that were rented out as living facilities, including a large unit that Mark and his girlfriend, Shan, were sharing down the hall. I waste your time with all of this detail in order for you to fully appreciate the tale I'm going to spin for you now.

Not only had Mark not changed his aesthetic influences, he had not changed his work habits. Mark wanted to start work "some time in the morning" and work until "we finished some time that night." So there would be no established hours and we would most probably be working six day weeks. For this, my payment would be $200 a week.

Steve Burg arrived at the studio, said hello to Mark, took a quick tour, then drove me back to his apartment. It was truly three rooms above a garage in the back of a main residence off of Fremont street. The main room was where Steve slept and lived, basically. Like our dorm room, the place was filled with books, spaceship models and bric a brac. Next to

A cartoon drawn by Mark illustrating how much mold work we were doing at the beginning of the project. Ghostbusters had just swept the nation, hence the reference.

this was a very small kitchen. I could see that this served more as a painting studio than an eating facility. Finally there was a very small bathroom with a sink, shower, and toilet.

He asked how I planned to sleep and I produced a long, thin drawstring pouch I had packed with me. Inside of it was a camper's cot. Basically canvas suspended between interlocking metal frame pieces. The idea was that I'd put it together at night, sleep on it, then put it away before I left for work, preventing any precious space from being wasted. And so the adventure began. But first, there was one last ceremony that needed to be performed before Steve and I would call it a night and prepare for the following work day. We walked half a block to Yum Yum Doughnuts and ate apple fritters. Then, the day could officially end.

Unlike me, Steve was working for a fairly regimented visual effects house, VCE, which was run by CalArts alumnus Peter Kuran. Steve had to drive from Alhambra to Hollywood in the morning traffic and would get home sometime after 8:00 pm most days. The apartment was so small that I couldn't help waking up when Steve did. I made coffee, took a shower, got dressed and began the nearly two mile walk to Mark's studio.

By the time I arrived, Mark, Bart, and Ed Ferrell were already there.

Ed was a weird dude. Not, Norman Bates-creepy-weird, but more like if you took Jeff Bridges' depiction of

"The Dude" from *The Big Leb-owski* and raised him in the Deep South. He didn't have the long-hair, hippy mental-ity as much as he just didn't seem like the kind of person who wanted to work in mov-ies. He was tall, stocky, spoke with a Southern lilt and was fairly unflappable. He credit-ed this to having spent most of his time working on a fish-ing boat outside of Wilm-ington, North Carolina. If he could handle the Atlan-tic Ocean and working on a

A stack of arm casts we did on our-selves while waiting for actors to be-come available. We fabricated gloves on these.

fishing boat, then making rubber monsters for movies would be much easier in comparison. However, I think the most significant thing Ed Ferrell did for the project was to give Mark Shostrom a nickname, and not just any nickname. This nickname would follow Mark for the rest of his career; Ed referred to Mark as "Cappy" (which was short for "Captain" - In Ed's eyes, Mark was the Captain of the ship).

At first, Mark didn't mind, but as the years went on, he did his best to shake the nickname, but it is as much a part of him as his flesh and his skeleton. Mark *is* the Cappy.

However, east along Mission Street was a liquor store Mark frequented called, "Cappy's World of Liquor." It was not unusual for me to be asked to make a run to the liquor store for Mark since I was technically the youngest with the least amount of experience. The request would sound something like this -

The head casts of the zombie actors sit on a table in the South Pasadena sun.

Mark: "Little guuuuyyy? Little guuuuyyyyy? Time to go buy the Cappy his beer and cigarettes." Ten bucks would be pushed into my hand and I'd walk down the street to buy Mark's life-blood. He lived on beer and cigarettes. The third component of the "Cappy-Diet" was coffee. Mark would generally wake up around ten or eleven o'clock in the morning, drink coffee and smoke cigarettes until roughly four or five in the evening, then switch to beer, getting more and more drunk as the night progressed until he passed out in the wee hours of the morning, only to repeat the process the next day–every day.

But amidst all of this "fun" there was work to be done.

Mark had already sculpted an impressive maquette of a Ghost Soldier using a human skeleton model kit as the base. He then sculpted rotted flesh and draped tattered cloth onto the body which he had painted with acrylic paints. Last, but not least, he glued wispy hair on its head.

My first "publicity photo" (jk). Highly influenced by photos I had seen of Rob Bottin.

While actors playing cadets and zombies were being scheduled for life casting, Mark had me do a few production illustrations. One was of a cadet being attacked by the Ghost Soldiers; the other was of the demise of the mysterious female lead character, Melanie. At the end of the film it was revealed that Melanie was not only over 100 years old, but that she was being kept "young" by her son who was possessed with supernatural powers - the same power that reanimated the Ghost Soldiers! I did a piece of artwork that "aped" Dick's demise of actress Catherine Deneuve from *The Hunger*.

Knowing that we would need zombie gloves that would run from the fingertips to the elbow, we chose to cast our own arms instead of waiting for actors to become available. Mark hired Lisa Jensen to not only costume the zombies, but to sew spandex gloves that served as the foundations for us to construct the ghost soldier arms. I don't know how Mark met Lisa, but she was infinitely patient with us all and very enthusiastic and committed to dressing the Ghost Soldiers as they were finished. But we're getting ahead of ourselves.

Two cadet actors arrived first for life casting. The first was Bobby Di Cicco who was the romantic male lead in *1941*. We cast his head for a bullet hit wound that needed to be sculpted, molded, and cast in elvacite plastic. Next was actress Anne Bancroft's son Bradford Bancroft. Bradford was scheduled to be stabbed in the stomach with a Ghost Soldiers' exposed, shattered radius and ulna forearm bones. We cast his chest to run a piece that could be stabbed in extreme closeup. Shortly after, the extra-actors playing the Ghost Soldiers began arriving.

This was my first lesson in the "truth" of Hollywood. The Casting Director, working from Mark's instruction, began sending thin, elderly actors to play the Ghost Soldiers. I'm not being age-ist here; however, I knew what

these performers would be asked to do would not be "acting" as much as it would be sweating inside of a latex body glove for hours at a time. However, these folks wanted the job! No one was holding a gun to their temples; they actually were excited

Bart Mixon makes a few final touches before he molds his "Ghost Soldier."

by the idea of dressing up like zombies and stumbling around in the dark! Actors!

After-life casting the first two, the Casting Director caught on and sent us younger, thin performers. Although we did head casts on all of them, we body cast three, one of whom was the only female performer to be cast. Plaster was poured into arm and head casts, but for the body casts, we used expanding rigid polyurethane foam.

Now for those of you who have no clue what expanding polyurethane foam is, give me a minute to explain. The best, quickest example I can provide is the spray insulation sold in a can at hardware stores. This, basically, is what is known in the effects industry as "rigid foam." I don't know this for certain, but I would guess that since this spray insulation is sold over-the-counter at hardware stores there are strict levels of consumer toxicity that are monitored to prevent litigation. The foam is produced as two chemicals (an "A" and a "B" component) are mixed at manufacturer recommended ratios. The chemicals begin to foam, expand, and then set rapidly. Simple, right? Well, not quite.

As the chemicals begin to foam, they release toxic gasses. This was described to me as an isocyanate gas). We did our best to only pour the chemicals outside in the alley between the buildings, but, as you can imagine, I spent a lot of time mixing, pouring and watching to make sure that the frail plaster bandage body molds filled completely because there would be no second chance.

The next day when I woke up, I felt strange. I went into Steve's bathroom and caught my reflection in the mirror. I noticed patchy, red discolorations on my face. I didn't make the immediate connection and returned to Mark's studio.

Upon seeing me, Mark explained that I must be worried, and that occasionally he fell victim to "worry rash." I thought nothing of it and joined Bart and Ed back in the alley to cover the foam bodies with a layer of polyester resin to fill in the open foam cells and strengthen the casts.

At some point, Bart asked me what was wrong with my face. I told him that Mark diagnosed it as a worry rash. By the gestures and noises that Bart offered, I sensed he did not agree with Mark's observation. Ed took a closer look and suggested that I might be allergic to something.

I had never been allergic to anything in my life, from ragweed pollen to bee stings to penicillin. What had caused this reaction? It was about then that Bart mentioned the cyanide-based gas in the foam. I stopped and went back inside to speak with Mark. My face had gone from bad to worse. Now tiny pustules began developing and the patches began to intensify.

"You must *really* be worried about something!" Mark said. I was upset, as you can imagine. I told him that I was sure that I was allergic to the foaming urethane and that I didn't want to pour it anymore. It took a little fighting, after all, pouring polyfoam was a very typical task given to novices but I was able to convince him to at least give me a break until my face healed.

However, it was to get *much* worse before it got better. My face had swollen on one side and amber fluid seeped from the patches. It was disgusting. Since there really was no mature mind amongst us and I feared having to tell my parents that I had been "injured" on the job so soon after starting it, I went to the local pharmacy and tried different topical ointments until one seemed to work and the healing began albeit very slowly.

Shortly thereafter, all of the head forms were poured, the body forms were mounted on stands, and sculpting could begin. It became clear that we would not be able to build our Ghost Soldiers the way Dick Smith and Carl Fullerton had painstakingly made the living mummies for *The Hunger*. Instead, ours would be latex slip masks, bodies built up with latex bone pieces glued to a spandex body suit then dressed with foam latex (more on that later). The hands would be fabricated directly out of foam latex as well.

While Bart and Mark grabbed head forms to begin sculpting, Ed molded a full-sized plastic skeleton arm, poured up a urethane plastic cast, cut it apart and hinged it to produce a mechanical skeletal arm and hand. I was given the task of sculpting "rib forms" on one of the bod-

Holding a beer, calamine lotion smeared on my allergic reaction, I stop for yet another photo while sculpting the only zombie I did for the show.

The sculptures lined up ready for molding!

ies.

"It doesn't have to be accurate" Mark explained, "It just has to have the form that we can build up on."

The creative part of the work finally commenced. I was sculpting away one night, it had to be around ten, when I heard a loud BANG from the room where most of the mold work was being done. I was wearing my head-phones (and yes, listening to a cassette tape, if you must know) and had just put them back on when -BANG- the sound rang out again. Then suddenly, BANG....BANG, BANG....BANG!

I couldn't imagine what was happening but I noticed that no one was in the room with me. I left my sculpture and walked into the room to see Mark, who was wearing a paper dust mask on the top of his head like a beanie. In the elastic of the mask on either side of his head were two long, flowing bunches of hemp. Imagine thin, tangled, dry hay we normally used as filler for stone molds to add thickness and strength to the plaster. He looked like a demented witch-doctor. On the opposite side of the room, he had posted one of the Ghost Soldier performer's head shots to the door and was throwing hand fulls of water-based clay at the photo. BANG! Bart and Ed, sans Mark's get up, had joined him, gleefully throwing clay and watching it flatten and stick to the wall.

I can't imagine how anyone else in the building put up with the noise. But that was just the beginning.

One night, a water fight broke out. It started with everyone firing spritzer bottles at each other and degenerated into filling and throwing *buckets* of water on each other. I guarantee that this activity most probably started around midnight and went on until one in the morning. The next day, the landlord, Randy, came to the studio concerned that there was a broken water pipe somewhere. The water had seeped through the wooden floor into the commercial space below and had ruined a $300 hand-made wool sweater and to make matters worse, the shop and sweater belonged to Randy's wife.

He poked around making sure that all of the plumbing was sound and left the studio and a giggling bunch of idiots. Oh, but my friends, that was just the beginning and this was only my first show!

I could tell the story of one of Mark's cats, escaping from his apartment at two o'clock in the morning and he and the crew chasing it into a vacant unit that Randy used as storage. Mark grabbed a broom and was trying to shoo the cat out from behind some boxes, got frustrated and swung the broom in a wide arc, shattering one of the windows. He immediately had us run downstairs, sweep up the glass, bring it inside, and dress it on the floor like it was an act of random vandalism.

All of this was balanced with the outbursts of Mark's famous hair-trigger temper. We would watch him screw 200 watt bulbs into 60 watt clamp-light fixtures only to have the bulbs burn out immediately. In determined frustration, he kept trying every bulb in the package burning them out until he picked up the light fixtures and threw them out of the door, smashing them against the opposite wall in the hallway. I had seen these fits *many* times and they were never easy to deal with. If we were lucky and they happened around dinner time, the rest of us would leave and let Mark sit and spin.

My "Ghost Soldier." The thought was that it would be a "base" that cotton and latex, etc. could be built up on to make it into different looks. We never did it. The skull was so big it became cartoonish!

When we returned, he always acted hurt, like we had betrayed him for not wanting to sit and witness his extreme behavior.

128

I was able to sculpt one of the Ghost Soldier masks. The rest had been divided between Mark and Bart, but I had trouble with the concept and ended up sculpting something that looked like "Skeletor" from the "He-Man" toy line. In contrast to Mark's excellent sculptures, it was fairly embarrassing.

When people ask me the best way to learn Makeup Effects, I tell them the best way is to learn on the job. I learned so much working on *Ghost Soldiers* as I picked up skills, not only from Mark but from Bart and Ed as well. Taking classes is a close second, but nothing beats learning right on the job!

Mark left it to me to paint most of the suits and gloves. I painted a few of the masks; however, Bart and Mark set aside a couple of the better masks that they wanted to paint for themselves. Any gaps between gloves and body suit, or masks and body suit were camouflaged either with Lisa's costume pieces, or by moss and dirt spray-glued over the trouble spots.

What do you do when you don't have a shop oven to vulcanize foam latex? You build one out of plywood.

Foam-latex built up suits bake in the make-shift oven.

The film was directed by Armand Mastroianni, who had built a reputation for himself with the film *He Knows*

You're Alone, which did well with horror audiences during the "Slasher" years of the early 1980s. Mark sent him photos and would have conversations with him on the phone, but I don't recall Armand ever stopping by the shop to check our status. I know I wasn't introduced

I ended up painting most of the suits with pax-paint and sponges.

As suits and masks were painted, they were paired prior to finishing.

to him until we began shooting on location in Malibu Canyon.

I had never worked on a movie set before. As a child, my father, my siblings and I were guests to the set of the musical *Tom Sawyer* as part of a press junket, so I was a bit familiar with the look and the trappings of a film set but working on one was a completely different experience. It reminded me of being dropped onto a battlefield with no basic training beyond what could be read out of a manual. I knew my job and what I had to do, but had no idea how my job would affect anyone else.

The other three had set experience, but so much of what I did was hang back, wait to be told what to do, then rush in and do it. If that wasn't daunting enough, all of the shooting took place at night, which meant we'd arrive in the late afternoon and come home in the early morning as the sun came up.

I got to experience L.A. traffic, but in reverse. As we drove out west from South Pasadena to Malibu we joined commuters going home from work, and as we drove back east, we sat in morning traffic as everyone else was rushing to work. Thank God Mark was exhausted on the way back or his road rage would have been epic.

Mark wears a "Ghost Soldier" suit at the studio complete with wardrobe made by Lisa Jennsen.

I don't recall how many nights we were on set. I know it was at least one week but most probably two. The old adage "hurry up and wait" has been proven on movie sets for decades and much of our time was spent sitting in a trailer with the Ghost Soldier performers partially dressed in their costumes, waiting for someone from production to tell us to prepare one, two, or all of them for a shot.

We wrapped *Ghost Soldiers* (which became *The Supernaturals*) in early November of '84.

By this time, James Cummins had returned from location in Spain, where he had been working on a movie entitled *The Falling* (which was eventually released as *Alien Predator* for obvious reasons). We had lunch together and he told me that now that I had real film experience, he would hire me on his next project.

Outwardly, I was very gracious and thankful. Inwardly I thought to myself: Real Film Experience?! Are you

kidding?! I had to run down to the bank to cash my checks before they bounced on the days when Mark remembered to pay me. On one check, Mark had written "Two hundred big ones" rather than "dollars." What I had experienced could hardly be described as a "film" experience, as it was bedlam. However if this was the initiation I required to be considered a "professional," then so be it.

A zombie sketch I did after the shoot. I was inspired!

CHAPTER 16

House (aka House- Ding, Dong, You're Dead)

...every step he took was a step up...
The Hudsucker Proxy

I had returned to New Orleans for the holidays since there was no point living on Steve Burg's floor or hanging around with Mark Shostrom waiting for the next project. James Cummins and his friend Rick Brophy had driven me to the airport and on the way there, James said that he was talking to some people about a new project that would start early in 1985. He advised that I shouldn't settle down when I returned home.

Spending the holidays with my family after working on my first motion picture was a bit like returning from a successful battle - I suppose in some way it was. I answered a million questions over turkey dinners and at family gatherings, but James' advice sat like an imp on my shoulder.

James answered one of the biggest questions I was wrestling with: How could I leave Tracy again? His suggestion was for her to come out with me; he'd give her a job on *House* to help start us off. She agreed; her family opposed, and we left.

The details are sketchy, but I do recall getting on a plane in New Orleans and getting off at LAX in Los Angeles and being met by James Cummins and his roommate, Rick Brophy. James was tall with a thick, round head of brown hair; Rick was shorter, stockier, and a bit older than James. I have no details how they met, but my understanding was the Rick was a struggling actor. He was taking lessons from character actor Clu Gallagher at the time and he was going to "produce" projects for James and would be acting as a business administrator for the creature effects of *House*.

When we arrived at their one-story home in Glendale, California, it was immediately evident that this was going to have to be a very short-term situation. There were two bedrooms and one bathroom but one of the bedrooms had been converted into a studio? Gym-type thing? There was a bed in there that was James', I guess, but James slept on a cot in the same room with Rick. We were shown a pull-out sofa bed where we would sleep in the living room. It didn't occur to me at the time (I know, I know, I know) that James and Rick were gay. If they had just come out and said it to Tracy and me, then I believe

things would have been *much* easier for all of us, but as it was they were "just friends."

Life with James and Rick was strange for other reasons. James was adamantly anti-television, which I completely under-

Tracy Fletcher and James Cummins at his Glendale home, shortly after Tracy and I had moved from New Orleans.

stand, so he liked to fill his time doing more creative things. There was a piano in one of the rooms and James would ask Tracy to play for him while they both sang. Other times, James would play his guitar and sing folksy type music; James Taylor and Linda Ronstadt were favorites of his. The reason we had this time to play out this weird sleep-over camp experience was that *House* had been delayed, and for how long was unclear.

James had showed us several of his production designs that had won him the contract. James' style was primarily watercolor paintings that had been augmented with pencil - a technique he taught me that I still enjoy from time to time. They all reflected his unique ropey-form sensibilities. He had painted concept designs of the demon-children, the witch, the war demon, and finally the zombie version of *Big Ben*, a Viet Nam soldier who comes back from the dead to torment the protagonist of the film. At this point in his career, James was truly an up-and-coming force in makeup effects and I had no idea that *House* was a prized job that several established makeup effects studios had been pursuing.

After a few weeks, James received a start date when a portion of his budget would be delivered so that the job could commence. However, it was during the doldrums that Tracy and I began to meet James' collaborators (from *Strange Invaders*) like mechanical designer, Bill Sturgeon, of whom I was aware, because of his previous association with Rick Baker, and sculptor, Brian Wade.

Starting the project meant doing a few things: a studio space had to be secured, materials and supplies had to be purchased, and a crew had to be hired. For the better part of a year and prior to moving into Glendale, James had worked in Marin County, California for makeup effects artist Chris Walas on the film *Enemy Mine* so James invited a few of his former co-workers to come down to Los Angeles to work on *House*. It didn't take long for the word to get out that an effects movie was seeking a crew and Rick Brophy began receiving calls and setting up portfolio interviews for prospective candidates at the house.

It was very strange that James should invite me to sit in on many of the interviews. I wasn't a supervisor (for sure!) and I certainly didn't command the level of talent that many of the artists had as they brought their portfolios to James' house for review. But came they did, and it was interesting to get that perspective of the portfolio interview process at this early stage of my career.

I don't know if James had a strategy in mind when he began interviewing people. It seemed that at first, artists like Earl Ellis showed up with their portfolios. It was clear that James was searching for two things. He wanted individuals who had varied/exemplary talent and personalities that he could tolerate. Believe it or not, I can recall just about every single interview that was conducted. For the sake of brevity, I'll only describe one that would have an affect on my career and story.

One rainy afternoon, two gentlemen from Northern California, both with their portfolios appeared seeking employment on *House*. The first was Tony McVey, a sculptor whom had proven himself by working with stop-motion luminary, Ray Harryhausen. In addition to his portfolio, which was exciting because of the nature of his work, he had brought along a carpet bag. After he turned the last page of his portfolio, he reached into the carpet bag and presented two stop-motion puppets: A Tyrannosaurus Rex, and a traditional Medieval Dragon (neck and head only). My heart stopped. I had never held a stop-motion puppet in my hands and this opportunity transcended the interview that was being conducted.

Tony informed us that only the extremities (head, hands, feet) had been sculpted/molded/cast and everything else was built up: meaning that using upholstery foam and thin sheets of latex cast in a flat plaster mold of reptilian scales, he carefully built up the muscle forms then covered them with the latex skin. He had skillfully gathered the thin, scale-y, latex skin in natural wrinkles where they would occur which only added to the realism of the piece. It was impressive to be sure. I hoped that I would have the opportunity to work with Tony because it would have been my plan to pester him for information constantly, but it was not to be. Tony's pay rate was outside of what James could afford, so Tony would be spared my incessant questioning for the next ten weeks of his life; he was safe.

The second gentleman was Richard Snell. I don't know what happened during that interview, perhaps having just been turned down by Tony McVey left a bad taste in James' mouth, but whatever the reason, James was not responding well to Richard. I didn't get it at all. Richard's portfolio featured clean sculptures, some light mechanics, skillfully painted maquettes. He even had an over-sized mechanical dragonfly for which he had done all of the sculpture/molding/casting painting as well as the mechanical design and construction. James was unimpressed by any of it, and was not disguising that fact.

Richard, unfazed by James' reactions, continued.

Reaching into a paper bag he had brought with him, Richard snapped a pair of beautiful fangs he had made into his mouth. Richard revealed that his grandfather was a dentist and had taught him how to make exquisite custom teeth that were, by casual observation, better than any fangs/teeth I had ever seen. James sat, unmoved.

Richard was not to be ignored and went into what I call "full-salesman mode." After James became dismissive of Richard's sculpting, mechanical, and dental skills, Richard reached back into the bag and handed a wig to James. Richard went on to say that he was a "wig master" having constructed custom furnished wigs to many important clients including Dolly Parton. James held the wig in his hand, examined the tiny knots that held the individual hairs into the delicate netting, and handed it back to Richard. James had been swayed a bit, but not quite enough to bite.

However, Richard wasn't done, not by a long-shot. He reached into his bag and produced a small, black case. He opened it and produced something that was unheard of at that point: custom painted, opaque soft contact lenses.

To put this in proper context, you have to understand that before that time, custom contact lenses were predominately made by one company in Los Angeles under the supervision of Dr. Morton Greenspoon. They were made of hard plastic, hand-painted and sealed with a thin layer of acrylic. They were expensive to make and painful to put in an actor's eyes.

And there sat Richard Snell, with the first comfortable alternative to the process. If there had been a game show-type board, it would have started flashing "WIN!" Richard opened a small bottle full of saline solution and "poured" an orange lens with a vertical cat eye pupil painted on it and put it into his eye. It was impressive. He then went further and put a pair of lenses into James' eyes. James went to a mirror and looked at his orange cat eyes and smiled. Richard was hired on the spot.

As Tony and Richard left, Rick Brophy asked James why he had hired Richard. James said that the soft-contact lenses alone were reason enough, but Richard did have skills that were needed for the project, even if James didn't like him. It never got better between James and Richard.

Within a couple of weeks, James and Rick had rented a shop space. It was located at what was called the "Golden Mall" in Burbank, the home to struggling boutique shops, questionable eateries and liquor stores before the grand re-gentrification of the 1990s. Homeless people shuffled around like zombies from a George Romero movie in contrast to the nearly non-existent foot traffic from shoppers.

The space itself was not rated as a manufacturing zone (which is what, technically, makeup effects studios are), which was evident by many things. First of all, it was located upstairs, over a used/collectible book shop. Next, most of the floors were carpeted. At the top of the stairs was a large landing that must have been designed as a reception or waiting area for whatever business *should* have been conducted. There was one corridor that ran the width of the building from front to back. On either side were rooms with wood paneling that had probably been used for offices. James assigned room-functions (sculpting, mold-making, etc) and then assigned people to these rooms.

Since the space was empty, the first order of business was building tables.

The tables, made primarily of 4' x 8' plywood on top of a 2"x4" wood frame were designed by Larry Odien who had blown us all away with an excellent portfolio that demonstrated unparalleled skill in both the art and mechanical departments. A native Californian and an ex-surfer, Larry was easy-going, enthusiastic, and an effective and frequent problem-solver. Under Larry's direction, the rest of us cut wood, drilled holes and bolted (rather than using screws or nails) the heavy-duty tables that would be burdened with large sculptures and even larger molds.

Once all of the tables had been put into place and a small wooden foam oven was built, we were all assigned duties and rooms and the work began in earnest.

While we waited for actors to be cast for the demon children, the witch and the zombie-version of *Big Ben,* whose living incarnation would be portrayed by actor Richard Moll, we began working on things that didn't necessarily need access to the actors in order to begin. Steve Burg, Howard "Howie" Weed, Brent Baker, Bill Sturgeon and I began sculpting creature gloves for a scene where the protagonist, Roger Cobb (played by William Katt) would be threatened by primarily unseen creatures on the other side of a medicine cabinet.

After a couple of days of casting each other's arms, we began sculpting. Meanwhile in the lobby area, Tracy and Barney Burman had been set up with a long metal armature for a tentacle that would join the medicine cabinet creatures that would attack Roger Cobb. However the most impressive of these projects was a marlin fish wall trophy that was to come to life.

Tracy works on the back-bone tentacle sculpture. She would be the first to say that she's not a sculptor.

If there was one person that I would have to shine a light on and dump praise upon during *House*, it might have to be Eric Fiedler. Where it came to that marlin, Eric was an impressive one-man band.

A shot from the set of HOUSE of the Marlin supervised by Eric Fiedler and painted by Mike Spatola.

Once he received a fiberglass marlin taxidermy form, Eric went straight to work sculpting. Within a short few days, he had the sculpture completed. He made a quick mold of the eye area then began the process of making a large resin eye that was expertly painted. He molded the sculpture in fiberglass, cored the mold (again, using fiberglass) molded the core (I could go on and on). After a beautiful and quick paint job by Mike Spatola, it looked amazing.

While Eric was fishing (get it?), and the rest of us were working on creature gloves and tentacles, the heavy-hitting sculptors, Brian Wade, Earl Ellis, and Larry Odien were working on "War Demon" parts. A visual metaphor for the horrors of the Viet Nam War, this demon ap-

A latex and polyfoam casting of a "War Demon" arm hangs on a studio door warning of what lies inside.

The "War Demon" neck sculpture by Brian Wade. Photo by Bill Sturgeon

I sculpted the "War Demon's" torso complete with skeletal hands that were supposed to be serving as ribs. All of this detail is lost in the film when you see it briefly.

peared to be made up of the faces of the dead, skeletons and weapons all jumbled together in what was loosely termed "monster stew."

James sculpted the head while Brian worked on the neck area and Larry and

Earl sculpted the thin, long arms. After I finished sculpting and molding my arm, I was put on the torso area of the War Demon.

Eventually three little people were cast to play the demon children. Actors Jerry Maren, "Little" Elizabeth Barrington, and Felix Silla arrived at the studio for head, hand and foot casting. I was given the task of sculpting Felix Silla's mask, which was exciting for me because as a

The latex "Demon Child" mask worn by Felix Silva.

Mechanical designer, Larry Odien, works on the eye mechanism for the main "Demon Child" puppet.

Larry Odien carefully glues the skin on the "Demon Child" puppet.

The completed "Demon Child" hero puppet sculpted by James Cummins, painted by Mike Spatola and wearing a wig made by Richard Snell.

huge nerd, I knew Felix had portrayed the robot "Twiki" in the television series *Buck Rogers*; one foot from stardom, as they say.

Howie Weed sculpted the mask for Jerry Maren, and Brent Baker worked on Elizabeth's mask. James sculpted a hero puppet version of a demon child which Larry Odien ended up mechanizing. Meanwhile, exiled to a small room working on his own, Richard Snell worked on a demon child puppet in a spitting water expression that (in my humble opinion) looked great. But I can still recall James being hyper-critical of it and then watching Richard, dejected, carrying the sculpture back down the hall

Howie Weed enthusiastically makes a mold.

Mike Spatola's paint station. "Demon Children" masks are being painted while the witch suit is being completed prior to painting in the background. A witch leg is on the bench having its paint design finalized. Photo by Bill Sturgeon

A bench in the mechanical shop. The hero-mechanical witch head wearing its test skin has the animatronics tested prior to final "skinning." Photo by Bill Sturgeon

A pair of witch suits (one dressed for a post-decapitation) sit in the painting room. The spitting "Demon Child" puppet sculpted by Richard Snell is seamed and ready for paint in the foreground.

to his room to continue working on it.

A Venice Beach street performer named Peter Pitofsky ("Just remember, Pit of sky!" he would say) was cast to portray the witch. We did head, arm, body, and foot

Hero skins of "Big Ben" and the Witch are completed and ready to be glued on to their mechanical masks.

casts of him as well as director Steve Miner's friend, Curt Wilmont, who was cast as the undead Big Ben (fans of the movie are sometimes shocked to learn that it wasn't Richard Moll in the monster suit!).

Now with multiple body, head, and arm casts being produced left and right, *House* truly began cranking along. As pieces were finished, many of them were painted by the very talented Michael Spatola, a veteran of Makeup Effects Lab in Van Nuys. His ease and talent matched his speed and it never ceased to amaze me how quickly he could paint something of quality without the final product looking labored or messy.

James eventually stopped sculpting because his time was spent roaming through the shop, supervising everything from sculpture, to mold-making to casting, seaming and patching, to mechanics and painting. This meant that Earl Ellis would sculpt Big Ben's head and the witch head, while Brian Wade sculpted Big Ben's chest and gloves while Brent Baker sculpted his legs. I wish I could recall who sculpted the witch parts; if I had to guess I would say Larry Odien?

Larry was given the task of mechanizing a radio-controlled dismembered witch hand. What was impressive was that he fabricated a mechanical finger joint, molded it and poured multiple copies in urethane resin in order to assemble the mechanism, while making it lightweight!

It would be wonderful to say that everything proceeded easily until we needed to go to set, however, once Steve Frakes, Barney Burman, and Brent Armstrong molded the six foot-long body of the War Demon and then began to run latex rubber, soft urethane foam and fiberglass

Brent Baker and Steve Frakes prepare to open the 6 piece cement mold of the "War Demon's" body. The mold was so big and heavy that when we were finally kicked out of the building, it was left behind for the landlords to throw away!

Making the mold of Big Ben's chest sculpted by Brian Wade.

"King" James Cummins confers with Brent Baker, Steve Frakes, and Barney Burman over the "War Demon" mold.

The molding area of the shop (this was upstairs, mind you). On the table on the left is the flying demon being prepared to be molded, Big Ben's torso and the War Demon's neck molds have been completed (note drying cracks in the surface) and the completed, stone Marlin mold is suspended in a frame so that it could be rotated during the urethane casting process. Photo by Bill Sturgeon

Anton "Tony" Rupprecht trims the flashing off of a latex War Demon arm.

Steve Frakes gets help rigging the War Demon body section on a frame to begin painting and assembly while James Belhovek smiles in the background. (Note: the prominent figure at the front of the War Demon body was sculpted using a face cast of Richard Brophy, the shop supervisor).

Mechanic Bill Sturgeon makes adjustments on the animatronic Big Ben mask.

James Cummins and Eric Fiedler suit up Curt Wilmont in his Big Ben costume while Brent Baker looks on.

James Cummins glues the seam closed between Big Ben's foam latex mechanical mask and neck.

Curt Wilmont strikes the iconic pose of Big Ben. Artist, William Stout, would produce a publicity illustration for the film with Big Ben in this pose.

James Belhovek poses with the Flying Demon he mechanized. It was sculpted by Steve Burg.

into the six piece stone mold, it was impossible to disguise what we were doing in that office space. In short, the place began to smell of fiberglass fumes, and I believe the book store owner beneath us complained to the landlord.

We were forced to make a hasty exit. With no possibility of renting an industrial space, we retreated to James and Rick's backyard to complete the project.

Having saved some money from our dual incomes, Tracy and I were able to move into a small one-bedroom apartment in neighboring Eagle Rock; however, with no car, we both had to take public transportation, which in Los Angeles added at least an hour to any commute.

The bus dropped us off a few blocks from James' house and Tracy and I would walk to his backyard, where plywood sheets set on top of saw horses served as tables. Mike Spatola and Steve Burg painted witch pieces in the shade of the trees while James Belohovek and Anton Rupprecht completed

James Cummins sitting in my first Los Angeles apartment holding a house-warming gift.

a flying demon puppet complete with flapping bat wings.

We were only in the back yard a few days before we began to go to set, and I was lucky enough to be included with the set crew. Having only been on an outdoor location for *The Supernaturals* I had no idea what working on a set would be like.

I'm not sure with whom I drove during the first days. My guess is it was that James initially drove to Raleigh Studios in Hollywood. Inside a sound stage the production crew had built a very authentic interior of a house (to match the actual house located in Northern California). As wasteful as it might seem, building such an ambitious set rather than just shooting in a practical location is a very wise move.

On a location there are logistical problems such as parking, bathrooms, staging (preparation) areas for the different departments, and *noise*. In addition, no matter how careful and well-meaning a film crew is, their presence and efforts tend to be a bit destructive. Nothing can

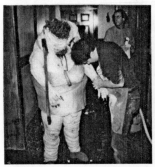

On set, suiting up The Witch, post-decapitation. I think Brent Baker was in the suit at this point. I played the Witch hand that gets flushed down the toilet.

Tracy Fletcher and I on the stairs of the HOUSE set.

Howie Weed puppeteers the Demon Child puppet.

Brent Baker (to the extreme left) sits patiently as Bill Sturgeon makes some last minute adjustments to the War Demon puppet on its shooting day. Bill had not slept the night before, poor guy.

The War Demon is tested to make sure it fits through the door!

Another photo of this ambitious puppet.

trash a location faster than a film crew and production frequently is left holding the bill to restore, and in some cases, improve, the location's appearance. Lastly, having a set means that some of the room walls are "wild" meaning that they can be removed so that the camera and crew can film into a room from a distance so that more of the room can be seen within the frame. To illustrate this, next time you are in a small room, take out your camera and stand against a wall and see how much of the room you can fit into the frame without panning it back and forth and you'll understand the advantage of removing a wall and moving the camera backward.

Obviously, Eric Fiedler's fish had to be installed right away because not only was it a puppet, it was set dressing and had to be established prior to coming to life and being shot with a shotgun. However, the first thing I recall shooting were the monster arms and tentacle. A group of us wearing the monster gloves stood on a wooden platform outside of the stage while actor, William Katt, opened the medicine cabinet door in the bathroom set. As soon as the door opened we reached through and began grabbing at him. Since there was no mechanism in the tentacle, once we had a hold of his arm with the monster arms, the rubber tentacle was placed around Katt's arm and filmed being pulled off. Then the film was printed in reverse so that it appeared that the tentacle was coming out of the cabinet and wrapping around his arm.

Again, in the interest of brevity (because I could probably write a small book just about the shooting of *House*), I'll limit my stories to one of the more interesting moments which had to do with the filming of Big Ben.

For those of you who are new to *House*, the character Big Ben was a soldier who had been captured, tortured and killed in the Viet Nam war. He returned from the grave as a living corpse bent on revenge to menace protagonist Roger Cobb. Since the War Demon was

Me, on set, with director Steve Miner (with the folded paper in this back pocket) and James Cummins on the first day we shot with Big Ben.

still under construction in James' back yard, I was left to supervise putting actor Curt Wilmont into the Big Ben costume, with the help of Anton "Tony" Rupprecht and Lauren Vogt.

This was a very educational experience.

Having no car meant that Tony would pick me up on his motorcycle outside my apartment in Eagle Rock. Together we would ride into Hollywood and to the set. A small area was cordoned off on the stage for us to dress Curt, rather than a traditional dressing room or makeup room.

Curt Wilmont was not an actor, nor was he a suit performer. Rumor had it that he was the tennis pro at director Steve Miner's tennis club; however, it was understandable why Curt had been offered the role. He must have stood at least six feet-five inches tall, and was thin and lean-muscled. However, Curt learned quickly that playing a monster in a movie was not just work. It was hard, uncomfortable, and in some ways thankless.

The suit consisted of foam-latex pants/legs that covered him from foot to upper thigh, a torso that went from his belly to his upper shoulders, a foam-latex neck piece, gloves, and a radio controlled mask that was glued around one of his eyes. He wore one of Richard Snell's milky white contact lenses. On top of all of this, he wore shredded Army fatigues and helmet; for a novice, it was challenging.

Like many actors, Curt wanted to "be seen" on set as much as possible which translated into not wanting to wear the uncomfortable mask until the very last minute. This often resulted in a very impatient production crew.

After his first day in the suit, when we removed the mask, Curt complained about the mask's custom-made fiberglass under-skull digging into the side of his nose.

Using a motor-tool grinder, Tony noted the area that was causing the discomfort and ground away at the fiberglass until it was in danger of losing its structural integrity. Lauren then lined the area with a layer of moleskin padding. The next morning, though, when we tried to put Curt into the mask, he couldn't tolerate the pain for longer than a few minutes, and it was very clear that there was an area on the side of his nose that was being rubbed raw by the under-skull but at this point, there was little we could do about it.

Thinking quickly, Tony excused himself and returned with a small cup of what appeared to be water. He told Curt that it was a "pain-killer" given to him by the set medic. He applied the liquid to the side of Curt's nose with a cotton-tipped applicator and it seemed to work. Curt could get into the mask and perform with little to no complaining.

And so it was for the next few days that Tony would go to the medic, come back with a cup and a new ritual was born in order for Curt to get into the mask. It all worked smoothly until the last day.

We only had a shot or two left of Curt wearing the mask and were about to put him in the head when Curt stopped us and asked us for the pain-killer before we started. Tony stalled and tried to talk Curt into wearing the mask, but Curt felt that it wasn't going to happen without the liquid salve. Tony grabbed me by the arm and pulled me aside.

"We have to convince him to put the mask on," Tony said to me.

"Why don't you just go to the medic and get some more pain killer?" I asked.

Tony leaned in and whispered in my ear, "I didn't get that from the medic and I'm all out of coke (cocaine)."

I was stunned. "WHAT!" I whisper-hissed into his ear. "You've been giving this guy coke every day for the past 4 days?! Are you insane?!" Tony just shrugged and said that it was the only way he could think of to get Curt to put on the mask.

I recall sending Tony to just get a cupful of plain water and pantomime the ritual. It was effective for a while, but I recall during the last shot, Curt turning to Tony on set and saying out loud, "I don't think this is the same stuff because my nose is starting to hurt again." Fortunately, it was the last shot before he was wrapped.

The primary Big Ben on-set team: Anton Rupprecht, Loren Vogt, and yours truly.

A little part of me would die if I learned that Curt Wilmont's life had spiraled down into cocaine addiction after working with him on *House*.

CHAPTER 17

Contrast – My Makeup Effects Lab Days

It ain't what you know, it's who you know in this business.
Long-standing Hollywood philosophy

For the first time in my life I found myself jobless after a gig. However, I was still in Los Angeles, and not alone. Tracy, too, was unemployed and we were getting our first lesson in being "grown up." She took a job in downtown Glendale at Carl Fischer Music, which was more suited to her interests since she was studying to be a classical vocalist. I, on the other hand, had no idea what the next move was. But I quickly discovered that old Hollywood adage "It isn't what you know, it's who you know" was the modus operandi of motion picture employment.

I received a call from Mike Spatola who asked me if I was interested in doing some work at Makeup Effects Lab on the remake of Invaders from Mars. Even if I could have afforded the luxury of choosing my next job, I would have RUN to work on *Invaders from Mars* since it was the remake of one of my favorite childhood sci-fi adventure movies.

The plot, in a nutshell, is that a little boy witnesses the landing of an alien spacecraft beyond his backyard. As adults (including his parents) go to investigate, they return as emotionless entities controlled by the Martian Supreme Intelligence.

The next day, I hopped on the series of buses that would carry me from Eagle Rock, through Glendale, then Burbank, finally dropping me off in Van Nuys where Makeup Effects Lab was located. The building was set back from the street, flanked on either side by automotive garages of some sort. I walked up to the door and rang the bell. An office worker opened the door and I explained that I was a friend of Mike Spatola's, and was there to meet Alan Apone and Doug White, the owners of Makeup Effects lab.

Now, to be truthful, I already knew about the company and their reputation. Makeup effects artists are nothing if not gossips (it's true...don't deny it) and I had heard a lot about the work they had done on *Metalstorm: The Destruction of Jarad Syn* and *Friday the 13th Part 3 in 3D*. Not that the work was necessarily bad, it was just widely accepted that it fell short of the Rick Baker standard. However, I was a novice, I needed the work, and I was happy that Mike Spatola had stuck his neck out to get me an interview.

Mike was paged to the front desk and brought me back to meet Doug White first. Doug was plump, wore glasses over squinty eyes, and had dark brown curly hair that already had wisps of gray beginning to show. He smiled a lot and chewed habitually on a plastic straw as we spoke. I showed him my portfolio and he toured me around the shop showing me work they were doing for various projects. He was very amiable and introduced me to Alan Apone, who instantly struck me as the exact opposite of Doug.

Alan was swarthy, in good shape, and exuded an alpha-male sensibility (which was probably how he became the 'star-request' makeup artist for Don Johnson). He was polite, looked through my portfolio and then offered to take Mike Spatola and me to lunch. We drove to a nearby restaurant and sat in a large booth. That is where the real interview took place.

Alan began asking me where I had worked previously. I began telling him of my limited experience with Mark Shostrom and James Cummins. At the mention of their names, Alan literally answered, "Mark Shostrom? I fired that guy!" and then told an anecdote about a show Mark had worked on at M.E.L. and the resulting "sacking." The same was said of James Cummins. Again, Alan, just stopped short at the mention of James' name and said "James Cummins?! I fired that guy!" and recounted that story to me as well. However, it didn't stop there...

Earl Ellis, Brian Wade... nearly any name I mentioned, Alan, mouth full of French fries, would say, "I fired that guy!" and tell the story. It seemed amazing that *anyone* worked at Makeup Effects Labs. However, Alan did like Mike Spatola and Mike liked me, so I was okay with Alan and got hired.

That was a Friday afternoon; I was to start work bright and early on Monday. Now, I had been told that I had been hired to do work on *Invaders from Mars* but what I didn't understand was that bigger studios had multiple contracts going simultaneously. When I arrived, Doug White handed me a mechanical arm they had built for a film called *Boarding School* (starring David Carradine). The plastic finger joints were all broken. New plastic joints had to be installed and the urethane "skin-flex" skin repaired.

Okay.

I was not a mechanic and it felt a little outside of my wheelhouse but I was willing to give it a shot. Beneath a painted bust of the character 'Baal' from *Metalstorm*, I began grinding the plastic pieces. The noxious smell of burning cyanoacrylate (superglue) began to fill the air. Of course, being twenty-three years old, I was not wearing a dust mask or eye protection, and it wasn't long before a small piece of plastic shrapnel shot into the corner of my eye. I jumped up from my stool, bent over and starting blinking my eye hoping that the irritant would just wash out of my eye naturally, but it wasn't working. I needed eyewash.

Remembering the location of the bathroom, I rushed in to open the medicine cabinet expecting to find first aid. I swung open the mirror to discover a pornographic photo of a nude woman and nothing else. What the hell? I closed the cabinet and began splashing my eyes with water. It was my first indication of how strange Makeup Effects Labs was.

After my eye was free from the plastic piece, I asked Tony Rupprecht (who was also working there) what had happened to the mechanical arm I was repairing. Tony told me that Friday night, Doug had been playing with his new B.B. Machine gun and had shot a fluorescent light fixture down from the ceiling. It crashed down onto a work table and smashed the arm. Wonderful.

With the arm repaired, I joined the rest of the crew who were preparing for some additional photography for a film entitled Neon Maniacs. Not only were we going to have to put actors into prosthetic makeups, but there was a scene in which a '*Neon Manic*' was killed by having his flesh dissolved. To accomplish this effect, Alan Apone had purchased cases of pink and blue cotton candy. He wanted us to do a test where we would press the cotton candy on the outside of a skeleton and attempt to paint it. Then, once cosmetically sound, splash it with water to see if it melted realistically.

Another young makeup effects artist named Mike Smithson and I were assigned the task. Mike had been sculpting miniature horns for some project I was unfamiliar with but was now helping me press cotton candy on the outside of a painted plastic skeleton.

Mike Smithson was one of the first artists I had met who demonstrated a level of professionalism that would forever become an example of how makeup effects artists should present, but more importantly, *market* themselves. His business cards and portfolio pages were beautifully designed, classy, and clever. His sculptures were very clean and precise and he was friendly and accommodating.

Where I was dubious about pressing fluorescent pink and blue cotton candy onto the skeleton, Smithson saw it as more of a challenge. He did his best to form muscle shapes, and when it was done he suggested lightly spraying the outside with temporary hair color (which had an alcohol base) from a distance so that the paint would almost be dry when it hit the surface. Once based, the rest was colored with powders. It wasn't great, but it was acceptable (by M.E.L. standards).

I'm not a makeup artist, which is a fact that confuses many people. To clarify, I don't have a makeup kit with colors, powders, glues, etc. I've always been a makeup effects artist, meaning I have a sculpting/mold-making kit, an airbrush and compressor, hand tools and something similar to a makeup kit that has some colors and glues in it, but not enough that I could go to set and put characters into prosthetic makeups daily. The next day on set for *Neon Maniacs* it looked like Alan Apone, Mike Spatola, Bruce Zalava, and Doug White would be handling the makeup responsibilities where Tony Rupprecht and I would be responsible for the makeup effects stuff.

To put things in proper perspective the "Neon Maniacs" each had a distinctive personality: A Samurai, a Native American, a Caveman, an Archer, etc – well, they were like the *Village People* of motion picture slashers. All of them (except Decapitator) were covered in foam latex prosthetics. As Doug was talking to me about putting together kits to bring to set, I pointed to a discarded, poorly cast foam latex appliance that was lying in a garbage can. "Is this a rejected appliance?" I asked. Doug looked, reached into the garbage can and pulled the piece out of the trash. "No!" he replied, "who threw this away, this is a *hero* piece!"

The piece was rinsed off in the sink, squeezed out like a sponge and stacked with the other prosthetics in a cardboard box to be applied to an actor the next day.

Not quite up to Rick Baker standards.

The next day I arrived at M.E.L. very early in the morning. We packed the cars that were going down to a studio in Hollywood (Raleigh again?) with the set kits, prosthetics and cotton candy that Alan had started referring to as "spun glucose."

While the rest of the makeup artists worked on the various Neon Maniac faces, I assisted by painting the accompanying character hands. At one point, a production assistant popped into the trailer and asked if anyone was free to play Decapitator for a shot. Alan and Doug sent me.

I was fitted into a heavy costume with lightweight plastic blades on my arms that were made to look like deadly weapons. I stood holding one of the blades up, and on action swiped rapidly in front of the camera lens. We did several takes from different set ups but when I saw the film, I would be dipped if I could see even ONE shot that we did that pick up day. Ah, show business.

Finally, it came time to melt the maniac and Alan turned to me on set and asked for me to grab the spun glucose. "The cotton candy?" I feigned ignorance. "*The spun glucose!*" Alan answered. Whatever all those other guys must have done at M.E.L., it must have been pretty bad because I didn't get fired. Tony and I pressed the cotton candy all over the skeleton and attempted to paint it the way Mike Smithson had shown me, but it really didn't work that well. The water hit the cotton candy and it did melt into bright pink and blue rivulets but was it successful? Who could tell? It was a low-budget movie entitled *Neon Maniacs* for corn's sake; did it matter?

Eventually, the actors had their prosthetics removed, set kits and sticky skeletons were packed back in the cars, and I took a late bus home back to our apartment in Eagle Rock.

The next day, I was finally handed my assignment for *Invaders from Mars*. Two life casts were taken of actors who had to appear to have Martian mind-control needles stuck in the back of their necks. Before the plaster casts were to be molded, I was asked to go in and clean up the casts, removing small air bubble 'warts' on the outside of the cast, filling small bubbles and re-sculpting missing skin texture. As I was cleaning the cast, Alan interrupted with a new job.

A rock video needed some werewolf pieces, specifically a right hand and two feet. Alan pointed to molds on a shelf. His instructions were to take two molds of *Primeval* caveman feet, and an arm mold from *Toby's Gorilla* and pour them in casting latex. Then I was to go upstairs and get the four-way stretch fur-fabric and glue it to them, finally finishing them off with dental acrylic nails.

Now, where to begin? Let's break down the instructions and get to the root of it all. Re-using molds was an industry standard from the very beginning. I, being a novice, didn't understand it at the time. Once I pulled the *Primeval* foot molds off of the shelf, I began to have my doubts. *The Primevals* was a television docu-drama done in the early 70s that was an attempt to accurately depict the lives of cavemen. Tom Burman and The Burman Studio had executed all of the makeups and M.E.L. had acquired the molds during a Burman Studio garage sale.

The caveman foot molds were big... basketball players' foot big. The toes were thick and gnarled, and the sculpture ended at the ankle. The werewolf feet I was supposed to be making were to extend all the way up to the knee. I guessed I would accomplish that with the four-way stretch fur. In any case, these werewolf feet were going to be *big*!

On the other hand (pun intended) *Toby's Gorilla* was

a low-budget childrens movie about a boy and a gorilla. M.E.L. had built the suit and Larry Odien, had been a key artist and technician on the film (I recalled seeing the photos in his portfolio when he met with James Cummins). The gorilla hand sculpture was nicely done, was, believe it or not, smaller in proportion to the big feet, and extended to just below the elbow. It was useable, but looked nothing like a werewolf's hand.

But...orders were orders. I went to work.

I put the molds into the foam oven to dry them faster and began to cut the fur fabric and construct tubes that would be like socks of fur. This meant sewing. I'm no seamstress (or sempster) but I knew how to wield a needle and thread like Victor Frankenstein, and in no time crude fur legs were created, waiting for their latex feet.

By Thursday evening, I had two brown-painted feet with fur legs, and a brown-painted hand with a furry arm waiting for the nails that I would make the next day, prior to the client picking them up for a weekend shoot.

The next morning, Alan was out of the shop; he was playing golf, which I understand was a passion of his. I was constructing toe and fingernails out of clear dental acrylic when Doug showed up saying that the client was there to pick up the pieces. I still had nails to glue onto the feet, but the arm was done. Doug took it out to show the client to stall them while I finished.

I glued the last nail onto the toe and waited for Doug's return. I waited.....and waited....and waited....Something was wrong.

Suddenly Doug burst in the room holding the arm saying, "Why does Alan always do this to *me*?!" He went on to explain that the client had not asked for *werewolf* feet and arm, they asked for *vampire* legs and an arm that were to *transform* like *An American Werewolf in London*!

What?!!!

Doug began scrambling around trying to figure it all out and then told me I had to work through the weekend to fix everything, but he wasn't sure how to do it. I looked around at the panic, the crappy work, the stacks of pornography and realized I wasn't M.E.L. material. I resigned before Alan had the opportunity to fire me.

Not quite up to Rick Baker standards

CHAPTER 18

Contrast: Stan Winston Studios

Something tells me I'm into something good...
"I'm Into Something Good" Herman's Hermits

July 12, 1985. I wish I could say that I remember that date and that it will forever be burned into my memory, but I would be lying.

Neither Doug White or Mike Spatola seemed overly concerned about my rapid exit from M.E.L. Perhaps they knew that when Alan returned from the back he'd fire me and say that I had misinterpreted his directions. I had to make the long bus ride back to M.E.L. to pick up my last paycheck on Monday. Again, I was unemployed.

That evening, I got a call from Bill Sturgeon. He was working at Stan Winston Studios and said that they were looking for people to come into the mold shop on *Aliens*, the James Cameron-directed sequel to the hit film *Alien*. I called Stan Winston studios the next day and set up a portfolio appointment for the following day: July 12, 1985.

I was nervous and excited. Stan Winston had been in the fandom zeitgeist for years, all the way back to that television movie that had frightened me as a kid, *Gargoyles*. I knew him as primarily a makeup artist having done work for *The Autobiography of Miss Jane Pittman* and having been the sole competition against Rick Baker for the first makeup Academy Award. I mentioned to James Cummins (who was still unemployed after *House* but didn't seem too concerned about it) that I was interviewing at Stan's.

I knew James had worked at Stan's prior to the breakout work on *The Terminator*. James had contributed to earlier, smaller films like *Dead and Buried* and *The Exterminator*. James told me he had been fired from Stan's because of some shameful tom-foolery that will be omitted from this text. The bottom line is that James summed up Stan like this to me: "He's a really nice guy, just never get in between him and his money."

I thought that was strange advice but I filed it in the back of my head, reviewed my portfolio one last time and nervously went to sleep after calling the Department of Transportation and writing down the numbers and times of the buses that would take me from Eagle Rock to Northridge, California, the location of Stan's studio.

It was a hot July day, and I walked the six blocks to the nearest bus stop and began my trek out to the San Fernando Valley. I caught the bus from Eagle Rock to Glendale and then from Glendale to Burbank, but then something went wrong. As we approached the bus stop, another bus was pulling away. It couldn't have been my connecting bus! It wasn't supposed to get to the stop for another twenty minutes!

I walked to the empty stop and looked at the sign. Several city buses stopped here, so maybe it had been another one. My appointment was for 2:00 pm and it was 1:15. Surely another bus would be by shortly.

Minute after excruciating minute passed. Other buses pulled up; they dropped off passengers who were picked up and taken to their destinations while I waited for my bus to appear. It finally did at roughly 1:45. I was hot, sweaty, and panicked. This bus took me to North Hollywood (not far from M.E.L., actually) and I looked at my black Casio watch; it was 2:00 pm. I ran to a pay phone and called the studio. Stan himself picked up and when I explained the situation, he told me to stop by the next day at the same time. I thanked him and returned to the bus stop to take the long trek home.

By the time I walked into the door of our one-bedroom apartment, Tracy was getting dressed up. "Come on, we're going to be late!" she said. When I asked, what for, she reminded me that we had tickets to go see soprano, Kiri Te Kanawa perform at the Hollywood Bowl. I was in no mood to go after what had just transpired; however, I took a shower, got dressed and took another set of buses to Pasadena, where we caught the Hollywood Bowl shuttle.

It became evident why Te Kanawa had been chosen to sing at Prince Charles and Lady Di's wedding. Although she looked like an ant to me from our cheap seats, her voice filled the air. Before long, I had completely forgotten the days frustrations. I became calm and happy again.

The next day, all the buses ran on schedule and I found myself approaching the front door of Stan Winston Studios behind two guys who looked like they had just come from a KISS concert. One of them was tall and blonde, the other was shorter and brunette and they both had portfolios under their arms. They went in about twenty seconds before me. Bill said they needed a lot of help, so I didn't get uptight or nervous that those two would be the last hired that day. I rang the front door bell. As the door swung open, I felt the refreshing blast of air conditioning and entered Stan's lobby.

I was greeted by a tall, thin young man with an effects-guy mullet wearing a short-sleeved white smock. I introduced myself and he shook my hand, "I'm Tom Woodruff." he said and then asked me to take a seat and wait for Stan. He then leaned into an office and told Stan I was there. "He'll be with you in a few minutes, okay?" Then Tom disappeared down a corridor. I looked around the lobby, where there were photos of the *Heartbeeps* robots, and of actor Rod Stieger as W.C. Fields from the movie *W.C. Fields and Me,* amongst many other images of Stan's amazing career. I saw Tom come back up the corridor and take the two heavy-metal guys down the hall when Stan appeared in the lobby.

As weird as this is going to sound, my first impression of Stan was that he was mature. I had worked with Mark Shostrom, James Cummins, Doug White and Alan Apone, but none of them looked as mature and focused as Stan. He shook my hand and took me into his office. Inside, opposite the big wooden desk were comfortable office chairs. Above the chairs, on a shelf were Stan's awards, which at the time consisted of Emmy and Saturn awards; this was all pre-Oscar. Next to Stan's desk was a sculpting stand that held a large green Roma Clay maquette of an ogre holding a huge ax. I was already blown away and I hadn't been past the lobby and office! Stan, standing behind his desk, asked to see my portfolio. I handed it to him and he began to flip through the pages rapidly like he was desperately searching for something, *FLIP, FLIP, FLIP!* All the time he was talking.

"What is your weekly rate?" *FLIP! FLIP! FLIP!* he asked. I answered that I got paid $450 a week, which is what I made on *House*. *FLIP! FLIP! FLIP!* "I'll pay you $500 a week, which is more than you asked for, so never forget that, okay?" Stan said and handed my book back to me. "Start tomorrow morning. We start at 8:00 in the morning and go to 6:30 in the evening. Clean up starts at 6:00, okay?" he said, and then called for Tom to give me a tour of the studio.

Tom took me past the windows of the makeup room where John Rosengrant and Shane Mahan were sculpting sections of what I could tell were some sort of H.R. Giger-esque Alien. It turned out to be the miniature Alien Queen for the film. Alien *Queen*? Also in the room was Willy Whitten, a thin, middle aged guy wearing a muscle shirt sculpting delicate spines for the queen. The work I had seen Mike Smithson do at M.E.L. was the closest thing I had seen, up to this point, to anything that matched the quality of what I was seeing in the shop. Along with the Alien Queen pieces, there were parts to another, larger creature. It sort of resembled a giant toad of some sort. There were only legs and gloves, but a small maquette showed what was the final design of the 'Drones' for *Invaders from Mars*. I truly felt like I was at Willy Wonka's factory because room after room revealed bigger surprises along the way; not to mention the full-sized Endoskeleton from *Terminator* which stood like a sentinel in the corner of the main workshop.

On a table in the shop was a plaster sculpting positive that had the clay face of a strange creature in progress. This was the face of the 'Martian Supreme Intelligence' that Stan himself was in the process of sculpting, and it was incredibly cool! My respect for this man shot through the ceiling like a Roman candle. Here was a mature business professional who was generous and a great artist to boot. I knew at that moment that here was a place I wanted to work at for as long or as often as I could.

Everyone was busy, but they seemed happy. The shop had inspiring photos of a legacy of iconic characters Stan had already created interspersed with movie posters that Stan had contributed to in some way. There was a line of cubbyholes along the wall of the shop with beautiful fake heads of character makeups Stan had designed and sculpted. And it was clean. *Really* clean. There was no garbage anywhere but in the garbage cans. The floors were swept and everyone was clean and presentable. At that moment, my mind drifted back to the stacks of nudie magazines and the prosthetics in the garbage cans at M.E.L. and my standard shifted again. *This* was now the zenith, the top of the ziggurat, the best of the best, and I had made it. I was to start work the next day!

CHAPTER 19

Aliens

Is all that we see or seem, but a dream within a dream?
Edgar Allen Poe

The next day, I arrived at Stan's at about 7:20 in the morning, not because I was so excited about starting my new job, but because of what happened on the first interview day. The next string of buses were scheduled to drop me off at the nearest corner to Stan's at roughly 7:55, and I couldn't risk being late. This meant that I had to get up every morning at 5:30, get showered and walk to the bus stop and be there no later than 6:10 in the morning. And yes, I would arrive at Stan's an hour and ten minutes later. Rapid Transit? No wonder everybody drives in Los Angeles!

Even though I had been introduced to just about everybody in the main shop by Tom Woodruff, now I was ushered across the parking lot to another smaller unit in the industrial complex, where a makeshift mold shop was in full operation.

No air conditioning. Utilitarian tables, blank walls, a stainless steel sink -all were fitted into the small unit where a half dozen young men were working. Among them, I was introduced to Howard Berger, Bob Kurtzman, Everett Burrell, and Steve James. The heavy metal guys I had seen the day before turned out to be Matt Rose and one

The main shop at Stan Winston's studio circa 1985. Pictured are Scott Wheeler, Rick Lazzarini and Everett Burrell. All sorts of goodies here, including the full endoskeleton from *The Terminator*, a puppet head from *The Frankenstein Factor* and maquettes sculpted by James Kagel for Stan's pet project, *Morgoolum*.

of his roommates, Mark Williams, who had been put into the main shop to sculpt the new Alien Warrior tail.

My first responsibility was to assist Steve James in extending a body sculpting form that was made of fiberglass filled with dense, rigid urethane foam. We made a plaster bandage body mold that stretched from the rib cage to the upper thighs. We then cut the form right above the hip area. The upper body form now extended from the head to the groin. We put the plaster bandage mold on the legs and laminated fiberglass into it, then filled the mold with more rigid foam. The result was that the leg form was now extended to the rib cage. That way the Alien Warrior body form could be sculpted overlapping from head to groin and the legs from the lower rib cage to the foot.

Okay, that previous paragraph may have been a bit boring and technical, but what is important to note is that it was some of the cleanest work I had ever done. Just being at Stan Winston's in the company of great artists pushed me to concentrate and do the best I could.

Meanwhile across the room, Howard Berger and Bob Kurtzman were making more stone sculpture positives while they were making their future plans. Apparently, they had been hired by another makeup studio, run by David Miller, who was prepping a new film entitled *Night of the Creeps.* They were excited, because they had been promised that they would have the opportunity to sculpt and design makeups rather than just sit in a hot warehouse making stone and fiberglass sculpting forms.

Whatever.

I was so happy to be at Stan Winston's that thoughts

of running off to work anywhere less p r e s t i g i o u s seemed like folly. The studio was busting at the seams with artists who were poised to break off and begin their own compa-

The Los Angeles mold shop for Aliens. Note the *Alien* back tube-vent being molded in fiberglass on the table. I was terrified to shoot too many photos at Stan's on that show.

nies including, Bob and Howard, who would form KNB EFX Group; Alec Gillis and Tom Woodruff, who would establish ADI; Rick Lazzarini, who would establish The Character Shop; Tony Gardner, who would become Alterian Studios; Kevin Yagher, who opened his own studio; Everett Burrell, who would start Optic Nerve; Brian Penkias, who started his own effects studio, and mechanic Dave Nelson, who established Animated Engineering a few years later. It was the compression, this concentration of talent that was like the beginning of a supernova.

It would soon explode, creating competing shops all over Los Angeles that had business models and quality control similar to that established at Stan Winston Studios.

But working alongside these very talented people wasn't the only perk. A huge crate was delivered to the mold shop, and inside were two original suits built by artist H.R. Giger for the first *Alien*. It was an instant education. Unlike the meticulous, perfect work I was seeing around Stan Winston's, this suit looked like it had been cobbled together hastily using whatever was lying around an appliance repair

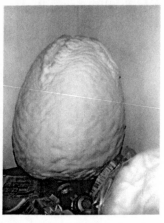

A latex and polyfoam casting of an Alien egg.

store. This is not to say that it wasn't absolutely impressive. It is to say that there are many roads to the same goal and sometimes it's better to take the road less traveled because the alien from *Alien* was just about the most iconic film creature of the day.

We took alginate casts from sections of the suit, made plaster positives, remolded them in silicone and then made fiberglass positives that would be sent to Pinewood

Everett Burrell and I paint resin "Gel Coat" onto an Alien suit piece to begin the fiberglass mold.

Studios where most of the fabrication and finishing work would be done on the Alien Warriors.

The next day was Saturday, and to meet the demanding schedule, a mold of a plaster section of the Alien's back had to be poured in silicone so that a fiberglass positive could begin the following Monday. Since I had just started work that Friday, I was immediately chosen to come in, because there would be no overtime issue (yes, Stan actually paid *overtime*!). I would be joined by Bob Kurtzman and we would be supervised by Tim Lawrence, who was the mold shop supervisor.

I could spend pages describing the technical process involved in making a poured flexible silicone rubber mold, but it would be very boring. All you really need to understand is this: silicone rubber is expensive. Like, $200 a gallon expensive! Bob and I started pouring the silicone into a pour spout made from a cardboard paper towel tube and checked the filling process by blocking tiny 'bleeder' holes with little balls of clay. As the silicone pushed through the tiny hole, we'd block it with the clay and continue pouring. Then we noticed that a ribbon of silicone had begun pouring out of the *bottom* of the mold!

Bob grabbed some water-based clay, fashioned a rope out of it, and pushed it into the space where the silicone was leaking; however, the hydraulic pressure was too much and the plaster shell that was holding the silicone lifted off of the plaster sculpting positive and flooded out onto the shop floor! Hundreds of dollars of silicone flowed out creating a four foot wide puddle on the ground.

It was just at this moment that Stan appeared at the shop door, mouth agape. He might as well have walked in to see a stack of dollar bills, *his* dollar bills, burning on the shop floor!

James Cummins' warning rang in my ears...

"Just don't get between Stan and his money."

Oops.

Fate was on my side that day because not only was this Tim Lawrence's last day, since he, too, was going to Dave Miller's shop the following Monday, but he had just made the same mistake a day or two earlier. Stan took him outside the shop and spoke directly with him while Bob and I began mixing pottery plaster and forming ropes with sisal fiber to seal off the gap, so that we could begin the pouring process again.

By very late in the afternoon, we had finished not only pouring up the mold but scraping the silicone off of the shop floor and dumping it into the trash can. Way to start a first week. I was going to walk back to the bus stop when Bob stopped me and offered to drive me home, easily a twenty minute drive, even

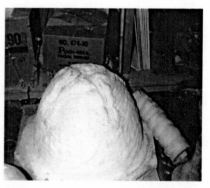

A fiberglass casting of the top of an Alien egg. I could never figure what this was for, but my best guess is that it was used as a sculpting armature to sculpt "open leaves" to simulate Alien eggs after the face-hugger inside had already jumped out.

though he lived just a few miles from the shop. That sums up Bob to this day; he'd give you the shirt off of his back.

The following Monday, Bob, Howard, Tim, and a couple of others had left the shop for the greener *Night of the Creeps* pastures, leaving me to open Saturday's disaster of a mold. I pulled the plaster and sisal fiber off of the bottom of the plaster shell and attempted to pry the plaster mold apart to reveal the set silicone and remove it from the plaster back positive. It wasn't budging. It was stuck. As I pried, chunks of plaster would crack and pop off, compromising the mold's structure. Stan came by, saw me covered with sweat, prying on the mold and asked about the progress. After hearing what was going on, he suggested I just break the plaster back positive into pieces, since we now had a silicone mold of it. That sounded better. I grabbed a mallet and a chisel and began trying to break apart the plaster back positive without destroying the mold.

After about two hours of diligent work, I had managed to break out about a third of the thick plaster. Stan came by again and told me to pitch it into the dumpster. "I've spent too much money on this mold already." he said. I picked up the mold (which must have weighed about 25 pounds) and threw it into the garbage. All of that silicone, plaster and time was wasted.

Meanwhile across the parking lot in the air-conditioned main shop, art work continued on both *Aliens* and *Invaders from Mars*. I had learned that there was a group of artists working for Stan who were on the payroll year round (unlike most of the employees who were all transient free-lance workers). These permanent employees were referred to as "Lifers" meaning that they were working for Stan *for life*! The Lifers were John Rosengrant, Shane Mahan, Tom Woodruff, Jr., Richard Landon, and the most recent addition, Alec Gillis. Most of them had joined Stan during *Terminator* with the exception of Alec who had been hired later.

The two who were sculpting the Alien Queen body and head were John and Shane, respectively. John had a bushy brown mullet, piercing eyes and rarely smiled, he was all business. Shane, on the other hand, was short with nearly platinum-blond hair piled high on his head. He wore no socks and leopard-print slip-on shoes. Unlike John, Shane was always looking for the opportunity to tell a funny joke or a story accompanied by voice impersonation. Tom Woodruff, Jr. was tall and thin which made him a great candidate to follow in the footsteps of one of his childhood idols, Janos Prohaska, who had made and performed in animal and creature suits primarily in the 1960s and '70s. Tom, like Shane, was very funny, but his humor was much more dry and clever. Richard Landon was also tall, and was not without a sense of humor; however, he was a fan of science and engineering which gave him the resources to offer detailed explanations of how and why things worked, both in creature effects and in larger spheres as well.

And finally there was Alec Gillis. Alec, self-described, was the "high school football star who was secretly the president of the science fiction club". Through the years, I would see all manner of women swoon when he walked into a room; however, when I met Alec he was already engaged to his long-time girlfriend, Alaine, whom he eventually married. Alec was somewhere between Shane and Tom in his humor. He was not afraid to put on silly voices and say and do silly things, but then would turn around and fire off clever puns that could elicit groans from even the most patient of audiences.

On a different tier were Rick Lazzarini and Kevin Ya-gher. It was clear that both of them seemed to be high up on the ladder. Kevin, Rick, and Alec were friends prior to them all working at Stan's. I had met Rick at Mark Shos-trom's in '84 and then I had heard about the infamous *Neon Maniacs* letter where, Rick had described himself and Mark as "literally geniuses" (because, in his defense, Rick *was* a member of M.E.N.S.A.) after the show had been awarded to Makeup Effects Labs. Rick was some-what reactionary, where Kevin seemed very confident yet distant.

Rounding out this cast of characters was Dave Nelson. Dave, originally from Manchester, England, was an in-credible animatronics designer and engineer. He had an almost intuitive eye for building mechanics that didn't just move foam latex around, but would somehow cap-ture the subtleties of organic movement. Not only was Dave a bit more mature than the rest of us, but he was part of a yacht sailing crew, so he had to leave early every Wednesday to drive to the marina to take the boat out. And since he was English, he had asked Stan to observe tea time at around 4:15 pm every day. Trust me when I say that I can't imagine another shop in Southern Cali-fornia in the summer of 1985 that was observing English tea time every day!

Under Stan Winston, this group served as the project leaders in some capacity or another. Since most of my days were spent in the mold shop, I wasn't around when Tony Gardner, Bill Sturgeon, or even Kevin Yagher left the shop; I just came in the next day and they had moved on. We would hear rumors of smaller projects that they were working on (I believe Bill returned to Rick Baker's shop) but that is the way the business worked back then. You had a job until the job didn't need you any more and then you were dropped back into the talent pool to find another situation as soon as possible.

Even though Shane was a Michigan native, he had taken to Southern California living and would often skateboard back and forth between shops. This board came to be used by nearly anyone who had to move between the two shops and soon Stan, himself, decided he would try it.

I watched him get on the board just outside of the main shop and start to push off toward the mold shop when the board shot out from under him and he hit the pavement. SMASH! I ran up from one direction, and Alec, who was walking from the other direction, ran to see if he was okay. Stan, being Stan, said, "You know what they say when you are thrown off of a horse? You get right back up on that horse!" By then, a small group of employees had shown up and Stan put his foot back on the board, pushed off and BAM! He hit the ground again. This time, he didn't seem too jovial. We helped him to his feet, he handed the board back to Shane and hobbled back into the main shop.

For the next week or so, Stan only wore stretchy warm up pants and would take delight in pulling the waistband down to show off the grapefruit sized mass of purple contusions he had acquired from his spills.

As *Aliens* pieces and molds were crated and shipped to England, the work flow shifted. Less work was required on *Aliens* and now, huge fiberglass molds appeared, courtesy of two specialty mold makers, the Reter Brothers. These were the parts of the Martian Supreme Intelligence and the Martian Drones. The Supreme Intelligence was made up of a huge head mold, tentacle molds, and a long body mold. The drones were massive body molds, large head molds and both front and back legs.

Stan, ever the illusionist, never felt 100% comfortable making creatures whose physicality could be summed up as human. He used to reference the original *Alien*, saying that for most of the film its broad-stroke form was kept secret, so it was nearly impossible to tell that it was a man-in-a-suit until they revealed it toward the end.

Stan and the team had come up with a design for the operators (puppeteers) of the Alien Queen to be strapped into a fiberglass body pan that held them nearly back-to-back. The forward arms of the two men became the tiny Queen arms, while the rear arms would operate the large mechanical arms. The entire body pan would be supported by a crane and the feet would be operated externally, via rod puppetry, while the head and neck were entirely mechanical. It was ingenious to say the least.

The creature design was done by James Cameron, and a copy of his color pencil illustration hung in the shop. Stan had attempted a design earlier, and had worked to integrate aspects of the beginning stages of the Alien creature (the face-hugger that launched out of the egg, and the chest burster that launched out of its host's rib cage), but Jim was nothing if not particular, and set off to do some concept illustrations himself.

This personality trait of Cameron's was evident as Stan already had framed illustrations Jim had done for *The Terminator* hanging on walls in the studio.

One of the aspects of working in that shop I can never

forget was the music that seemed to be playing all of the time. Shane was fond of ex-Police drummer Stewart Copeland's solo album, *The Rhythmatist*. Although I only worked in the main shop from time to time, it seemed that album was played continuously and was only interrupted by the album *Brothers in Arms*, by Dire Straits, that Dave Nelson would put on at any opportunity. In my memory, this became the soundtrack of Stan Winston studios circa 1985; to this day, if I hear a cut from either of those two albums, I'm transported back in time to the sulfurous smell of Roma plastilina and the incessant hum of the mill.

Eventually, John, Shane, Richard, and Tom left the shop and Northridge, California, for Pinewood Studio in England to begin the construction of the Alien Warrior Suits and the Queen herself.

Alec Gillis and Rick Lazzarini would leave after the work on *Invaders from Mars* was completed. However, to finish off this chapter on *Aliens*, we need to speak a bit about Rick Lazzarini and the mechanical face-huggers.

As you will learn, while the core crew left for England and then the rest of us went to work on set for *Invaders from Mars*, Rick was left in the shop with the task of mechanizing chest-bursters. Unlike the first film, *Alien*, this time the chest-bursters would be featured in their own scene having to scuttle around on the floor and jump at potential hosts in an infirmary.

Rick began trying different methods of locomotion: electronic servo motors, cable controls, rod puppeting. None of them worked. Jim Cameron even suggested using a gas-powered motor and a complex gear system to run the face-hugger but it was ineffective as well.

Every evening after working on set, we would return to the shop to discover Rick still there. Having worked by himself all day long, he was a bit frustrated and suffering from isolation. One night, we returned from set to discover that Rick had taken a micro-torch and carefully burned off just the faces on several photos displayed in Dave Nelson's open tool box. Idle hands...

Eventually Rick figured out a pulley system; the face-hugger rode on a wire while being pulled by a second wire. As the figure was pulled, a wheel inside of the body turned a complex series of mechanisms that made the legs move realistically. If you pulled it slowly it looked like it was creeping along like a tarantula; if you pulled it quickly, it looked like it was scampering.

Unlike the rest of the crew, Rick volunteered to go to England to continue his work on *Aliens*. It is still common that whenever you bring an American crew to a foreign country, the number of foreign workers is limited, because (not only is it expensive) but the local film commission wants to employ the greatest number of local workers. Rick was not in Stan's labor budget, but bought his own ticket instead. I didn't go to England, but I would have thought it was a good idea since Rick's mechanical design had required so much research and development that risking it in the hands of someone else might have brought unnecessary trouble to the project.

Upon the crew's return, the Rick Lazzarini stories were priceless, but you'll have to wait for Rick to write that book.

CHAPTER 20

Invaders from Mars

Much Ado About Nothing
William Shakespeare

We are creature makers. When we are hired as independent contractors to make monsters or characters for a film, that means that we are responsible for the creatures. Only the creatures. We're not responsible for the story, the acting, the directing, the art design, the costume design, etc.. I say this to most of the students I teach, and I just want it to be clear to all of you as well. But the bottom line is this:

The checks still cash. Turkey or hit, a paycheck is a paycheck.

After seeing the quality of the fake heads being made at M.E.L., I was really blown away by the designs that Stan and his team had done for *Invaders from Mars*. On tracing paper, his favorite illustration foundation, Stan had done illustrations of the Drones over photos of actors walking backward holding ski poles. That way, the knees of the creatures would bend backward with the intention of fooling the eye and hiding "the man in the suit" look that Stan was always trying to avoid.

Shane Mahan had sculpted a maquette of the creature

based on Stan's drawings and since the Drones were so huge, John, Shane, Tom, and Alec supervised the sculpting of the full-sized suit. But there was more to this creature than a man walking backward holding ski poles. Stan envisioned that the larger athletic suit performers would carry a little person, sitting back-to-back who would use their legs to operate the creatures' big jaws!

The custom backpack frame was designed and built by Rick Lazzarini. Body casts of a suit performer, Doug Simpson, and a little person (I believe it was Debbie Carrington?) were made and cast in dense, heavy, rigid urethane foam. Using measurements and photos of the sculptures, Rick approximated the size of the backpack frame, fit all of the straps and a very comfortable chair for the small performer to sit on. Decades before i-phones and digital video, a small analog video camera was fit into the nostril of the Drone while a small monitor with a mirror was rigged to the larger performer's chest so that they could see what was going on while they were walking backwards. It was ingenious.

As I mentioned in the last chapter, the large molds showed up and it was time to begin running skins. With the departure of some of our crew, new faces showed up including Matt Rose's roommate, Steve Wang, and another heavy-metal rock and roll guy from Philadelphia, Gino Crognale. I will be honest and say that I have no idea who figured out the material and method of running these large skins. It was probably too difficult and not cost effective to attempt to make them out of foam latex, so it was decided that they would be run (our term for cast) out of a tissue-thin urethane skin, backed by expanding soft urethane foam.

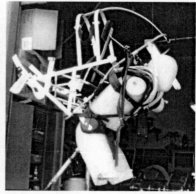

A "Drone" head casting fresh out of the mold.

The ingenious frame designed and built by Rick Lazzarini for the Drone performers. Note the chair on the back meant for a little performer to sit on on the back of the larger Drone performer.

Again, without getting too technical, there were some issues surrounding this technique. Expanding urethane foam is somewhat temperature sensitive and since it is the result of a direct chemical reaction, once the catalyst is introduced into the base chemical, there is a finite amount of time allowed to mix it thoroughly and get it into the mold before it starts to expand. The big mold pieces had to be bolted together by a series of screws and nuts that ran along the flange every 3.5 inches or so. This made opening and closing the mold a time consuming step.

Again, in stepped Rick Lazzarini. I have no idea where he got the idea, but he came up with a technique he termed "Octo-injection." Now, the word "Octo" here was not being used as its Latin root would suggest for the number eight (as in octopus) but rather to suggest that the injection method looked much like an octopus once it was set up and ready to be implemented.

So, what is an "Octo-injector" you ask?

It starts with a bunch of one inch holes drilled strategically inside the hollow fiberglass core of the mold. Into these holes, one inch plastic hardware nipples were glued into place. A five gallon bucket with a lid was drilled out as well and attached to the same number of nipples on the bucket in ratio to what was drilled into the core). The bucket was suspended above the mold assembly via a ladder and then clear, 1 inch inner diameter Tygon brand vinyl tubing was attached from the bucket (the octo-injector) to the core and attached with hose clamps.

There were two holes drilled into the lid – one would accommodate a clean, dedicated shop vacuum hose set to 'exhaust' while the other would fit an air compressor nozzle. Thus set up, casting a Drone skin went something like this:

The urethane chemicals were carefully stored in a refrigerator to retard the chemical reaction as long as possible. The Drone mold surfaces were lubricated with a urethane release. Then, using an industrial sprayer, the urethane "skin" chemical was tinted brown and then sprayed onto the surface of the mold. When two or three layers had been built up, the mold was closed, bolted and inverted so that the widest part was facing upward. The octo-injector was hooked up and then teams of workers were organized- mixers, pourers, and air pumpers. The chemicals were weighed out and then, like clockwork, the urethane was mixed in large paper buckets and handed to two people on ladders who poured the mixed chemicals into the bucket, then jumped off of the ladders. Then the lid was slammed on, the shop vac and compressor shot air into the chamber and the chemicals raced through the tubing and into the mold.

Easy!

After a couple of runs, we became more efficient. Efficiency led to familiarity which led to comfort, and finally routine. Nice of life to be around to remind everyone that you should never become complacent. During one of the runs, everything seemed to be working fine; however, once the chemicals were being poured into the octo-injector tank, the urethane began foaming prematurely! In a panic, the lid was thrown on, and the air pumped into the bucket. We watched as the urethane in the tubing started to foam and started expanding BACKWARDS!

Mark Williams stood on a ladder and tried to hold the lid down and force the foaming chemical back down into the mold and then...BOOM! The pressure forced the lid upward on a column of explosive expanding soft urethane that sprayed the chemical into the air like a volcano belching lava! We all ran as fast as we could but Mark ended up getting sprayed in his long bleached rock and roll hair! He was lucky that he didn't get sprayed in his eyes, and that it only took some strategic scissoring to remove the urethane drops out from hair.

We ended up casting three sets of heads and bodies (usable casts) while the rejects were saved to be used for painting tests and patching material. Urethane casts of the Drone maquette had been run and given to a few choice artists to take home and use for test paint designs. Among the artists chosen was Steve Wang, who was a newcomer to the studio, but not completely unknown.

Matt Rose and Steve Wang had won *Fangoria* magazine's "Ghoul Brothers" contest by submitting two excellent rubber masks they had designed, sculpted, painted and photographed. When they came into the shop, they were first identified as a team for having won this prize, and were even occasionally referred to at this early stage as The Ghoul Brothers. Matt's sculpture of the Alien Warrior tail was enough to get Stan's attention, but we were in finishing mode, and not sculpting/designing mode. Their time would come, but for the time being Steve was given a Drone maquette casting to do a prospective paint design. What he brought back was part of the basis of the final paint design.

Looking to a leopard frog as inspiration, Steve painted the majority of the body using this as a template. However, someone else had painted the fleshy top of their Drone maquette as a pinky-red external organ and the two designs were integrated to become the final paint design. But the Drones weren't the only Martians that needed artistic attention.

The Supreme Martian Intelligence molds had been run using latex and soft expanding urethane foam. Richard Landon spent hours carefully stippling latex into the bulbous lobes of the brainy body of the creature, creating delicate air bladders, both in the protruding blood vessels as well as the lobes themselves. This way the sides of the creature 'breathed' while the smaller blood vessels pulsated. When the bladders were finished, they were connected to air hoses that ran to a manifold operated by a keyboard (like a piano). You pressed a key and a particular bladder would swell. Apparently, Stan had done this for the air bladder transformations for the television show *Manimal* and it worked better than manually blowing into a tube trying to figure out which bladder was inflating! The challenge came from not depressing a key on the keyboard too long which would over-inflate the bladder and pop it.

Unlike the Drones, the Supreme was entirely a puppet. It's humanoid face was run in foam latex and blended onto the latex/polyfoam body. Beneath the foam latex skin, Dave Nelson had designed and built the most sophisticated eye mechanisms I had seen up to that point. The most impressive feature was that the lower lids were 'slaved' to the eye

Drying urethane sealer on a "Supreme Intelligence" tentacle.

movement so that when the Supreme looked upward, the lower lids followed naturally. However the most challenging aspect of the Supreme was that it was basically a large body at the end of a long tentacle-like tail. The idea was that it would push itself out of a small opening in the bulkhead of the Martian space ship and rest on a type of throne.

Dave engineered a sophisticated (and relatively expensive) system to operate the tail; however, the fact that it was

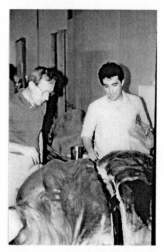

One of the highlights of my professional life. My first meeting with makeup legend, Dick Smith, who came to the shop to visit Stan. I had the pleasure of explaining how the Drone suit was being cast and assembled to him.

thicker at the head than at the back made it almost impossible for it to operate effectively. "You can't fight father physics!" someone had said to me after we had tried to test it at the shop, and the poor Supreme just drooped downward no matter how much force was applied to the big controllers that were supposed to lift it. The special effects supervisor, John Dykstra, suggested we "fly it" via exterior wires that would take the weight of Supreme as it made its way to its seat on the throne. "If anyone sees those wires," Dykstra said, "I'll give 'em their seven bucks back." So, the Supreme became sort of a marionette for its flying scenes.

Knowing that the Supreme had dialogue, the mouth was designed to be controlled by hand. Once it was sitting on its throne, the puppet's belly was opened up, allowing two puppeteers access to its mouth and its vestigial hands in the front, that were lovingly referred to as its "croissants."

I don't think I'll be ruining the film for anybody, but at one point the Supreme is riddled with machine gun bullets by the United States Marines. Artist Greg Figel sculpted a pained-face prosthetic that was attached to a hastily built secondary Supreme head/body casting that was attached to a simple latex and polyfoam tail. But more about that a little later.

My artistic contribution to the Supreme was unusual. The design of the top of its head was supposed to look like a clear membrane was covering thick, clear fluid, in which a network of veins ran over its large brain. Since it had to be so lightweight, a clear, plastic vacu-formed shell became the membrane, but the weight of a clear liquid was impractical. It became my task to take thin lengths of brass rod, bend them, solder them, blend the joints and then paint them like three-dimensional veins suspended in fluid. You barely see them in the film, but they are there!

As fans know, the eighties were a time of great blood-letting with films like the *Friday the 13th* series and *A Nightmare on Elm Street*. The result was that the film ratings board became sensitive to how much red, human blood they would allow to be shown before giving the film an "R" rating. *Invaders from Mars* was slated for a "PG," rating, so when the Martians were killed they would have to bleed something else besides red blood.

I'll be honest, I have no idea who came up with the concept, but it was decided that Martians bleed a combination of two fluids, one purple and one yellow. That meant that we would have to mix gallons of two different colors and dress them on set so that they wouldn't mix and just become brown.

Since the film *Alien*, slime had become synonymous with creatures, and it wasn't unusual to see all sorts of creatures slathered with clear methylcellulose, which is a clear food thickener famous for being rumored to have been the primary ingredient in McDonald's shakes. (Note: they weren't called "milkshakes" for years.) It was a natural plant derivative that was mixed much like gelatin. I don't need to tell you that it was slimy and messy and sticky, and when it dried, it became white and flaky. A different route was decided upon, though, and we cast our eyes to a popular toy of the time: Mattel's Slime.

"Slime," as it was marketed to kids, was just that –slime. It was green, and jelly-like, and had a great consistency, but the best thing about it was that, with the exception of carpet and fabric, you could just scrape it off of any surface and put it back into the container to be used again and again! Because, let's face it, what kid wouldn't want to spend hours playing with green slime? Well, the answer turned out to be, "any kid" -because it was a huge hit.

With a little research and many long distance phone calls, we found the company that mixed and distributed the base of this slime, and were able to purchase about twenty gallons of it. Using latex paint tints, we were able to color it the desired purple and yellow. I must confess, that in its raw state, the slime had a peculiar look not unlike a fluid exclusively produced by male animals.

Once one of the Drone skins had been painted and the network of velcro closures were put in place (they were designed so that the head could be detached from the body quickly), the Drone performers were invited to the shop for a test run. Doug Simpson put the suit on first and when he strolled into the parking lot, surrounded by excited and enthusiastic Stan Winston employees, we all saw the potential of the design and the creature. Stan even invited Tom Burman by the studio to show off this latest marvel.

Meanwhile, video tapes from the crew in England began to get sent back from the *Aliens* workshop that showed Tom, Shane, John and their new British colleagues hard at work sculpting the full sized Queen Alien. Needless to say, it was inspiring!

Eventually, the Drone suits were completed. The Supreme Intelligence and all of its guises were completed, and they were all loaded into a truck along with tool boxes full of maintenance materials and equipment to be shipped to a set which was located at an abandoned Naval facility in San Pedro, California.

It was during this summer that Tracy and I were finally able to buy a car, and we had our experience with our first used car salesman, Alec Gillis. Alec was looking to get rid of his old Honda Civic to upgrade to a Volkswagen station wagon, so he sold us his old car for about $500. The problem was that it was a five-speed stick shift, and neither Tracy nor I knew how to drive it. After a few disastrous attempts in the Stan Winston parking lot, Rick Lazzarini, - bless him, - sat me down and explained *exactly* what happened when the clutch and the gas pedals were depressed, and why the engine would stall, etc.

I wish I remembered that speech verbatim, because whatever it was, I walked right out into the lot, got in the car and drove it without a hitch. I drove it all the way home, gave the speech to Tracy and *she* was able to drive the car like a pro! The Sheas now had wheels!

One set of wheels.

This meant that Tracy, who had recently enrolled at Cal State Northridge, in the Music Department, would have to drive me from Eagle Rock to Stan Winston's early in the morning, where I would hitch a ride with Scott Wheeler to ride down to San Pedro. Then, at night, she'd have to drive all the way back and pick me up!

Even though it was a hassle, it was better and more efficient than trying to time buses the whole way there and back.

The drive down to San Pedro was easily forty miles, and we'd make the trip just as the sun was rising over Los Angeles. At this hour traffic was just beginning to back up and it still took close to an hour and a half to get to the docks of San Pedro and the Naval building.

Invaders from Mars was produced by the Cannon Group run by Menahem Golan and Yoram Globas. I don't know how they found the building, but my guess was that it must have been very inexpensive. Inside the massive main room, giant interior sets had been built to simulate the interior of the Marian space craft, as well as the characteristic tunnels that the creatures supposedly made in order to kidnap humans and transform them into emotionless, mental slaves of their Martian hive.

The on-set, Stan Winston crew holding room. Supervisor, Alec Gillis, downs a beverage while Everett Burrell, Scott Wheeler, and Brian Penikas make preparations to the suits.

Sculptor, Greg Figel, and myself on the set for Invaders from Mars. Greg was a longtime Stan Winston artist originally from San Diego, California.

The physical effects company run by Phil Cory was responsible for rigging the Drones and the Supreme with "squibs" - which are small explosives used to simulate bullet hits. Because of the unusual manner of rigging these creatures with the squibs, Phil Cory's crew asked for a test. They were given a Drone suit, in which they cut a hole, placed a bag of their mixture of Martian blood, and then attached a small electronically triggered explosive.

The whole thing was covered with a paper towel that was painted to match the color of the Drone's skin.

3....2...1...POW! The squib was detonated and an unimpressive dribble of colored fluid appeared at the tear in the paper towel. This was bad because Phil's crew had used glycerin as a blood base, and now the spongy urethane was saturated, having absorbed the glycerin. In defense of Phil's crew, had they used clear corn syrup (which is the base of most motion picture blood), it would be just as sticky and messy; however, it would draw flies since it was a sugar, and no one would want that.

Armed with this new knowledge, it was determined that the blood bags would be inverted allowing the hydraulic pressure to dump all of the blood out of the bag; however, the inside of the drone suit was in danger of becoming structurally unsound as the glycerin being absorbed by the urethane foam would add weight and weaken the cell structure. That meant that the entire inside of the drone skin would have to be sealed with a flexible urethane skin, and guess who that job fell to? You guessed it.

While a crew measured small batches of the raw chemicals, I was wrapped head to toe in plastic garbage bags, wearing a respirator and eye protection. The chemicals were mixed and handed to me while I was halfway inside of the suit, brushing the entire inner surface with the fast-setting ure-

When you are about to crawl into a Drone suit and brush layers of sticky, messy urethane sealer on the inside, you've got to be prepared!

thane. And this had to be done on two suits!

I emerged from the suits with toxic urethane drips and drops clinging to the protective plastic. I was cut out of my cocoon and joined the rest of the crew in setting up the two adjoining rooms we were assigned in the facility. And that is what they were, just two empty rooms without tables or chairs or running water. By the look of the ancient, horrible wall paper still yellowing on the walls, these must have served as administrative offices of some sort. As was the fashion in that day, one of the rooms was set up primarily as an Art Department room while the other was set up as a Mechanical Department room. Huge stands had been built that suspended the Drone suits from above by a pin that fit into the aluminum frame. These stands were lifted via a large forklift to the second floor of the Martian spaceship set when the Drones had to perform there.

A Drone suit is suspended from a frame on a fork lift. The suits were lifted to the second level of the set in order to suit up the performers so they wouldn't tire themselves walking the lengthy ramps of the massive set.

Above and outside the main Martian throne room set, the Supreme sat on a scaffold, ready to be lowered out of its portal and onto the throne. The way that the Art Direction of the set had been designed, the throne would hide puppeteers who would operate the Supreme's mechanical tentacles, which were not actually attached to the main creature.

This version of *Invaders from Mars* was directed by Tobe Hooper, who had gained fame for his films *The Texas Chainsaw Massacre* and *The Funhouse*. However, most mainstream, non-horror fans are more familiar with his film *Poltergeist*. I wondered what to expect from Tobe.

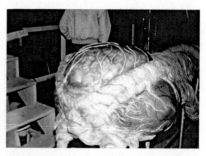

Greg Figel stands behind the Martian "Supreme Intelligence" on his platform above the Throne Room set. Greg had sculpted the main body of the creature while Stan Winston, himself, had sculpted the face.

Being a fan, I had seen numerous photos of Tobe on film sets looking tired and intense simultaneously. My memory of *The Texas Chainsaw Massacre* had been blurred, because I watched the film from between my fingers; it was just too intense and brutal for me. *The Funhouse* was strange, but I was such a fan of Rick Baker and Craig Reardon that I only recall the creature that they made for the film. *Poltergeist* was so obviously produced by Steven Spielberg that Tobe's fingerprints were less noticeable on that project. My friends and I as teens had also seen a lesser known film of Tobe's, *Eaten Alive*, at a midnight movie in

Alec Gillis confers with a Drone performer at the back of the creature suit.

New Orleans, and that, in my opinion, was less than successful.

So which Tobe would be at the helm of this film? I'll put it this way: Not the one I expected. Tobe seemed distracted nearly all of the time. He was short, always had a can of Dr. Pepper in his hand, and spoke with a low, growling Texas drawl. He'd be in the middle of giving direction or discussing something and he'd just stop in mid-sentence and say, "Right, man!" and then walk off, leaving whomever he was speaking to confused. He would get a bit frustrated and yell, which only increased his resemblance to *Looney Tunes'* Yosemite Sam.

It was not unusual for the Stan Winston crew to be in our rooms, waiting to prepare the Drones to be suited up and used while Tobe's voice boomed through the building over a bullhorn, directing child actor, Hunter Carson, with a system of numbered expressions that they must have rehearsed. "Face 4 Hunter! Face 4!" we'd hear Tobe yell, "Now, 9! 9 Hunter, face 9! Now 3 with a little 5! A little 5, Hunter! 5 Hunter, face 5! Oh goddammit! *Cut!*"

The Martian Supreme Intelligence sits on its throne waiting to be filmed.

Hunter Carson was a little blonde boy. He was the son of actress Karen Black, who was the lead in the film playing the school nurse, Linda. As miserable as Hunter seemed on set, Karen seemed not to be that aware of what was going on from one minute to the next. In supporting roles we had Louise Fletcher as Mrs. McKelch, the school teacher, and James Karen as General Wilson. Although actors Laraine Newman and Timothy Bottoms were also in the film, as Hunter's parents, we rarely saw them on set. We did do a scene with cult film favorite *Harold and Maude* star, Bud Cort, in which he was disintegrated by the Martian Drones.

However, most of our days were spent suiting up the Drone actors, Doug Simpson, Scott Wulf, Matt Bennett, and Lonny Low. There were two suits, and two actors per suit, so that when one team got tired, they could break, get out of the suit, and the second team would pick it up.

A Drone on a break. Randall Wulff stands with an electric fan to assist Doug Simpson in the suit.

At this point I need to sing the praises of Drone performer, Doug Simpson. Doug was a big guy, with a brown Tom Selleck mustache and an easy demeanor. But what set him apart from the other three performers was that he took his job very seriously, and understood that his performance would be limited or enhanced by the suit he was wearing. He would speak to Alec Gillis, who was the acting on-set supervisor for the film, and Dave Nelson about making improvements in the suits here and there, not just to make it more comfortable, but to enable the performer to move more easily or get in and out of it more efficiently. He became an

Doug Simpson in the suit. Note the video monitor on his chest.

integral part of the team, and began hanging around with the puppeteers.

As he did, we began messing with Doug in and out of the Drone suit. I know that I personally tortured him so much that when it was time to get him out of his suit at the end of the day, he grabbed me in one of his paws and wiped his sweaty butt with the back of my head! What a jerk! The entire drive back to Northridge from San Pedro, my hair smelled like Doug's butt crack. (Just remember Doug –payback is a bitch and it ain't over, pal!)

In spite of Tobe yelling at Hunter and me walking around with my head smelling of ass, we did have to shoot the Supreme Intelligence scenes. Unfortunately, for most of these scenes, the Drones worked as well. That meant that we had to suit up two performers, then run behind the throne, take our positions and puppeteer the Supreme. Then, when Tobe yelled "Cut!" we'd run in with apple boxes (wooden boxes furnished by the grip department) slide them under the Drone performers' butts, and open the back of their suits to get some cool fresh air.

Beneath the hollow throne set piece was room for at least three performers. Alec Gillis performed the little vestigial hands, while Everett performed the mouth. I was beneath the set with the air bladder keyboard. Hidden behind the throne, the other performers operated the long mechanical tentacles. Even though we had lit-

Everett Burrell looks on as Dave Nelson and Alec Gillis discuss a scene where a Drone eats "Mrs. McKeltch" played by Louise Fletcher.

Everett Burrell moistens a Drone nostril prior to shooting.

Stuntman, Steve Lambert, dressed as Mrs. McKeltch gets ready to be swallowed by a Drone.

tle television monitors, it was difficult to coordinate between all of the puppeteers.

In the first scene the Supreme Intelligence mocks David by using David's father's voice, saying, "Poor little guy....poor little guy." Normally this kind of work is done using an audio playback that the mouth performer listens to a number of times, and then can move the mouth in rhythm with the pre-recorded dialogue, but such was not the case. Tobe, himself, would read the line, and Everett would try to keep up (even if he was a half beat behind Tobe). The problem was that take after take, Tobe's performance was inconsistent, so Everett would be puppeteering as best he could while Tobe would say, "Poor little guy............" Then he'd forget his line, then remember and say, "......little guy." In the long run it didn't matter, because I'm positive that whoever supplied the Supreme's voice in that scene was forced to match Everett's performance while doing additional dialogue recording (ADR).

When it was time for the Marines to shoot the Supreme Intelligence, the "stunt" latex and polyfoam version wearing the "pained face" was brought to set. Phil Cory and his crew had spent the better part of a day carefully squibbing the puppet, and in doing so had cut large sections of the fiberglass under structure (or underskull as it is called in the business), to the point where its structure had been compromised.

Since it was supposed to rear up while being shot, Gino Crognale had volunteered to lie on a fulcrum inside the creature, in a sort of "Superman flying pose," while puppeteers would lift him up and down during the shot. To keep Gino from rolling off the long board, he had been duct taped in place. Meanwhile, the rest of us doubled up on the tentacles, since they would be flailing around during the shot.

Cameras rolled, action was called, and Phil Cory's crew began shooting spark and dust hits with air guns. Dust hits were fuller's earth put into fragile capsules that would shatter on contact with something hard creating a dusty impact. Spark hits, as you can surmise, worked the same way, except they would create a spark upon impact.

While we were moving the Supreme around during this cacophony of activity, fire began falling from the set around us. The set, having been painted with flammable paint, had been touched off by the spark hits. Thin, painted mattress foam dressed on the walls of the set ignited and burned like napalm as it fell in handfuls of goopy flame.

Recall, the throne area of the set was two stories tall, and behind the throne was easily an eighteen foot drop, so jumping was out of the question. While fire continued to fall around us, the puppeteers began rapidly evacuating the set. I picked up a fire extinguisher and put out Brian Penikas' foot as some burning foam struck it, but all of this time we had forgotten that Gino was still taped inside of the creature, unaware and still performing!

Later, Gino would tell me that he never heard cut, so he assumed the take was just going on extra long, until he saw the blade of Dave Nelsons knife appear and begin cutting down the length of the creature. "Come on, Gino, let's go, the set is on fire," Dave said to him calmly and the two were the last to abandon the creature and leave the set to the fire fighters.

Fortunately, no one got hurt and the set was put out and repaired quickly. Production moved away from the Throne Room and into the Needle Room to continue shooting, while the Art Department began their repairs.

The Drone performers, having become familiar with and somewhat nimble in their suits, had managed to do most of the shoot without carrying the extra weight of the little people performers on their backs, but as we moved into the tunnels, that changed.

We had been spoiled by not having to dress the little performers in the Drone suits. Now we would have to remove the head of the Drone, lift the little performers into their chairs, strap them in, re-attach the head, then ask the little performers to push their arms out of holes on the sides of the creature so we could slide their Drone gloves on. Then, the larger puppeteers, who would have been sitting this entire time, would rock forward bearing the new weight on their backs, and stand up, get into position and then perform once the cameras were rolling. Having the extra weight on their backs affected the larger puppeteers, and they would tire more easily and frequently.

Luckily, for close, insert shots of the creatures' small arms doing specific things, we were able to take the performers out of the suits and mount the head on a stand and just let the little performers, wearing the gloves, stand on a box and perform without being strapped into a chair on the other performers' backs.

One of the last sequences we shot in the Martian tunnels was a scene where a Drone eats M&M candies as a direct homage to Spielberg's "E.T." Since The M&M/Mars Candy company had not granted Spielberg and company the rights to use M&Ms, Reeses Pieces has been used instead. However, for whatever reason, M&M/Mars didn't want to have their candy featured in *Invaders from Mars* so the Art Department hastily changed them to W&Ws (get it? 'M' upside down becomes 'W'!). Using Super Glue, we attached hundreds of candies to fishing line and on "Action!" we pulled them up into the Drone's mouth. After a beat, the Drone then "vomited" the candy, along with foamy liquid

Director Tobe Hooper directs Drone action while Lonnie Low smiles in his Drone suit.

we made with methocel and dish soap. Maybe that was the problem. Mars Candy didn't like the idea that M&Ms made anyone or any *thing* vomit! For whatever reason, the entire scene was cut from the final film.

In Los Angeles during the eighties, the preferred swag was satin crew jackets (yes, satin crew jackets). I had seen individuals walking around town wearing their powder-blue satin *Thing* jackets, and when I was on the set of *House* I had seen director, Steve Miner, holding up a black satin crew jacket that had an intricate embroidery of illustrator, William Stout's publicity illustration. So cool!

Imagine our reaction when someone came to our room and said for us to a.) choose our jacket style either black satin or letterman style b.) our size and c.) whether or not we wanted our names embroidered on the front! Black satin crew jacket? *Hell yes*! I even got my name embroidered on the front in red! Looking back at how I must have looked running around Los Angeles wearing a black satin jacket with *Invaders from Mars* on the back of it....well...what can I say? It was the eighties.

When the movie finally came out the next year, I was back at Stan Winston's. A lot had gone down and I had worked on other movies, which are coming in the following chapters. We went to the premiere and no one left the theater jumping up and down with excitement. The film was okay. It would take repeated viewings of the film to attempt to determine who *really* was to blame for the failure of the film at the box office.

But it didn't matter. I had my black satin jacket, that became the subject of ridicule once the film was released, and John Dykstra never had to pay anyone $7 to my knowledge.

We didn't take the Drones back to Stan's shop at the end of the shoot. Somehow, Cannon Films had it in their contract that they owned everything so we left it all in San Pedro. The set would be left up, refitted, and redressed to become Skeletor's throne room for Cannon Films' *Masters of the Universe* movie based on Mattel's "He-Man" toy series.

Tracy drove me back to the apartment, and another bout of unemployment.

CHAPTER 21

Back at Shostrom's for From Beyond

Better to sleep with a sober cannibal than a drunk Christian.
"Moby Dick," Herman Melville

As was the pattern, the day after I had been laid off, I began calling around town to see who had work. I knew Matt Rose and Steve Wang were off to Rick Baker's for *Harry and the Hendersons*. I had stopped by their apartment during the *Invaders from Mars* prep and it became very clear to me that they were, above and beyond, more talented than most of the typical folks running from shop to shop looking for work.

Although their apartment should have been condemned as a health risk, the truth was that there were sculptures *everywhere*! Masks in progress, Roma clay maquettes, and tons of painted and unpainted Super Sculpey figures literally took up most of the living area. It was evident that Matt and Steve belonged in Rick Baker's prestigious sculpture department. However, I heard that Everett Burrell had made it into the mold shop and I thought that maybe I'd have a chance there, too.

I got Rick's number and set up an appointment then spent the rest of the day putting my portfolio together. I didn't have much, but I painstakingly labeled everything explaining exactly what my contribution to every project had been. I dropped Tracy off at work for a change, then drove to Rick's place, which turned out to be just down the street from M.E.L.. How ironic.

Rick himself met me at the door, and I took a seat on a couch beneath lines of incredible latex masks as Rick began to go through my portfolio. Unlike Stan Winston, Rick took the time to look at every picture, study it, and ask questions. When he got to the last page he said, "Well, of all of the people I've ever met, you have the most honest portfolios I've ever seen." Apparently, Rick had seen many portfolios that included photos of finished work only to discover that the prospective candidate had only cast the material or made the mold and left it up to the interviewer to ask informed questions.

Rick shook my hand, thanked me, and didn't hire me. I heard through the grapevine that he had hired Howard Berger instead, having known Howard for years.

As luck would have it, Mark Shostrom called to tell me that he was in the middle of a project and could use a little help. It turned out to be the second film by Stuart Gordon and producer Brian Yuzna, the duo behind the successful cult-classic *The Reanimator*. I had gone to see *Reanimator* with James Cummins at the Eagle Rock Theater when it opened. Personally, I didn't get it. The effects were crude and the subject matter turned out to be cruder. Yes, Shannon is a bit of a prude and the decapitated head performing cunnilingus on actress Barbara Crampton, was a bit much for me.

But everyone else loved it, and now the follow up was being made and Mark Shostrom was one of three studios supplying effects to the ambitious film. I wasn't thrilled, but I needed to work, so I did it.

Being back at Mark's after Stan Winston's was a bit of a shock. Gone were the regular hours, the clean shop, and the professional attitude. Instead, it was back at the monster party. This time there were a few new players. The first was David Kindlon, a mechanic who had arrived in Los Angeles via the New York City Muppet shop. Dave was a burgeoning genius. He had a lot of great ideas, a lot of good experience with the Muppets, but not a heck of a lot of experience with Hollywood creature effects. However, he was building an enormous creature that was the final incarnation of the ever-evolving Dr. Pretorious and doing a better job than any previous mechanic in Shostrom's employ. Mark was graduating into a higher caliber of product and Dave was helping him.

Also on board were Gregor Punchatz, an effects artist out of Texas, and Aaron Sims, an artist bedecked in punk rock wear. They were both entry level, and were assigned a lot of lab work. Filling out the crew was Bob Kurtzman, whom I hadn't seen since our disastrous mold at Stan's. Bob had found his new favorite place to work having been with Mark since *A Nightmare on Elm Street 2*.

I didn't get the chance to read the script, so Mark took me through most of it. Like *Reanimator* before it, *From Beyond* was based on the work of the classic horror author H.P. Lovecraft although I don't recall that Lovecraft wrote anything about decapitated heads perform-

The fiberglass mold of the Dr. Pretorious Monster is prepped for casting.

ing oral sex on victims. Shostrom explained that we were working on a couple of stages of Dr. Pretorius's transformation from human to something...from beyond! One stage was sculpted exclusively by Bob Kurtzman and was a huge, ambitious series of prosthetics that ran up one side of actor Ted Sorell's body onto his face, making it appear as though he was degrading into a mass of purple tumors. In the last stage, Dr. Pretorius was to become a huge, long-necked nightmare creature that would be accomplished as a puppet with multiple stages of mechanical heads. The design demanded Mr. Sorrell be able to sit in front of the puppet and have his head "blended" onto it with prosthetics! Like I said, it was very ambitious!

A layer of tissue-thin urethane skin has been sprayed into the Dr. Pretorious Monster mold.

The transformation was to be the result of the stimulation of the pineal gland, deep in the brain, by a "resonator" built by Dr. Pretorius, that affected him both physically and mentally. As a result of over-exposure to the resonator, a subject's pineal gland would shoot out of their foreheads like a tentacle with a bloody almond at its tip. My first assignment was to sculpt the extreme version of this for the Pretorius monster as the puppet was named.

My reference? A medical illustration of a prolapsed rectum. This horrible, wrinkled, pine cone of a mass was set upon a stalk made up of root-like strands unlike the simple, single stalk that the other deformed pineal glands rested upon. I sculpted and then molded the piece, which was run in foam latex.

My second assignment was to help Dave Kindlon with the fiberglass understructure of the final Pretorius creature. Okay. I was familiar with fiberglass but not an avid practitioner thereof. Dave reviewed the steps, and I began the process outside Mark's shop in the alley.

Bob Kurtzman, John Blake, and Dave Kindlon bolt the mold together prior to casting it in soft, expanding urethane.

A modest version of Rick Lazzarini's "Octo-injector" design for delivering large amounts of urethane into molds quickly!

While I was putting layer after layer of fiberglass cloth into the big, reinforced plaster bandage mold of the core, I saw a car pull up across the street from Mark's shop in South Pasadena. A figure wearing a long, black coat got out, leaving his female companion in the car, and walked to the front of the shop. I thought nothing of it and went back to work.

About twenty minutes later, Dave Kindlon appeared with iconic Makeup Effects Artist, Tom Savini at his shoulder. Dave introduced me to Tom and then went on to explain what I was doing; however, he did so like he was explaining it to a ten year-old. Very weird.

As it turned out, my lack of experience yielded a fiberglass core that had the thickness of a commercial motor boat hull. Five layers of resin and cloth became nearly a quarter inch of dense, rigid fiberglass that poor Dave had a hell of a time cutting!

My final contribution to *From Beyond* was the introduction of Rick Lazzarini's "Octo-injector" to Mark's studio. Since Bob had left Stan's prior to our casting Drones, he was anxious to learn the method, but because Mark had a fraction of Stan's budget, we had to cut some corners. Instead of clear, vinyl Tygon tubing, we used garden hose instead. This meant that we could not visually see the progress of the foaming process. Also, the construction of the mold looked like a mountain–very wide at the base and narrow at the neck. The first run we did, the expanding foam gathered in the neck and compressed, so that it lost most of its flexibility.

The next run, we turned the mold upside down and ran it with satisfactory results; however, there was a huge back pressure from the expanding foam, and another Octo-injector explosion resulted, this time with no one affected.

What it looks like when an Octo-injector backs up and explodes.

Post Octo-injector explosion: solidified piles of urethane litter the floor.

Dave Kindlon pretends to slit his own wrists in comic frustration.

While I was prepping the Octo-injector, I received a call from Tony Gardner who was working for ex-Rick Baker mechanic Doug Beswick. Tony was helping Doug with cosmetics for the miniature Queen Alien puppet, and asked if I was interested in returning to *Aliens*.

Continue working on *From Beyond* or return to *Aliens*? Hmmmmm. That decision took a nanosecond; I told Tony I would see him the following Monday, and then returned to inadvertently create another column of soft polyfoam exploding out of an Octo-Injector.

My Halloween costume in Fall of 1985 – The precursor to what would become "Evil Ed."

CHAPTER 22

Aliens at Doug Beswick's Shop

A candle that burns twice as bright, burns twice as quickly.
Dr. Tyrell, "Bladerunner"

I knew the name "Doug Beswick." Being a fan, I had seen photos of him in articles about Rick Baker, and seen him on television documentaries about creature effects, but the most recent articles and information about Doug had to do with a mechanical tyrannosaurus rex puppet he and his small crew had made for a B-picture entitled *My Science Project*. Doug had begun as a stop-motion animator back for Art Clokey, the creator of the claymation *Gumby* series and television's *Davy and Goliath*. Doug had met Rick at Clokey's where they became friends.

When Rick had established his effects shop, Doug came on board as the mechanic designing and building sophisticated real-time puppet controls instead of ball and socket animation puppets. Being invited to work in his studio (versus cold-calling and setting up a portfolio interview) was, to me, like having won the golden ticket. I was a fan of Doug's work, both practical (*An American Werewolf in London*) and stop-motion (*The Terminator*). His shop was located in Sun Valley, which was quite a haul for Tracy to drive me every morning; however, when

I arrived I had little idea of what (or specifically *who*) was waiting for me.

Tracy dropped me off at a small industrial park, and I walked through the front door to meet a sunny woman sitting behind a desk. She introduced herself as Vicki Beswick, Doug's wife, and then asked me to wait while she went in the back shop to get him. As I sat there, I took in my surroundings. Photos of *The Terminator* stop-motion Endoskeleton and the tyrannosaurus puppet were hanging on the wall. In a little plexiglass case, there was a tick (parasitic insect, tick) stop-motion puppet for a film Doug wanted to direct, entitled, you guessed it, *Ticks*.

Doug appeared at the door, shook my hand warmly and took me into the back shop. I immediately noticed that not only was Tony Gardner there, but so was Brian Penikas. Mentally, that was a relief; I already knew two members of his crew. But then I noticed another familiar face sitting at a work table. My old college friend now turned miniature builder, Jim Belohovek! This really was turning out to be a great experience and it was only the first day!

The last member of the crew, a stranger to me, was mechanical genius Phil Notaro and I don't use that word lightly in this case. Soft spoken and direct, Phil sat in front of an aluminum skeleton that I knew, based on its size and proportions, belonged to the Queen Alien.

Doug went on to explain that his association with Jim Cameron on *The Terminator* warranted Doug's contributing to Aliens in a similar fashion, but instead of contributing to the stop-motion work in post-production, Doug would supply two sophisticated puppets that were more like the tyrannosaurs he had built for *My Science*

Project.

Okay, as I've typed the above words I have just realized the irony of that situation and how something similar would play out nearly six years later! Doug's tyrannosaurus landed him the job on the Queen Alien and it would be Stan Winston's work on the Queen Alien that would land him the job building the tyrannosaurus for *Jurassic Park*! Don't you see the irony? No? It's just me? All right then, back to the story:

The job required that more than just the Queen Alien had to be built. In the film (as if you didn't already know this), actress Sigourney Weaver would be fighting the Queen Alien using a futuristic industrial vehicle called a "power loader." This anthropomorphic fork lift was being built full-sized by British effects wizard John Richardson, from a design by Jim Cameron. Our job was to build a miniature, mechanical puppet in scale with the existing miniature Queen Alien that had been sculpted earlier that summer.

Jim Belohovek supervised and built most of the miniature power loader. Using photos, mechanical drawings and measurements, Jim built sections of the intricate machine using wood and Bondo body filler. He would hand the pieces over to Brian Penikas and myself, and we'd make silicone molds of them. Depending on how the cast parts would be attached to the mechanisms that Doug and Phil were building, the molds would either be run out of thin fiberglass shells (no boat hulls here) or in a solid, light-weight urethane resin called "Feathercast." The cast pieces were returned to Jim who would do finishing work, or use them as reference for building surrounding pieces.

The only picture I have of myself working at Doug Beswick's on Aliens.

A miniature figure of Sigourney Weaver had been sculpted at Stan Winston Studios while I was there, but upon receiving the mold at Doug Beswick's, Tony Gardner was instructed to re-sculpt the figure to make it more nearly resemble the actress. Since most of the action would happen in quick cuts, the figure had few internal mechanisms to it; however, Phil built a very simple but effective "head-turn" into it that would subtly raise and lower her chin as the figure's head turned left and right. This little motion prevented the puppet's movement looking too mechanical. It was a little stroke of genius.

The legs and body were run out of soft urethane, but the arms, head and neck were run out of hot melt vinyl commonly known as the material that clear rubber fishing worms are made out of. Although it was translucent with great stretching and compression qualities, hot melt vinyl had its share of drawbacks. First of all it was *very* poisonous to mix and cast. Since it had to be heated up to such a high temperature, that presented dangers as well and extra precautions had to be made when casting the hot, noxious material. Finally, it was *very* difficult to paint; however, in years prior, the development and technical strides later made by platinum based silicones, hot melt vinyl was the best material to mimic actual human flesh.

The best part of working at Doug Beswick's shop was working for Doug himself. Doug was fairly quiet, but very friendly, enjoyed a good laugh, but most importantly, treated everyone there like valued family. He was honest, patient, generous, and enjoyed answering my millions of questions, both technical and about his past work. He could have told me to be quiet and get back to work on many occasions, but instead he'd quietly tell me how he had machined Endoskeleton cylinders on the lathe or how Pete Kleinow had animated the puppet, all very patiently. I remember him pulling a cardboard box off of a shelf and showing me the few Endoskeleton parts that had been sculpted by Willy Whitte. All of the rest of it had been painstakingly machined, which was why Doug did not have a finished stop-motion puppet in his shop. It was just too much work!

It didn't matter that we were such a small crew in such a small shop; impressive work was being done. I clearly remember Jim Belohovek taking wooden dowels that were the correct diameter, proportionately, to the full-sized power loader, cutting them into sections, spanning the gaps with aluminum armature wire, bending the wires until the shape matched the full sized roll-cage, and then filling the gaps with body filler, sanding the entire thing perfectly. It was then molded and cast. It might sound simple but I can tell you that it was challenging, especially knowing that the final piece would be delivered to Jim Cameron who had a very discerning eye.

Across the shop, Phil Notaro was stringing up his tiny, intricate mechanisms with thin, strong cables. When a specific "motion" was strung and ready for testing, he'd call me over to his table to demonstrate. While much of it was insanely cool, the details that got me the most were the delicate fingers on the Queen's over-sized hands, which were mechanized by using thin metal cable housing that was made to bend in one direction and return to its original position by its inherent nature. The other detail was that the Queen didn't have a hard, angled elbow joint; it appeared to be round. To facilitate this, Phil used a double elbow joint that would allow the arm to bend without getting a hard, unnatural elbow protrusion. And if all that wasn't enough, he had built a simple, tiny pneumatic Alien-tongue mechanism that shot out of the Queen's mouth and retracted rapidly. It was beautiful.

The Queen Alien's head was a combination of Feathercast and resin; however, the mouth area had to be cast in something clear to match what the Stan Winston crew was manufacturing in England. Clear dental acrylic was poured into the silicone mold of the front of the Queen's head. Not having a pressure pot or evacuator, I put the mold into a plastic bucket tied to a rope and swung it over my head until the viscous, clear acrylic flowed into the thin teeth using centrifugal force.

The black foam latex skins were run by Michael Burnett at his shop and, at the time, I recall being impressed by just how black Mike had been able to tint the foam without it seeming to have any adverse reaction to the material. In my experience, when foam had been tinted, it would have a pastel color of some sort, either a Caucasian flesh tone, or a pink undertone, but I had never seen foam latex that deep black before.

While we were working on *Aliens*, Brian Penikas was offered a job and left the shop; then Doug pulled in another project called *Assassin*, a television knock off of *The*

Terminator starring tough guy Robert Conrad, famous for *The Wild Wild West* and *Baa Baa Black Sheep* television series. As you might guess, the film had to do with a renegade humanoid robot that Conrad was trying to stop.

There wasn't that much to do. Earl Ellis came on board to sculpt an abdomen section of the actor playing the robot that would open up and reveal electronics beneath his skin.

It was during this time that James Cummins called and asked if he could use an alien I had designed and sculpted that I called a "Shrimp Head" creature you can take the boy out of New Orleans, but you can't take New Orleans out of the boy. James, bidding on the *Star Trek IV* aliens contract, thought "Shrimp Head" would be a good addition to the designs he was submitting.

Work finally became a trickle at Doug Beswick's and I was laid off. I was only at Doug Beswick's for a little over a month, but in that time, I had so much fun, and was happily involved with high quality work again. As bittersweet as it was, I knew that there was a possibility that I could be working on *Star Trek IV*, which could potentially be another fantastic opportunity!

CHAPTER 23

Star Trek IV: The Voyage Home

It's not personal, Sonny, it's strictly business...
Michael Corleone, "The Godfather"

James Cummins and I had stayed in close touch after working together on *House*. We were, after all, long-time friends. He had been happy to hear about Jim Belohovek working on *Aliens* at Doug's shop and kept up with all of my news; however, something was different. James was not the most motivated guy I ever knew.

Actually, James had a taste for the good life. He liked eating in good restaurants, frequently bought records, books, and went on vacations. When the bills came due, James would set his mind to finding work to acquire money to enable his lifestyle.

My original illustration of my "Shrimp-man" creature.

Star Trek IV was a project he felt he was uniquely qualified to work on. He knew Leonard Nimoy's personal assistant on the film, Kirk Thatcher, who had been one of the early concept designers on *House*. James had a very simple yet effective strategy for getting hired on films: He would sit down, do about four color illustrations and then knock out a sculpture that he would photograph. His style was so unique that, by and large, this strategy worked, provided production was comfortable aligning their vision with James' own.

Wanting my Shrimp Head alien as the basis of one of his proposed alien designs, he invited me to his house one Saturday to spend the day just sketching out concepts of different aliens.

I had also sculpted a maquette of this character in New Orleans.

I believe he had already met with actor/director, Leonard Nimoy, so he had some guidelines as to what the aliens should look like. "Think cultures, not creatures," James had said to me and I sat across from him for hours just sketching idea after idea after idea, anything I could think of, while "Jukebox James" kept the James Taylor tunes playing in the background. He probably felt like we were just two twelve year-old kids drawing aliens one Saturday afternoon, and to James I'm fairly certain that is what he wanted to feel. I, on the other hand, felt weird. I wasn't being paid. Eric Fiedler had coached me about "the business" when we worked together on *House* and he advised me to *never* work for free, always get something from the deal. I was providing James with something I learned was, in many ways, more valuable than money: I was giving him my *ideas.*

When I hit something that resonated with James, he'd stop, take the drawing, and then re-draw the alien in his own style including my Shrimp Headed guy.

But I pushed these feelings down because we were friends and I was helping. I wanted James to get the job because I knew he needed the money, and I also knew he would hire me back and that meant more work. I left James early that evening to pick Tracy up at Carl Fischer Music in Glendale. He thanked me, hugged me and said good bye. I wished him good luck with the meeting and left.

I had no idea that exchange would be one of the last friendly, civil exchanges James and I would share.

James called me a couple days later and told me that his meeting with Mr. Nimoy had not gone well. After looking at James' drawings, Leonard had said, "This is *Star TREK*, not *Star WARS*! *Star Wars* is about alien creatures and monsters, *Star Trek* was about *people!*" And just like that, James was out of the picture. He was very disappointed and I felt horrible for him. However, I was also faced with the stark reality of unemployment. I had to find work, and soon.

And just like that, my phone rang.

Ironically, it was Richard Snell, the artist from *House* who had worked so diligently to get hired. He had just been awarded the *Star Trek* contract and offered me a job. I was flabbergasted. What a sudden and unexpected turn of fate! Recalling my coaching from Eric Fiedler, I quoted the highest price I'd ever been paid to that point: $850 a week. Richard agreed to it without hesitating, adding that I was worth every penny. He gave me the address of the temporary studio he was renting in Van Nuys, California, and asked me to be there the following Monday.

"You can't take this job!" James Cummins said to me when I called him and told him what had transpired. "You're part of *my* team! Richard can't hire you off of *my* team!" I explained that I was teetering on financial collapse and needed the work. "If you're truly my friend, you won't take this job and will work with me to find a new job." I told James that I didn't think I could do that. I had an opportunity where I was going to be paid better than I had ever been paid before. I didn't see what this had to do with friendship.

James had other ideas. He interpreted this act as a violation of our sacred friendship and I was no longer his friend. We were done. At least until the invention of Facebook the next century.

Yes, it was rough to hear, and it was a very difficult decision to make. I heard my father's voice in my head warning me about working in motion pictures. I was too sensitive, he thought, and I was possessed of empathetic tendencies. My father was convinced that Hollywood would chew me up, spit me out, and send me packing to New Orleans a broken man. There I was, having made the decision to let a friendship dissolve in favor of my career. Was it selfish or was it self-preservation? I was too young to entertain such heady thoughts, and just focused on finally having a job.

Tracy drove me to my new work location, a crappy building on a crappy street in the crappy section of Van Nuys which is already a crappy section of the crappy San Fernando Valley. How crappy was it? I'll put it to you this way: there were street ice cream vendors on the sidewalks who would whistle as a signal that they had drugs to sell.

I walked into the modest building to find ginger-head-ed, freckle-faced Richard Snell smiling at my arrival. Already in the studio was Dale Brady whom I had met during my CalArts years while he had been working at Tom Burman studios. We were soon joined by Brian Wade and Craig Caton-Largent whom I had heard of but had never met. This was to be the Los Angeles crew; however, since the film was shooting by and large in San Francisco and the surrounding environs, none of us, except Richard, would be going to set.

In addition, we would be receiving alien designs developed by Leonard Nimoy's daughter, Nancy Nimoy very soon. But for the time being, it was going to be all about the ears.

Richard had already met Leonard Nimoy and cast his ears so that the famous pointed Vulcan ear prosthetics could be sculpted and produced. The challenge was that 'Spock', Mr. Nimoy's on screen persona shot roughly for-ty-five days, and one mold would not stand up to the re-peated foam latex runs without breaking down. Since the material required several hours to vulcanize in an oven (I'm sorry, I couldn't resist), we would have to get a perfect cast every day for forty-five days!

Richard decided he wanted to attempt something he called "gang-molding." We made silicone molds of Leon-ard's ear positives and silicone molds of Spock's ears. Then, using a copy of the stone positive we would put it into a copy of the silicone mold of the ear, creating, in theory, a new mold. No matter how many times we attempted it, it never worked. Silicone and stone both fractionally shrink while they are setting, and these tiny imperfections were enough to ensure that there would be thin spots or horrible blending edges in the foam latex castings.

Finally, after a few days of trial and error, Richard succumbed to the inevitable. Molten clay was poured into the Spock ear mold and a stone positive copy was pushed into it. When it cooled, the positive with the clay ear on it was removed from the silicone mold, it was re-tooled, and then remolded, creating several sets of specific Spock ear molds that had to be kept with their specific stone positives.

Of course, this work didn't require all of us to be involved. During our down time we would make fake eyes that we would use for the aliens we knew we would eventually be sculpting.

Actors began to show up for life casting. Actress Robin Curtis, who had stepped into the role of 'Lt. Saavik' in *Star Trek III* came in to have her ears cast so that we could produce her Vulcan ears. Richard met actor Mark Lenard, who portrayed Spock's father, Sarek, and cast his ears at his Los Angeles home. John Schuck, of motion picture *M*A*S*H* fame, came in for his life cast to play a Klingon ambassador.

Impatient for the new alien designs, in my youthful arrogance and exuberance, I produced a pencil drawing depicting updated versions of three classic aliens from the original *Star Trek* series: an Andorian (complete with white hair and antennae), a Telerite (a pig-nosed creature), and a Gorn (a lizard-like creature). Richard showed the artwork to Leonard who approved including the Andorian and the Telerite, but upon looking at the Gorn, said, "The Gorns are not part of the Federation."

Well, two out of three weren't bad!

Now, all of this time, Nimoy's assistant Kirk Thatcher would come bounding in and out of the studio like Tigger from *Winnie the Pooh*. Complete with a red, *Woody Woodpecker*-esque pompador wave of hair atop his head, Kirk had been assigned the task of being the liaison between Richard and Leonard. Always chipper, always chirping, Kirk bounced around from table to table like comedian Robin Williams talking a mile a minute and free associating while giving valuable insights into what Leonard was looking for from the shop.

I remembered Kirk from our brief meeting during *House* and he was so fun and supportive that for a moment, it didn't feel like we were sitting in a non-climate-controlled cinder block building; it felt like we were all in *Pee Wee's Playhouse*.

It fell to me to sculpt Saavik and Sarek's Vulcan ears using the approved Spock ear sculptures as guides. Meanwhile, Craig Caton began sculpting the Telerite and Dale Brady sculpted Andorian antennae. Brian Wade had gone missing. Rumor was that he had been working at Rick Baker's during the day and was going to come in at night, or sculpt at home and bring in completed sculptures. It was a strange arrangement that Richard accepted patiently.

Coordinator, Kirk Thatcher pretends to be a fake head.

One day, Kirk bounded in again, holding the coveted designs of the new aliens drawn by Nancy Nimoy: A cat-man, a frog-man, a lizard-man, an Asian-looking woman, and what looked like a welding mask. What had happened to *Star Wars* is about animals and creatures, *Star Trek* is about people? I guess it didn't matter at that point because they were approved, which meant we were free to begin sculpting.

I wanted to do the lizard-man since it looked most like a dinosaur. Richard wanted to sculpt the frog-man; Craig was going to start the Asian girl whom we referred to as "The China Doll," and with Brian absent, Dale claimed the cat-creature. Every time Kirk looked at the design, sculpture, or completed mask of the cat-man, he would say, in his best Robin Williams voice, "Cat man, doo!"

The Lizard Man puppet I sculpted for Star Trek IV: The Voyage Home.

However, there was one day that Kirk came in stripped of his contagious "fun-ergy." Instead he wore a grim expression on his face. "Didn't you guys hear? The Space Shuttle just exploded," he told us. None of us had. None of us were listening to a radio and there certainly was no television in the studio. None of us had received any phone calls; however, the news struck us all like a thunderbolt, and we turned on the radio to listen to the report.

They say you never forget where you were when a national tragedy strikes. I remember that day clearly.

For those of you too young to understand why this had such a significance beyond the horrific loss of life, you need to go back to the unveiling of the very first Space Shuttle, affectionately named *Enterprise* after the starship from *Star Trek*. At that ceremony, the cast of Star Trek were in attendance and from that day on, the Space Shuttle *Enterprise* had become part of the *Star Trek* lore, even being referenced in *Star Trek: The Motion Picture* as the "first" *Enterprise*. This fact intensified the tragedy within the production.

I learned something else that day: Hollywood pauses, but it never stops.

We took a break, listened to the news, a couple of the guys slipped out of the shop to smoke some grass, but then little by little we found ourselves back at our tables, working.

On a much lighter note, I experienced another significant milestone during that show. Richard was friends with a medical prosthetic artist named Allen Feuerstein who came in as a consultant on the show, especially where it came to artificial eyes. Allen brought with him a black-velvet-lined case that held medical prosthetics for patients who had lost facial features. The prosthetics, unlike the latex ones I was used to, were beautiful, translucent *silicone*! Not only were the sculptures impeccable, since they would have to be to fool the naked human eye but the translucency of the material made it possible for Allen to position tiny fibers that looked like capillaries within the silicone. They were amazing, but at the time had limitations. They weren't made to be blended into the skin cosmetically. Allen explained that normally they would be attached to something like glasses so that at a glance the patient looked like they were in possession of all of their facial features.

This was years before silicone appliances would become the mainstay of motion picture prosthetics!

I finished my lizard-man sculpture and made the mistake of molding it in Hydrocal (a plaster-like stone that sets rapidly). Because the sculpture was relatively long and thin, the Hydrocal *warped* and I was only able to get two latex and polyfoam castings before the mold became useless.

If that wasn't enough, one morning Dale Brady came in to find his cat man (doo) sculpture *missing*! Brian Wade, unhappy with Dale's work, had taken the sculpture home to finish it himself! It was a *huge* breach of shop ethics. To add insult to injury, a taxi cab showed up around 10:00 in the morning with the finished sculpture in the back seat and a pissy driver demanding Richard pay the fare!

As bad as it was for shop morale, I had my own problems; it had fallen to me to sculpt Nancy Nimoy's Welding Mask alien.

I admit that I had trouble with it conceptually from the very beginning. It looked kind of like a robot with a thin visor opening where human eyes would normally sit, but at the top of the head. Human hair cascaded down the sides. So what the hell was it?

After days of struggling with the design, Richard suggested that I sculpt it two ways. On the left side, I divided the features along the planes with seams, as if it was made up of large, shaped pieces of metal. On the right side,

I sculpted tiny little bulkhead plates, as if the mask was made of smaller pieces of metal that had all been built up to become the shape. We were told that Leonard Nimoy, himself, was coming by the shop to see everything in person and we'd leave the final decision up to him.

One of the last sculptures of the menagerie to be completed was the pointed-eared frog-like alien that Richard sculpted. It was composed of so many complicated shapes that it would require a multi-piece mold rather than a simple one or two piece mold.

Generally, molds are made by dividing the sculpture along high points by making walls out of clay or using thin sheet aluminum, referred to as "shims," but the day we molded the frog-alien I watched Richard make small mold pieces without the use of a wall! He just carefully applied the stone where he wanted it and as the stone thickened, he used artist's brushes to smooth the stone and create dividing walls. It was impressive!

Even though Richard had been good about taking photos of all of the sculptures and having them approved through Kirk Thatcher, Leonard and Nancy wanted to make a studio visit, or perhaps Kirk had talked them into it. In any case, the Nimoys were coming and I was thrilled to meet one of my childhood heroes.

Leonard and Nancy arrived, escorted by Kirk who fluttered around making introductions and narrating their tour. I admit to being a bit star-struck when I met the actor/director, because, for the life of me, I don't remember saying much. However, I do recall Nimoy speaking quite a bit. He gave us insights into some of the aliens we had made to that point; he explained their roles as intergalactic ambassadors, etc.

Meanwhile, at another table, Nancy, smiling, was standing and looking at the Welding Mask-alien I had sculpted. Leonard joined her and I heard him softly ask, "Is this what you had in mind?" She nodded. "You can mold this," he told Richard.

If I had attempted to speak, it probably would have sounded like Porky the Pig, but either Richard or Kirk (probably Kirk) asked Leonard what the idea behind the welding mask aliens was. Were they robots? If so, why did they have hair?

Nimoy went on to explain that these aliens were energy beings not unlike the Organians from the *Star Trek* episode "Errand of Mercy." The shells we were sculpting were to be worn by these energy beings to assist them with interacting with other physical forms of life. And there you go! We molded them and you can see them (much to my embarrassment) in the final film.

As the work died down, the shop disbanded, and as Richard Snell took the aliens and prosthetics north to San Francisco to work on set, I returned to South Pasadena to join Mark Shostrom for a new project.

CHAPTER 24

Evil Dead II: Dead by Dawn

Who delivered the Medical School cadavers to the alumni dinner?
Dean Wormer, "Animal House"

Yes, I had received a call from Mark "The Cappy" Shostrom informing me that he had just been awarded the contract to produce the makeup effects for *Evil Dead II*, the sequel to the first film of the same name directed by Michigan's own Sam Raimi, starring Bruce Campbell, and produced by Robert Tappert. The three of them had been friends growing up. They had made *The Evil Dead* in Michigan for very little money and had unwittingly created what had become a cult horror film. What they had lacked in funds they more than made up for in creativity relying not just on frantic kinetic camera moves, but with unique low-budget effects produced by Tom Sullivan.

Now, before I continue, I'm sure that Mark Shostrom, or Howard Berger could write an entire book on the shooting of *Evil Dead II* on location in North Carolina. I didn't go, for reasons I'll explain later. This chapter will focus only on what happened at the shop in South Pasadena.

Tracy and I were still sharing one car; she would drive me from Eagle Rock to South Pasadena and drop me off at Mark's studio. His studio was on Fairview Street, right off of Mission Street and it was still a mess. Don't bother Google-mapping it; the building has been long since torn down. Molds cluttered tables and floor space, empty beer cans and snubbed out cigarettes sat on the corners of tables, and in the air hung the familiar smell of Roma clay, foam latex, and paint.

I was back where I had started.

Aaron Sims, whom I had met on *From Beyond*, was also there to assist with the designs. Mark gave me a copy of the script to read later but described several of the effects that we were going to make, including the possession of the lead character, Ash, who would be portrayed by Bruce Campbell; the "Linda Zombie" (Ash's girlfriend returned from the dead), "Evil Ed" whose mouth was to grow huge after being possessed by the "Evil Force," and "Henrietta," a bloated, naked zombie that would be played by Sam Raimi's brother, Ted.

Mark had done a few drawings on his own. Knowing that Henrietta would require the most amount of work and be the most challenging, he focused on that while Aaron drew sketches of possessed Ash and Ash's dismembered "Evil Hand." I did one preliminary drawing of Henrietta's face, but Evil Ed became my responsibility from day one. I was intrigued by the whole over-sized mouth illusion. The only example of this kind of design had been executed by Steve Johnson, an ex-Rick Baker protege who had achieved an over-sized mouth prosthetic for the character Amy in *Fright Night*.

Now, you must understand that I'm a huge fan of Steve Johnson's work and Amy's makeup specifically. I didn't want to just rip him off. I began to think about the virtues and drawbacks of the makeup. The virtues were obvious, but the biggest drawback of the design was that the prosthetic's corners of the mouth sat obviously outside of the actress' mouth by about an inch or so on each cheek. To hide her face underneath the teeth and stretched lips that seemed to smile impossibly, they had simply painted the actress' face black. Shooting the makeup backlit and in shadows completed the illusion.

What could I do that would effectively hide the actor's face beneath an oversized mouth with teeth? For some reason, a lamprey jumped into my head. A lamprey is an eel-like fish with a round mouth lined with rows of small pointed teeth. They are truly disgusting. I bounced the idea off of Mark, and he seemed to respond to it.

With no reference photos of the actor who would portray Ed, I drew one of my signature white-on-black drawings of the design. I don't want to sound like I had created this drawing technique, but ever since my CalArts days, I had become more comfortable drawing with white Prismacolor pencils on black paper when drawing creatures, rather than in the more common black graphite on white paper. Other illustrators like Ron Cobb and James Cameron had also done it, but without an Internet and relying solely on books and magazines. I hadn't seen their drawings. I just did it one day. My college roommate, Steve Burg, credits me with having shifted his illustration style after watching me draw white on black. Try it sometime, it is very effective.

Mark collected the art to show Sam and Rob and told me that we were to start the following Monday. Mark, Aaron and I would be joined by a few others including Howard Berger and a new Pittsburgh transplant, Mike

Trcic, who was rumored to be an excellent sculptor. Bob Kurtzman and Dave Kindlon were both still in Italy working on set for *From Beyond,* but they would be joining us later in the schedule.

We all gathered in the front of Mark's shop and discussed the breakdown of the duties. For some reason that escapes me, Howard was viewed as the senior make-up effects artist, so the task of transforming Bruce Campbell into all of his possessed guises. Aaron was going to sculpt all of Ash's possessed hand effects and sculpt a long, snake-like neck that the possessed Henrietta would grow just prior to having her head cut off with a chainsaw. When Ash's girlfriend, Linda, gets possessed by the Evil Force, she, too, is decapitated but returns from the dead as a chainsaw-wielding zombie to be sculpted and painted by Mike Trcic. Mark himself would transform Sam Raimi's brother, actor Ted Raimi, into the possessed Henrietta and I would handle the Evil Ed duties.

Our first actor to be cast would be Ted Raimi, and since he wasn't going to show up until the next day, we spent much of our time prepping for his arrival. Mark's shop, from the front to the back, consisted of a small reception area and office, a main shop floor, a narrow middle room that ran the width of the building and a little warehouse area in the back.

Mark hardly ever used his office since it was crammed with magazines and books and God knows what else stacked on whatever furniture he set in there. The office looked like he had been doing business for forty years or so, but we had done *The Supernaturals* in his old studio around the corner only a year or so before! There were two bathrooms, but one of them was so incredibly filthy and unusable. I can recall that the blackened toilet bowl looked like it had just become a dry receptacle for old cigarette butts. The back warehouse area had big wooden shelves that I'm sure had been built by Bob Kurtzman, on which sat stacks of old molds from earlier efforts.

When I returned home from work daily, Tracy couldn't believe how much I reeked just from working there. It seems incredible to me now that somehow this was seen as a "professional" studio. I think that having worked at Richard Snell's (which was smaller, sparser, and had the feeling of a temporary work space) had prepared me with an adequate mental adjustment that prevented me from the direct comparison between Stan Winston's uber-shop vs. Mark's hell hole.

I was very happy for the work, but I longed to be back at Stan's, for sure.

Ted Raimi had been cast to play the possessed Henrietta primarily because of the physical action the character would be required to do. The actress playing Henrietta prior to possession was Lou Hancock and it was decided that instead of torturing Lou, Sam would much rather torture his little brother. Mark's design for Henrietta was a big, bloated, rotting corpse with sparse hair. In contrast, Ted was thin and in good shape, which meant that the Henrietta suit would have to be large and Ted would need full facial prosthetics in an attempt to make him resemble Lou Hancock.

This meant Ted would have to endure a full body cast, a head cast, hand casts, foot casts and dental casts. The head, hands, feet and teeth were all cast in flexible medical grade alginate.

The body cast, however, is usually done by applying plaster bandages onto an actor wearing a body stocking that has been liberally coated with petroleum jelly. Because Mark wanted to pull multiple casts out of Ted's body mold, it meant that the normally fragile plaster bandage body mold would be reinforced with burlap strips dipped in plaster and supported by wood two by fours. I'm confident that prior to this and after it was executed, no one ever did to any actor what we did to Ted. Sam's torture of his brother started with us.

One of the faux-pas of making a body-sculpting form is to keep the actors' arms down at their sides and their knees locked. If you can imagine a finished creature suit constructed this way, you might see the problems that would occur when the actor bent his knees or lifted his arms above his head. The knees wrinkle unrealistically like a pair of pants and the armpits of the suit rip out. That is why we cast Ted with his arms horizontal to the floor with his elbows bent slightly, while his knees, too, were bent.

Ted came into the shop and was immediately funny and friendly. He took a quick tour around the shop while Mark explained the life-casting process to him. Mike, Aaron, Howard and I were busy prepping materials to begin.

We began with the body cast, since it was so difficult. Whenever an alginate life-cast is performed, the mold must be filled immediately with plaster, otherwise the cast shrinks as moisture evaporates (think of those "Grow Animal" toys that swell in a glass of water). We handed Ted a black leotard to wear and prepared for the arduous casting.

We had two wooden stands that looked like they were part of a 17th century criminal punishment device. Ted rested his arms on them so he wouldn't have to bear the coming weight of the cast. He stood on a pad made of mattress foam, while Howard and I began brushing his body with warmed petroleum jelly (and people wonder why I say that I dislike life-casting). Once covered, Aaron and I began dipping lengths of plaster bandage strips into the water, while Mark and Howard carefully pressed them onto Ted's body.

Once Ted was covered with the plaster bandage, we began reinforcing it with the burlap dipped in pottery plaster. Plaster sets by an endothermic chemical reaction...I believe lye is involved, but I'm not a chemist. This means the plaster begins to heat up; the thicker the plaster the hotter it gets. By the time we had finished building the two-by-four frame around the burlap/plaster shell, Ted was roasting!

As soon as the plaster set, we were able to peel Ted out of the mold. All of the petroleum jelly we had applied to protect him had been absorbed by the porous plaster bandage surface, and the leotard stuck a bit to the cast, leaving tiny little fibers in it. Ted took a break while we let the cast completely cool.

Then it was time for the second half, the front half of the mold.

We laid the back half on the ground on its wooden frame and then carefully lowered Ted into it. Although it sounds like it would be more comfortable, it wasn't. Now that Ted's body was being held in a strange position, we had to work fast.

However, with Ted lying down, gravity was on our side, and we were able to finish the mold faster.

So for those of you who are new to all of this, let me explain some quick vernacular:

A **mold** is a *negative* impression of something from which you make a positive; think of it like a cake pan.

A **cast** is a *positive* that comes out of a mold; the cake that comes out of the pan.

I say this because when we referred to life-casting an actor, it meant that we were making negative molds in order to get positive casts (cakes, if you will) of the actor's head and body.

The next step was to mold Ted's head. A latex bald cap was glued tightly to Ted's head, greased with petroleum jelly, along with his eyebrows and eyelashes, and then thick, yellow alginate was spread onto his entire head, front and back. Extra care was taken to keep his nostril holes open while the material flowed around his nose.

Once the alginate was set, it was quickly covered with a plaster bandage mother mold. And when that was set, voila, the mold was made and it was handed over to have plaster poured into it.

Ted, since he would be completely covered as possessed Henrietta, endured the most life-casting torture. The other actors, Bruce Campbell and Rick Francis, as he was known, (he went back to his original last name 'Domeier' afterward), only needed their faces and teeth cast (although Rick did have his finger tips cast so that I could make finger extensions). Denise Bixler, who played Linda had to submit to a nude alginate body cast because a rotted puppet of her was going to be made based on her anatomy. I can't describe the process because I wasn't there, due to the invasive nature of the process. Only Howard, Mark and Mike did the casting on a Saturday morning.

When we cast actress Cassie Wesley, who played Bobbie Jo in the movie, we didn't realize until after Cassie left that we would have to make a Bobbie Jo dummy, and that we had neglected to cast her legs. Tracy turned out to be a perfect substitute; she agreed to the casting and that's how Tracy's legs ended up in *Evil Dead II*.

During the early days of the project, we were told that after the character Linda returns from the dead she would be doing a dance that was to be accomplished (pre-cgi) through stop-motion animation. I recommended my old employer, Doug Beswick, for the job. I remember Rob Tappert worrying that Doug would be too expensive to consider, but I reassured him that Doug *wanted* to do stop-motion, much more than he enjoyed makeup effects. They contacted Doug and he took the job!

And so, with white plaster castings of our actors sitting on tables, the sculpt-a-thon began. Mark had his work station set up toward the front of the shop. A black, fiberglass form of Ted Raimi's body stood on a stand where Mark would begin sculpting the enormous costume and the Henrietta likeness makeup. When the possessed character's neck grew, her head would become distorted and animal-skull-like, an effect that Mark referred to as "the Pee-Wee head," referring to the comedian Pee Wee Herman's film *Pee Wee's Big Adventure*, which featured a startling transformation from a heavy-set woman, Large Marge, into a shock creature. Aaron Simms began sculpting the big neck on a table in the same room as Mark, while Shostrom himself would sculpt the Pee Wee head.

Richard Dormier's head cast poured in clay ready for me to transform it into "Evil Ed."

I used the term Pee-Wee four times in that paragraph. Shocking.

Howard Berger and I were set up in the middle room, which was the cleanest, since it was normally used for running foam latex. I had my plaster Rick Francis cast on my desk, and Howard had three Bruce Campbell face casts on his. It was a peaceful co-existence, since Howard and I enjoyed each other's company and shared a love of movie score soundtracks. In the back warehouse, Mike Trcic began sculpting the Linda possession puppet from a clay casting out of Denise's body mold. To this day, I'm not sure if it was Mike's decision or Mark's, but her rotted, skeletal arms were to be sculpted not in clay, but dark brown micro-crystalline wax, which is infinitely more difficult to sculpt than clay.

A shot of my original sculpture of the Evil Ed prosthetics.

Another shot of the prosthetic sculpture prior to it being cut, floated and molded into three pieces: The forehead, the lower face, and the lower lip.

The sculpture of the Evil Ed puppet. Stan Winston saw this photo in a French horror magazine and hired me back to his studio.

It probably wouldn't have mattered even if soft, flexible, silicone had been more readily available back in those days; to make molds we needed to run rigid casts. Mark couldn't have afforded it anyway. We did make a silicone mold of a skeleton, as you might recall from my *Supernaturals* chapter, but it was way too expensive for Mark's budget. We turned instead to a flexible urethane from the Smooth-On company.

We had made a Smooth-On elastomer mold of Rick Francis' head and I painstakingly cast a clay form out of it to sculpt a fake head of him in his Evil Ed guise. In the film, Evil Ed would be struck in the head with an ax cutting off a large section that would fall to the ground. After I had roughed out the prosthetic makeup for Rick, I set up an armature and began sculpting Evil Ed's fake head.

Evil Ed's teeth are removed prior to his molding.

However, there were two other duties required before Ed's look was finished. I sculpted finger extensions, which were the rage in the 1980s. Finger extensions were just that; sculpted extra joints attached to the ends of an actor's fingers to make his/her hand look long-fingered and sinister. In keeping with the multiple sets of teeth concept, I sculpted some of Ed's fingers with the appearance of having multiple fingernails growing, a detail that is completely missed in the film.

Sculpting one of Evil Ed's finger extensions.

The other duty was the dentures. The entire illusion of the oversized mouth depended upon the success of the sculpture of the dentures. I'm a huge fan of illustrator Basil Wolverton, and one of his most renowned features has been described as "plank teeth" which look like they have the characteristics of old wood planks. That became the inspiration for Ed's teeth, instead of the sharp, pointed teeth more reminiscent of a lamprey fish.

At least that's the way I described it to Sam Raimi when he and Rob Tappert came by the studio to check out our sculptures a couple of weeks into the build. We had most of our sculptures roughed out, with the exception of Henrietta. Mark would ping-pong back and forth between sculpting the head and sculpting the body. Neither was very complete by the time Sam came in to check them out. True, it was a monumental task for one person to attempt to complete alone; however, some of it did have to do with Mark's work ethic.

Howard and I had been conditioned by Stan Winston. We liked to get into the shop by 8:00 in the morning an leave by 6:30, after the daily half-hour clean up. On the other hand, it was typical for Mark to arrive somewhere around 11:30 in the morning. Some days he'd want everyone to stop work and join him at the local coffee house for breakfast; other days, he'd show up and start making his morning coffee while the rest of us filed out of the shop at noon for our lunch break. The latter would sometimes trigger that famous Shostrom anger, and we'd walk away while we heard Mark throwing things around the studio.

Later, we'd return and he would calmly state that it frustrated him that the first thing in the morning (from his perception) his crew would be walking out of the door. Luckily, since most of us were on normal hours, he couldn't focus his anger on any individual, and he learned to accept it.

Mark somehow dragged himself out of bed the morning of the shop visit and led Sam through the shop, introducing us and letting us talk about what we were doing. Sam loved most of what he saw; the only note I can recall was to Howard Berger in reference to Bruce Campbell's possession makeup.

"Witchie-poo" was how Sam described the chin he wanted for Bruce, referencing the infamous witch played by actress Billie Hayes on *H.R. Pufnstuf.*

It was always a great feeling to have a client pleased with the work you were doing. As Sam left and thanked all of us, it was time to take a break and visit Cappy's World of Liquor for a reward of chocolate milk and Hostess pudding pies, deadly factory-made pastries filled with chocolate or vanilla custard and glazed with chocolate on the outside. I'm ashamed to say that this was a regular custom for us, as disgusting as it sounds. Mark stuck with his usual regimen of coffee and cigarettes until 5:00 and then beer and cigarettes through the late night hours.

With sculptures approved, we began molding our appliances and running foam. I still had the puppet head sculpture of Ed to finish and with the clock ticking down, I decided to take a short cut and cast flexible acrylic ears out of the Smooth-On mold of Rick Francis and stick them to the sides of the head so I could concentrate on the face. Truth be told, I was twenty-three years old and not a very good sculptor; I agonized over what would take most experienced sculptors hours.

Although it sounds like we were a well-oiled machine, nothing could be further from the truth. Mark was easily distracted, and many times, the rest of the studio was encouraged to join in his escapades. We shot many goofy videos; some were just one-off gags, others were more elaborate. One, in particular, was a re-creation of the Evil Force from *The Evil Dead*, barreling through Mark's shop back to front, eventually finding Mark standing in the street. We would spend hours shooting these videos, many times while Howard, who had opted not to participate, would yell, 'Some of us have *work* to do, here!" While it was true, the work (well, *most* of it) got done on time.

Bob Kurtzman returned from Italy and the *From Beyond* shooting. He brought tons of photos from set and we were all surprised to see that Director of Photography, Mac Ahlberg (or director Stuart Gordon) had decided to light the makeup effects using strong red and blue fill lights. These are lights designed to 'fill' in shadows cast by the primary lights. The result was reminiscent of comic book coloring, and both Bob and Mark were disappointed since much of their intricate paint work was obliterated by the light.

Most days, Howard and I would come to the studio a bit early in the morning, open all of the prosthetic molds from the day before, prep the molds by cleaning them out and releasing them with foam-latex mold release, then run foam and put the molds back into the oven to bake all day. The appliances' quality was evaluated and then they were stored in plastic bags and tacked to a big cork board.

Mark finished the Henrietta sculpture, and Don Pennington, who had been instrumental in creating the dolphin puppets for *Cocoon*, was hired to make the fiberglass mold. Unlike the rest of us, Don was in his forties already and was a bit cantankerous. I'm sure that if someone had hired me to work in that hell hole after working on *Cocoon*, I would have been cantankerous as well. However, Don was a professional and set out to make this large fiberglass mold, pretty much on his own. I'm fairly certain that at specific points in the process, Bob had jumped in to lend a hand.

Mark had arranged a makeup test day, and since it was understood that I would not be going to North Carolina, Bob, who would be applying the makeup on set, would assist in the Evil Ed test.

Rick Francis arrived and was very cooperative while Bob and I glued and colored all of the foam latex prosthetics. I don't think we took the time to glue all of the finger extensions down, but when I finally popped Rick's dentures into his mouth, all of us were amazed by the illusion. It really looked like Rick's mouth was huge and there were rows of ragged teeth that continued onto the roof of his mouth.

Now, no matter how hard Rick tried, he really couldn't

speak, and he tended to drool a lot with his fake teeth in, but these were small matters compared to the success of the design and makeup. I was elated along with everybody else.

Bob Kurtzman paints the appliances during our test makeup in South Pasadena prior to shooting.

Richard Dormier in all of his glory as Evil Ed...well, sans the white lenses.

With the makeup test completed, my last task was to complete the two Evil Ed puppet heads needed for the film: One was to be used for a couple of gags that Rick would be unable to do, such as turn his head around 180 degrees, kind of like Dick Smith's gag in *The Exorcist* and eating some of Bobbi Joe's hair. The second puppet was called Chop Top and it was to be used after Ash had cut a hefty section of Ed's head off, revealing a shriveled brain remaining in his head.

The ill-haired Evil Ed puppet.

The chop-top puppet complete with its "Pee-Wee" brain.

I had sculpted the puppet head in a strange expression on purpose. One side of it's face looked angry and the other side surprised. That way, when the head was chopped, the surprised side remained while the angry chunk lay on the floor, complete with eyebrow expression thanks to Dave Kindlon. I fabricated the shriveled brain, referred to as the Pee Wee Brain because of its size, not because of the comedian, by using a large syringe and pumping out squiggly noodles of foam latex onto a foil-covered piece of wood. After it gelled, I was able to sculpt the shape using wooden sculpting tools covered in baby powder (to prevent snagging and sticking). It was baked and then painted. However, Mark had a brilliant idea for the dressing of the inside of Chop Top's puppet head.

He had me mix up a liquid vinyl called Elvacite from the Dow-Corning company. Dick Smith had made bleeding vein bladders for *Scanners* using this material. It was my understanding that Elvacite was formulated for airline seats, but don't

A section of Ed's head mechanized by Dave Kindlon.

ask me how it was utilized. In any case, using a one-inch chip brush and a hair drier, I made Elvacite webs that stretched from the inside walls of Chop Top's skull to the Pee Wee brain. The affect was that this little brain was being suspended by a network of neural webs.

My only disappointment was that due to the schedule, the hair work on the main Ed puppet was rushed, and the result was unsatisfactory. However, the guys assured me that they would do what they could on set. I helped pack the boxes to be shipped to location, and was surprised to see all of the raw materials and equipment that would be going out there, since much of the Henrietta suit was still unfinished along with the Pee Wee head. That work was to be completed in North Carolina.

As I left the crew that would be gone for months to shoot *Evil Dead II*, I thought I was done with the film, but fate had other plans for me.

CHAPTER 25

Evil Dead II Part 2
and more fun at Cosmekinetics

*You had best unfuck yourself or I will unscrew
your head and shit down your neck!
Gunnery Sergeant Hartman, "Full Metal Jacket"*

While we were working on *Evil Dead II* at Mark Shostrom's studio, we knew that other special makeup effects companies had been hired for other tasks. Tony Gardener, with whom I had worked at Stan Winston's and Doug Beswick's studios, was building a giant puppet head for the end of the film at his own studio, which he had recently opened. Moreover, Ellis "Sonny" Burman, Jr., the son of legendary Hollywood prop master Ellis Burman, and brother to makeup effects man Tom Burman, had been hired to build several action props, including Evil Trees, a demonic deer trophy, and the iconic chainsaws that Ash used to dispatch the possessed.

I had received a call from my friend, Scott Wheeler, who was working for Sonny Burman at their company, Cosmekinetics, which coincidentally was in the same industrial park as Stan Winston's studio.

He asked if I was available to come in and assist with finishing some of the props, including running foam latex in the Evil Tree molds. Without work, and in search of another paycheck, I happily agreed. I had no idea what I was about to experience.

When I think about Sonny Burman, I think of a capitol V because that was his shape. Sonny was ex-military having served two tours in both the Korean and Viet Nam wars. He was tough as nails and to say he was a bit intimidating would be an understatement. My first impression was that I wouldn't last long. I had no real exposure to the military, and I thought that the moment I stepped out of line I'd receive a dishonorable discharge, or maybe just be shot. I couldn't have been more wrong.

Sonny turned out to be one of the most, if not *the* most fair employers I have ever had. He certainly was one of the most honest. All he asked was that you work for the 8 hours he had you during the day. Talking, joking, all of that still happened, but with Sonny's presence in the studio it just didn't happen to the same level as other places.

Besides Scott and me, the only other person who was around was Sonny's business partner, Bob Williams. Unlike Sonny, Bob was more civilian, and spoke with a calm sarcasm. One of his favorite terms to describe something that was of questionable quality was "Micky Rodentia" (as in: "That eye mechanism is Micky Rodentia"). This was Bob's take on the expression "Micky Mouse" to describe something that was impractical and was better suited to a cartoon.

There was one last occupant of Cosmekinetics, but it wasn't human. The final resident was a pet rattlesnake which was kept in a terrarium up on a shelf. I swallowed my intense fear of snakes (rattlesnakes in particular) and, fortunately, never heard the snake buzzing in his glass tank.

The layout of the shop was familiar, since I had worked in the satellite mold shop at Stan Winston's, which had been just down the row of one-story units. There was a small reception area that served as a small display area. On a shelf sat a life cast of actor and ex-football star, John Matuszak, which featured the ingenious mechanisms built by Sonny and Bob and used for the character Sloth from *The Goonies*. A beautiful maquette of a werewolf, sculpted by James Kagel for *The Howling II* was on a sculpting stand across the room and interspersed between them were motorcycle and motocross magazines.

The main shop space was larger than Mark Shostrom's shop, and had work tables in the center, while the heavy machinery was pushed against the walls. At that time, a large Evil Tree prop sat toward the large open bay door, made from latex, soft urethane foam, and backed with fiberglass chop strand, a material made by using a "gun" to rapidly shoot fiberglass strands into wet resin. Lined up on one table, were a set of identical prop chainsaws that were in their final stages of finish.

As requested, my first order of business was foam running, and this was a challenge because Sonny had no foam room. Foam latex, especially quality foam latex, can be difficult. It is affected by temperature and humidity. Without spending paragraphs explaining the chemistry, much of it has to do with the amount of ammonia remaining in the base of the latex and how the other chemical components react to this ammonia level that results in either a mess or a success. Even Mark Shostrom had his cramped clean(ish) room that was cooled by a window air conditioner in order to run foam.

Needless to say, after a couple of bad foam runs, Bob and Sonny stepped in to help out. Their answer was to use a portable Ph Meter to test the alkalinity of the foam just before I added the gel. The problem was that I had no idea what the proper alkalinity should be, and I don't think they did, either. I'd be refining the foam mixture and one of them would run over with a small black plastic case, holding a wand attached to the case with a wire. They would dip the glass end of the wand into the foam and check the digital readout and then read me the numbers.

It was helpful, I'm sure, but it just meant nothing to me. As I cleaned gelled foam-latex out of the mixing blades, I began to think about Mark Shostrom hovering over the mixing bowl and *smelling* the level of ammonia before he gelled it. I went out, bought a bottle of ammonia from the grocery store, and ran the foam again. Just before I added the gelling agent, I smelled the foam instead of calling Sonny and Bob over with their Ph Meter. It smelled like rubber with no smell of ammonia at all. I poured a tiny amount of ammonia into the foam and then added the gel.

Success! And from that moment onward, I could, with fair accuracy, predict the success of a foam run based on how the latex smelled just prior to the gelling stage.

Now that I had figured out the foam latex issue, I ran the Evil Deer Trophy used in the Laughing Room scene with little to no issue. While I was running around doing most of the lab work, Scott Wheeler was busy doing the finishing work. Scott was a long-time employee of Sonny's, having assisted with *The Howling II*, both in the shop and applying makeups on set.

While we were putting the finishing touches on puppets for *Evil Dead II*, Sonny received a call about another job. He asked if I was interested in driving up north to Steve Martin's Working Wildlife, to see a new litter of Puma cubs.

We would be building artificial Puma cubs to be carried by animal-star, "Benji" for his new film, *Benji the Hunted*. As crass as it sounds, I was in no mood to be unemployed any time soon, so I drove the 40 miles or so north of the San Fernando Valley to the animal compound.

And to be clear, this was not *the comedian*, Steve Martin's place, but another Steve Martin who had made his career training animals for movies.

After negotiating the winding, narrow road through the hills, I parked my car and walked the rest of the way up to the main building. As I rounded the corner, I came face to face with a trainer walking a black leopard on a leash! Leash or not, the sight of a big cat like that without bars or a moat between us was thrilling.

I met the trainers, who took me to the kitten's pen, which was set up on a sunny porch. While the little pumas croaked (I don't know how else to describe the sound they made) and tumbled around each other, the trainers would take one out for me. I measured it with a tape measure, wrote the figures, then photographed each one as best as I could.

Back at the shop, Scott had finished packing the *Evil Dead II* props for shipping and had decided to take a couple of days off before he, too, left for location in North Carolina. This left me with the task of making the puma

Shannon Shea

cubs. It seems incredible to me now that I was only 23 years old and given this task!

A phony baby Puma for Benji the Hunted.

I built an armature so the head sculpture could be removed from the body sculpt. That way, I could mold the body and run it in foam while I finished the facial details of the sculpt. Sonny came out from his office and told me that he had promised them "something" in a week, and that I should concentrate on delivering that puma puppet first.

The pieces were sculpted in a pose that suggested that it was being carried by the scruff of its neck and then molded in dense pink "Tool" stone. Bob built a little armature that I suspended in the center of the mold using fishing line. The result was a little foam-latex puma cub body with jointed arms and legs. I ran the head out of latex and soft urethane foam (since it had no movement to it), glued it to the body and sent it off to the trainers.

One morning just before noon, Sonny appeared on his blue, BMW motorcycle with a small box. On the outside of the box was printed, "Somebody loves me" and "I've found

Demonstrating how Benji, the dog performer, should be carried.

a home." I was unprepared for what Sonny said to me as he took off his motorcycle helmet.

Sonny's Marine Sargent timbre broke the silence of the shop. "Son, today is the day you lose your fear of snakes!" he said and grabbed me by a shoulder and led me to the rattlesnake. I could feel the panic begin to squirm around my insides. He opened the top of the terrarium and the rattlesnake began its ominous buzzing. Although I trusted Sonny 100%, I thought I was going to be sick. He withdrew a small white mouse from the pet store box, and held it by its pink tail over the snake.

"Once you see how a snake eats, you'll learn to respect it. And once you respect it, you will no longer fear it. Now, I want you to watch!" He dropped the mouse onto the floor of the tank opposite the buzzing snake and then Sonny held me by my shoulders forcing me to watch what was about to happen.

Unfortunately, I can't describe what transpired after that between the snake and the mouse, because unknown to Sonny, I had my eyes closed. I heard a quick shift in the terrarium and a tiny squeak, and by the time I opened my eyes, the mouse's head was already in the snake's mouth.

I felt a heavy, proud pat on my back. "See? How bad was that?" Sonny asked. "Thanks, Sonny," was all I could muster as he walked up to his office, and the snake continued swallowing the mouse.

Poor mouse. Someone did love him and he had really found a home...but it was in the belly of a rattlesnake.

To this day, I still don't like snakes, but don't tell Sonny. I wouldn't want to go through that again.

We received a call from the *Benji the Hunted* production office with new instructions for our fake puma cubs. Bob Williams was building a mechanical puppet that pivoted at its neck and could lift its rear legs, but they didn't want this version any more. In its place they wanted a new version with a hollow belly that they could stuff weights into for training. Apparently, once Benji got a hold of our little puma training puppet he shook it like a rag doll. They didn't want him to do this with the real puma kittens and they believed that by increasing the weight of the figure, it would stop Benji from shaking it while getting him used to carrying the real kittens.

I built and finished two kitten figures, one with the hollow belly and one that was just a latex and foam figure. Both had the armatures in the arms and legs that prevented the limbs from bending unrealistically and looking like rubber. With Scott Wheeler in North Carolina, and no one else in the shop, I was left alone to do all of the cosmetic work myself.

One afternoon, as I was dumping one of the shop garbage cans into the industrial park's community dumpster, I had an impromptu meeting with Stan Winston.

He smiled when he saw me, called me over and gave me a big hug. He asked what I was doing and I told him that I was working at Sonny's. This was a prickly subject because Sonny had been sub-contracted by Stan to do a lot of the parts machining and on-set puppeteering of the Endoskeleton for *Terminator*. Sonny felt that he had been instrumental in the creation of the robot puppet and Stan felt that Sonny had been hired as any vendor was and paid for his services. They had worked together years before on the television movie *Gargoyles*, which was Sonny's project on which Stan had been hired to assist in the building of the background suits.

Whether any of this bothered Stan one way or the other was not evident. Instead he asked me if I had been responsible for the Evil Ed puppet sculpture he had seen in a copy of *Mad Movies* a French industry magazine that had run a story about Mark Shostrom and had featured a photo of my puppet sculpt (thank, Mark, for giving me credit!). I told him that I had sculpted the puppet and the makeup.

"Can you start working for me next week?" he asked. I didn't know what to say. On the one hand, I was finishing up *Benji* and potentially could not have work, but on the other hand, Sonny had been really good to me.

Sonny completely trusted and supported his employees. I heard evidence of this one day when the *Evil Dead II* production called with some sort of complaint about Scott Wheeler on set. What their complaint was, I couldn't tell you, but I heard Sonny's response, and it was not pretty. Sonny started ranting to them on the phone, again in his very frightening Marine sergeant voice: "You will *not* disrespect any one of my employees, who are representatives. *Do you understand me*?! I hire skilled professionals and I pride myself on a mutual respect of the contract that we both have signed! Scott represents me and *you will not speak to him in a disrespectful tone!*"

Holy shit. I had *never* heard *any* of my employers back me the way that Sonny backed Scott. It was witnessing that interaction that made me respect Sonny Burman more than any of the people I had worked for previously or would work for in the future. He was a stand-up guy like no other.

Stan followed me back to Sonny's shop, which wasn't making me very comfortable. I had no idea how those two would get along once they were in the same room together. But I rolled the garbage can into the shop, and Stan went into the office to speak to Sonny about my future employment.

Stan stopped by the big bay door before he returned back to his shop. "I'll see you next Monday." he said and walked away. Sonny appeared at the office door. "Shannon?" he called and waved me in with a hand gesture.

I followed and sat across from him in his office. "Stan has offered you a job. The decision to take it is yours," he said. "We don't have much going on here with the exception of a television series that is going to start shooting in the next couple of weeks. We built the puppet for the main actor and there is a job doing on-set maintenance on the puppet if you want it."

He slid a photo of a goofy, hairy, puppet with obvious black paint in its ears to simulate depth that hadn't been sculpted into it. It looked awful. It was *Alf*. I, of course, had no idea that *Alf* would be a hit show that would run multiple seasons and have an animated series spin-off.

To me, the thought of spending my days gluing ripped ears and futzing with frayed fake fur on a television set sounded dreadful. I thanked Sonny and asked him if he minded very much if I returned to Stan Winston's. He shook my hand and told me to call him if I was ever laid off. If Sonny had a job, he'd hire me back.

By the time we were finishing *Leviathan* at Stan Winston's a couple of years later, Sonny was moving out of his shop. Being in the same industrial park across from

Academy Award winning Stan Winston must not have helped Sonny's business, and that was a shame.

I never spoke with Sonny again, not even to say hello in the parking lot, because I never saw him again. He went back onto the makeup union roster and eventually ended up doing prosthetic makeups for *Star Trek: The Next Generation,* or so I understood.

The following Monday, after Stan's visit with Sonny, I parked on the opposite side of the parking lot and returned to Stan Winston studios. I was home! Or so I thought. I swung the door open and saw all of the familiar faces returned from England and their *Aliens* experience. I was happy to see them but... something had changed.

CHAPTER 26

Black Widow and Amazing Stories

I don't get no respect, no respect at all.
Rodney Dangerfield

The gods had returned to Mount Olympus. Well, most of them had. One of the very first changes I felt when I walked into the rear shop door at Stan Winston's was the absence of Alec Gillis. He had taken a leave of absence to assist his friend, Kevin Yagher, build a mechanical demon puppet for the film *Trick or Treat* (not to be confused with *Trick 'r Treat*). The second thing I noticed was that there were fake heads of actor Christopher Lloyd all around the shop.

It turned out that the Stan Winston crew had just completed work on an episode of the Steven Spielberg produced television show *Amazing Stories* which, as the title suggested, featured half-hour fantasy, science fiction and horror tales. In addition, the show boasted collaborations with big-name directors such as Robert Zemekis, director of *Back to the Future*, and Joe Dante, director of *Gremlins*.

The episode they had just completed was entitled *Go to the Head of the Class* which turned out to be an hour-long Halloween special directed by Zemekis. In the story, Christopher Lloyd played a sadistic school teacher who fell under a frustrated student's clumsy voodoo spell and ended up losing his head. However, instead of being killed, the decapitated teacher continued to torment the student with his living head.

Stan Winston Lifers, John Rosengrant, Shane Mahan, and Tom Woodruff had each sculpted specific expression heads of Christopher Lloyd that were mechanized by Dave Nelson and Steve James (both of whom had returned as well). Richard Landon had constructed a dismembered puppet body for specific shots where Lloyd's body would sit up sans his noggin.

Stan Winston, the man, in his office circa 1986.

But that job was completed; what was currently being worked on in the shop was completely different.

On one of Stan's work tables sat two fiberglass molds that could be quickly identified as the body and head of a pig. In addition, on one of the mechanical tables, an aluminum framework held servo motors, gears and cycle chains that powered a pair of mechanical legs.

The show was a new thriller film entitled *Black Widow*, featuring actress Theresa Russell as a serial killer who lured in wealthy men, married them, then murdered them. The FBI agent who worked to catch her was played by Debra Winger. So why the hell would they need a pig?

Apparently, in the script there was a scene where Winger would be chased by an aggressive wild boar, after following Russell to Hawaii. For shots where the pig would be just inches from Ms. Winger, the safe alternative was an artificial animal. I had gone from pumas to pigs in a matter of weeks.

However all of this was just superficial information; there was something more subtle hanging in the air there – exclusivity. The lifers who had returned from England had been forged into a very tight brotherhood that excluded even Dave Nelson, who was from Manchester, England. The others would spend most of the days discussing their triumph on the *Aliens* set and their off-work antics in Europe.

And a triumph it was. In the pre-computer days, Stan had sets of photo albums in the front office of the shop that anyone could page through (and I did). He had tons of behind the scenes photos that went all the way back to his work at the Walt Disney studio when he appreticed under makeup artist Robert Schiffer. A new album sat on the shelf in the front holding on-set photos from *Aliens*. What the creature crew had accomplished was truly impressive. It is difficult to describe my feelings when I first saw a photo of the full-sized Queen Alien suit perched atop her titanic egg sac with her back spines extended out radially. I was stupefied. Stan caught me staring at one of the photos, teary-eyed and asked me what was wrong. I replied, "I'm nothing," at which he laughed and said something diplomatic like, "It was a team effort and we all shared credit for bringing the Queen to life."

But that wasn't true.

The Lifers certainly didn't feel that way. They strutted around the shop like they had been accepted into some sort of fraternity that could only be infiltrated had you shared the *Aliens* on-set experience. Was I envious? Of course. Who wouldn't be? But it wasn't just *feeling* like I had missed out on something special, it was the *constant daily reminders* that I had not only missed out on something special, but there was no way that I would ever be accepted, because when the on-set filming had wrapped, the door was closed. No new members need apply.

Even Shane, who was more low-key than the others, would try to engage me in conversation and ask if I had ever had experiences in Europe and then would go on to describe his off-set experiences in English pubs, etc. I hadn't been out of the country. I didn't even have a passport. It was then that I realized something important: I truly hadn't worked much with any of the Lifers except Alec.

I had been in the mold shop on *Aliens* and *Invaders from Mars* until the crew left for England and they rarely came back to the rear shop. Now, I was getting to know them better.

The sculpting on the *Black Widow* boar had been done, obviously, and I was assigned to the foam latex room to begin running skins. Having mastered the craft in more difficult situations, being in a 68 degree enclosed room would be much easier than my more recent tasks at Cosmekinetics and Mark Shostrom's.

Stan's preferred method of filling molds with foam latex was injection with an enormous syringe commonly referred to as a "gun" or "injector." These injectors had threaded aluminum front and rear caps that attached to either side of a threaded clear acrylic tube. An aluminum plunger with two rubber O rings pushed the foam out of a tapered aluminum tube tip that was threaded into the front cap.

Corresponding holes were drilled into the cores of the molds so that the foam latex could be injected into them. Because foam was being injected into a closed mold, there was less of a chance that air voids would occur from closing a mold already full of material. Also, since the mold was closed when injected, the seams on the foam pieces would be more delicate and easier to remove.

I was left alone to prepare the molds and run the foam, but injecting was a two-person operation, so I sought the assistance of one of the Lifers. More often than not, the molds would be injected, and the injector opened before the foam latex could set in the threads of the injector, which made it difficult to disassemble.

On the occasions where it set in the injector after the molds were filled, it became a chore to unscrew the aluminum caps, which now had foam latex cementing them in place. I had been advised to make sure that once the molds were filled, that I immediately disassembled the injector, so that I could do most of the job without assistance.

However, foam latex is unpredictable and a sudden change in temperature or humidity can affect the material. During a particular run I found myself, again, with an injector full of set foam latex; the aluminum caps were frozen in place.

John Rosengrant came into the room, surveyed the situation and slapped me on the side of my head, then yelled the reminder that I had been instructed to open the injector prior to the foam gelling. I was so red-faced and flushed that I lost the ability to explain that it had

been an unavoidable accident. Instead, I had been transformed back into a frightened eight-year-old kid facing
his angry tyrant father. Eyes bugging and veins bulging
in his neck and arms, John grabbed his end of the injector and together we twisted it open. With one more acerbic stream of words, he stomped out of the foam room.

Understand that I had worked with ill-tempered people before. I couldn't count the amount of times I had
watched Mark Shostrom throw things around his apartment or the studio in rage. Bob Kurtzman was famous
for losing his temper and screaming in the shop. However this was the first time I had ever been struck at work.
Ever.

As I cleaned the foam room and prepared for another
run, I wondered what I should do. I had just been hired
at Stan's and the thought of reporting John's action and
threatening a lawsuit, which, in retrospect I should have
done, seemed to carry with it the potential of a dark stain
on my work reputation. It might prove to make it more
difficult to keep my job at Stan's or find work again else-
where. I would be labeled "a whistle-blower," a pariah.

I took a deep breath and resumed weighing out chemicals.

Since all I had to do was run the boar head and body
molds, I was done running foam in a few days and delivered two sets of skins: one to the mechanical department so they could complete their mechanisms and test
them against the resistance of the foam latex and a second to the cosmetic department so that the skins could
be seamed, painted and finished.

Dave Nelson, and the mechanical crew had completed

the running rig, which turned out to be a glorified wheelbarrow. The mechanical boar sat out on the end of a substantial aluminum boom arm while at the rear, two thick inflated tires smoothed the ride as the boar was pushed forward. Its chain-driven front legs would simulate the pig's gait and the speed was adjustable from trotting to all out running - another impressive feat for Dave Nelson and Steve James.

Whether it was because Dave didn't go to England with the rest of the *Aliens* crew, or that he and I had been in the trenches of San Pedro for *Invaders from Mars*, he told me that he was doing his best to include me with the puppeteers needed to perform the boar in Hawaii. I had missed England and North Carolina, but now it looked like I would be joining this crew for a shoot in Hawaii!

Before I had time to figure out how I was going to break the news to Tracy, Stan emerged from his office to inform us that the pig sequence had been cut from *Black Widow*; however, we had just been hired onto a new episode of *Amazing Stories* titled "Miss Stardust."

The plot was fairly simple: A con-man organizes a beauty pageant to earn quick money, but soon finds himself in a quandary when an angry alien promoter insists on the inclusion of three intergalactic contestants. Our job was simple: Build the three contestants and the alien promoter.

Alec Gillis returned to the studio and joined John, Shane, and Tom to design the aliens. In a short while we were joined by Matt Rose, fresh from Rick Baker's shop; Dave Kindlon, the mechanic I had worked with on *From Beyond* at Mark Shostrom's; Stan's teenaged son, Matt, and Lindsay MacGowan, who had come from England after working with Stan and the crew as a local hire on *Aliens.*

Matt Winston loved his father and was enthusiastic about the work happening at the shop. Stan had relocated his family (Karen, Matt and daughter Debbie) to England during the shoot and Matt had the opportunity to witness the on-set shooting. He was so keyed into *Aliens* and director James Cameron that if he heard the words "alien," "James," or "Cameron," Matt would look up wide-eyed from whatever task he'd been assigned and ask, "What about Jim Cameron?!" or "What about *Aliens*?" Tom and Shane would tease Matt, purposefully dropping a buzz word or two into their conversations just to have Matt react. Then, they'd tell him to mind his own business!

On the other hand, Lindsay MacGowan was diminutive and quiet. Without car or family in Los Angeles, Lindsay had taken a crappy apartment in neighboring Van Nuys and got to work either by bus or by the generosity of one of us. I'll never forget, however, one of his first days settling into his new Los Angeles lifestyle; he was grabbed by two policemen who threw him to the ground, mistaking him for a criminal reported in the area. After they realized they had made a mistake, one of them said to him, "Welcome to Los Angeles."

This episode of *Amazing Stories* was a tongue-in-cheek comedy directed by our old friend, Tobe Hooper, and would star one of my childhood idols, actor Dick Shawn! The designs of the alien contestants, one each from the planets Jupiter, Venus and Mars all reflected the comedic influence of the script.

Musical comedian "Weird" Al Yankovic had been cast

to play the alien beauty contestant promoter, so he came in for a head and hand cast. Shane had taken over the design and sculpting responsibilities and Kevin Yagher, who had just attained his makeup union status), would do the on-set application. Shane's approved design transformed Yankovic's countenance and head into an enormous head of lettuce!

Armatures were built and sculpting assignments were handed out. I ended up sculpting Miss Venus' facial tentacles which turned out to be sleeker versions of the mutated pineal gland I sculpted for *From Beyond*. I also attempted to sculpt her hands, but I did such a crappy job, that Tom had to jump in and re-sculpt them in a day.

It was evident from that time that Alec and Tom enjoyed collaborating. They sculpted the majority of Miss Venus together, and when Alec began sculpting Miss Jupiter's head, Tom worked on her body. Matt Rose sculpted Miss Jupiter's delicate hands and arms, while Lindsay and I each sculpted one of Miss Jupiter's legs.

The Miss Venus puppet as it was displayed in Stan's original shop in Northridge, CA.

Miss Mars and Miss Jupiter, because of their proportions were completely mechanical puppets, while Miss Venus could accommodate a performer who would manipulate the harp-playing hands.

When it came time to paint the puppets, Miss Jupiter in particular, Matt Rose gave me an impromptu painting lesson that I not only still recall, but pass onto my students. He had me look at the palm of my hand and note the fine blue and red blood vessels that were running through it like lacework. He demonstrated that by painting layers of blue and red washes in that particular vein. The pattern result was an illusion of skin translucence which is difficult to achieve on the opaque surface of foam latex. It was excellent advice and is a painting technique I use and teach to this day.

Dave Nelson and Steve James built most of the facial mechanisms for all three puppets while Dave Kindlon built the arms of Miss Jupiter and the legs of Miss Mars. Richard Landon built the arms of Miss Mars and his use of differential gears in the shoulders would determine Matt Winston's and my puppeteering positions on the show.

I learned another lesson in physics on that show. Even though Miss Mars' arms, made of foam skins and mechanical armatures, only weighed a few pounds apiece, they were about thirty inches long from the shoulders to the fingertips. For the shoulder mechanics, Richard used differential gears that would automatically disengage when too much force was exerted on them in order to prevent the gears from stripping.

Miss Mars on display at Stan Winston studios.

The result was that as Miss Mars lifted her arms from the shoulders, the force due to the leverage increased, the differentials disengaged and her arms would then drop lifelessly at her sides. In order to decrease the load, external wires were attached that ran from the puppet's wrists through pulleys mounted above the puppet that were counterweighted on the other end.

The episodes were shot on the Universal Studios lot, which meant that those of us working on set had to be in a union. At that time, unions had a firm grip on Los Angeles film production. No one was allowed to work on any set without being part of a union, whether it was special effects, wardrobe, makeup, etc. Stan, maintaining that we weren't creating creatures, but bringing performers to set, had all of us working *as actors.* That meant we'd all be working under a Screen Actor's Guild deal.

Screen Actor's Guild (SAG) was a much different animal in 1986. Motion pictures and

Miss Jupiter sits above the shop office at Stan Winston studios in 1986.

one-hour television dramas were still shot on film and the union (under then-acting president Patty Duke) was very powerful. Everybody in the world could appear in one motion picture or television show without a union card under a provision referred to as "Taft-Hartley." You would receive union pay scale, work union hours. SAG union residual payments were calculated as the movie/ television show was sold to foreign markets, cable or commercial television for broadcast or syndication, and on VHS tape, the actors would receive a royalty payment.

This sounds fantastic; however, with the exception of producers, directors, writers, and actors, no one else on set...no one else...receives residuals. Commonly called "the line." Everyone who does not share in the profits works "below the line" while the fortunate work "above the line." Imagine a studio full of below-the-line workers yielding to a bunch of motley puppeteers dragging cable controllers and boxes full of maintenance materials, knowing that the puppeteers were amongst the highest paid workers on set. It didn't make for a friendly environment.

The episode was shot on a couple of sound stages on the lot, so while Tobe Hooper and production were shooting all of the live action scenes, we were on another stage rehearsing with the puppets. Miss Venus required the least amount of rehearsal since the post-production sound department would add the futuristic harp music to match the puppeteer's movements. I would assume that it was Tom Woodruff in the suit, but for some reason, I remember seeing Steve James in the gloves – ah – failing memory!

For Miss Mars and her Middle Eastern-influenced dance, Matt Winston and I had to climb to the roof of the stage and step down onto a suspended platform over the puppet. Richard Landon rigged the pulleys and the arm wires were fed through and weighted. In addition, a long horizontal pole was rigged with two wires that took the weight of the puppet. Matt and I would lift the puppet and rhythmically move her left and right while the puppeteers on the ground coordinated her dancing moves.

Miss Jupiter required that we coordinate not just her

body but also her facial expressions to an audio playback. Later, I recognized the musical selection as the aria "Santo di Patria" from Verdi's *Attila* when Tracy happened to be playing a recording of it at home. Having this time to rehearse was a luxury, and I can only think of a handful of times when we puppeteers were afforded this luxury.

Meanwhile, Kevin Yagher had transformed Weird Al into a head of lettuce, and it was very effective. He even placed little black balloons behind Al's leafy ears that could be inflated/deflated rapidly to enhance the character's frustration with "Eeth men" (Earth men).

Miss Jupiter as she appeared on the set of the Amazing Stories episode "Miss Stardust"

While Kevin was on set, though, I witnessed him do something much more amazing than his makeup application.

Using only cuticle scissors, he clipped a perfect Teddy Bear out of a white latex sponge, the kind normally sold as wedges at the drug/cosmetic store. It was uncanny.

Stan had a different approach to his downtime. Walking past actresses dressed as beauty contestants, he would launch into his Jerry Lewis act, mimicking the famous comedian and pretending that he had a large erection in his pants that was affecting his ability to walk. He was shameless and hilarious!

When it came time to actually shoot the alien contestants, vaudevillian comedian Jack Carter played the emcee who introduced each hopeful with a wisecrack. Production waited while we set up each puppet to perform. While Miss Venus performed her harp routine, the rest of us began preparing Miss Mars.

Production took a break while Matt Winston and I climbed into the rafters and took our positions. Puppet control cables were run through holes cut in the stage floor, and the support wires were run up through the pulleys and connected to the puppeteering rod. Everything was going smoothly until we did a dry run-through before production returned.

We were in the middle of our dance when one of the counterweights snapped off the wire. It was almost like slow motion; as Matt and I watched, the wire slipped through the pulley and the 300 mg weight dropped to the stage floor, luckily missing everyone. POW! With the echoing sound of a gunshot, it hit and dented the stage floor, and everybody instinctively looked up. Had it hit someone, I'm convinced it could have killed them.

When it came time to shoot Miss Jupiter, I, along with my co-workers, received an education about rehearsal and shooting. We had gone through the trouble of learning a routine to the audio playback, having choreographed and coordinated our movements so that we all knew exactly what we needed to do at certain points in the aria. However, when Stan, Tobe, and the rest of the crew showed up, they watched what we had rehearsed (independent of any input), and decided that they didn't like it.

So, we performed by the seat of our pants, hearing Stan

shout out directions like "Lift her right arm! Higher! Look right! Look right!" My guess is that Stan, watching the video monitors was making sure that she looked her best through the lens of the camera, while we puppeteered to a dedicated video camera.

After we shot all of the intergalactic contestants doing their routines, we set all three puppets up on a backstage set where Dick Shawn had his final confrontation with Weird Al. It was such a pleasure to watch Dick work, and memories of him from *It's a Mad, Mad, Mad, Mad World* and *The Producers* made me grin like an idiot. My only regret is that I didn't ask him for an autograph. He died, doing a live stage show, a year later.

During one of our lunch breaks, Stan approached us to tell us about our next project. How apropos that we would be shooting on the Universal Studios lot, the home of the original *Frankenstein, Dracula, The Mummy, The Wolfman* and *The Creature from the Black Lagoon*. Stan had just been hired to provide the monsters for a new horror/comedy that featured all of the creatures mentioned. A project written and directed by *Night of the Creeps* writer/director, Fred Dekker. The show was called *The Monster Squad*.

CHAPTER 27

The Monster Squad

It's only with hindsight we can see things for what they really are.
"Before I go to Sleep" S. J. Watson

In the spirit of honesty, I didn't see what all the fuss was about. Sure, I was happy to segue to another job immediately without having to run around and look for work, but I didn't share the enthusiasm of the majority of the Lifers. Frankenstein? Dracula? Sure, I had seen the Universal movies and I thought that they were great for watching on Saturday afternoons instead of doing chores, but my passions were much more steeped in Ray Harryhausen or Toho efforts.

A guy running around wearing a cape and fangs was no match for a seven-headed Hydra or an atomic lizard destroying Tokyo. But that was me. The rest of the guys were chattering away, discussing what they thought would be "cool" interpretations of the classic Universal monsters. This was when Stan dropped the first bomb. *Monster Squad* was not going to be a Universal movie, which meant that all of the designs had to be reminiscent of but not be infractions upon the established Universal monsters designs, which the studio controlled and guarded with an army of lawyers. In addition, entertainment attorney Bela Lugosi, Jr. had contacted the surviving families of Boris Karloff and Lon Chaney Sr/Jr and had brought a suit to Universal demanding that the studio share in royalties based on the likenesses of the actors who had portrayed the monsters, and they had won!

In a nutshell, what it meant was the Frankenstein could not have the signature flat-top head and neck bolts, etc. Dracula could not have a pointed 'widow's peak' hairline. You get the idea.

We returned to Stan's Northridge, California studio and began preparing the studio for this new sizable project. During *Amazing Stories*, Stan had rented another unit directly across the parking lot intended to move the noisy mechanical department with its industrial mills, lathe, and band saws. In addition, Stan leased another unit, next door to the unit where we had made molds for *Aliens* specifically to house a large walk-in foam oven. With the preparations for such an ambitious project, new talent was hired including bringing about the return of Steve Wang, as well as introducing a new runner named Grant Arndt, an East Coast Dick Smith protege named Emilio Gonzales.

During this time, Stan himself began designing all of the monsters. Using his signature tracing paper and pencil style, he began looking at the work of illustrator, Berni Wrightson for inspiration. Berni had garnered a reputation for himself as an eminent horror comic book artist having contributed to DC Comics' *House of Secrets* and *Swamp Thing*. I recall having read that makeup effects artist Rob Bottin credited Berni for the inspiration behind his werewolves for *The Howling*.

I must admit that there was something kind of cool about seeing Stan sitting at his drafting table, surrounded by reference photos of himself making faces, wolves, comic book art, whatever inspiration he could get his hands on, sketching monsters. I didn't realize that it would be one of the the last times I would ever see Stan designing everything, if not the very last.

It was equally amusing that Alec took the opportunity to attempt to annoy Stan with purposefully dumb questions like: "Hey, Stan, was Paul Bunyan's shirt oversized plaid, or was it just yards and yard of regular-sized plaid?" or "Hey, Stan, can a seal kill you?" Stan, concentrating, would answer the question calmly without getting ruffled. I never heard the answer to the seal question, but Stan certainly didn't know the answer about Paul Bunyan's shirt.

Finally, Stan appeared with his approved designs and gathered us all together for a meeting to decide how the work flow would be divided. Again, my memory isn't clear on this, but I believe

Shane Mahan and I clowning around in front of the Dracula transformation puppet arm sculptures.

that even *before* that meeting, Stan had decided that Matt Rose and Steve Wang were going to be given the Gillman responsibilities. I couldn't be 100% sure, but I believe it had something to do with their recent participation with the build of the Bigfoot suit at Rick Baker's studio for *Harry and the Hendersons.* If they were good enough for Rick, they were good enough for Stan Winston!

Matt Rose had been one of the first sculptors put to work on *Monster Squad,* having taken the time to sculpt a detailed maquette of the Gillman, based on Stan's drawings. Tom Woodruff, had been pushing to perform inside creature suits, and the Gillman would be his debut.

Woodruff spoke up and said that he would like the opportunity to tackle the Frankenstein duties; Rosengrant wanted the Wolfman; Shane took the Mummy; which left Alec with the Dracula transformation and bat duties.

Next, just like in a schoolyard, teams were picked and unlike my school sports experiences, I was one of the first to be chosen...by John Rosengrant!

This created conflicting feelings within me. Here

John Rosengrant roughs out The Wolfman head sculpture.

was this guy who had once struck me and who had yelled at me whenever he had the chance, now choosing *me* over the rest of the crew. Was it because he thought I was talented, or that I would put up with his bullshit? I didn't have the luxury to entertain this line of thinking. Whether I liked it or not, I was part of the Wolfman team, along with Emilio Gonzales.

While we waited for the performers who would play the rest of the creatures, we cast Tom Woodruff and began making the molds necessary to produce head, body, hands and foot sculptures. Matt and Steve had obviously learned a thing or two while working for Rick, because they asked for the life casts to be prepared in a specific way.

Once we had molded Tom's body in plaster bandage, it was removed and then filled with rigid expanding polyurethane foam. They took a drill bit and taped off all of it from the base on, except a quarter of an inch at the

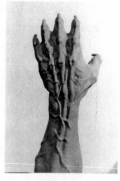

My original sculpture of The Wolfman's arm – muscled and vascular.

Another view of my original Wolfman arm displaying the wolf-like pads in the palm.

end. That way they could be sure only a quarter of an inch was being drilled into Tom's rigid foam body cast. Then the entire surface was drilled with these little holes.

Upon completion, the entire surface was sanded until none of the holes showed. Matt and Steve explained to me that doing this ensured that the foam latex suit was going to fit Tom tightly, and that there would be little to no areas where the suit would be baggy or wrinkle funny.

The next set of casts were of the three actresses who were going to play Dracula's "brides," unfortunate victims who would return from death as vampires. This meant more than tooth casts and vampire fangs. In Fred Dekker's script, they are dispatched by bow and arrow, and since the brides wore plunging necklines, Tom and Shane suggested sculpting foam latex prosthetics that would conceal the necessary plate on which the prop arrows would be mounted. The result was that Shane and Tom had to take nude chest casts of the three actresses playing the brides. I wonder if there was any coincidence that Shane began dating one of the three actresses after he took the cast?

Actor Tom Noonan was cast to play Frankenstein's monster. Tom Woodruff led the team that cast his head, hands and teeth while John Rosengrant led us in the casting of actor Johnathan Gries, who would be portraying the man who would transform into the Wolfman.

Michael MacKay was cast (figuratively and literally) as the Mummy. We had been told that Mike was very skinny, and he was, for sure! But what we didn't know until he appeared at the shop, was that he was about 5' 4" tall. That didn't make for an intimidating Mummy. However, Shane, ever the spin-doctor pointed out that real mummies, historically, weren't very tall and since he would be acting against kids, our Mummy would still be menacing.

I love Shane.

Since the part of Dracula had not been cast, three sculpting armatures were in different configurations, each one less bat-like and more human. Dave Nelson designed and built the mechanics of these puppet arms that featured stretching fingers and limbs that, when shot in reverse, looked like delicate bat fingers were shrinking and taking on human proportions.

It was during these early prep days that something very strange happened.

One weekend Tracy and I were invited to a birthday party that was to be held at the "home of wayward makeup artists." This was the name given to the house in the San Fernando Valley rented by Howard Berger, Bob

Kurtzman and Dave Kindlon. We arrived at the party and had been introduced to a young man from New York named Derek Devoe.

Derek was an accomplished sculptor and who had committed the same faux pas that most young make-up effects artists did in the 80s: they would bring their portfolios to every social function. At the mere mention of someone working at a specific studio, the portfolios would fly open and pages would turn! Tracy began referring to these events as "ass-sniffing parties" (like dogs getting to know each other).

As Derek flipped the pages in his book, he told me of his plan to come to Stan's, show his portfolio, get hired, and then become the top sculptor at the studio. I explained that it didn't work that way at Stan's and that the Lifers would always be on top of the food chain. Insulted rather than educated or discouraged, Derek assured me that would not be the case.

A couple of days later, Matt Winston and I were in the back of the main shop, when a car pulled up outside of the open loading bay door. The driver, wearing a purple latex pig mask hopped out of the car and walked directly to me, past Matt. He lifted the mask and as you expect, it was Derek pushing his portfolio into my hands. "Show this to Stan, it's my illustration portfolio," Derek told me then, pulling the mask down over his head; he hopped into his car and drove away.

What else was I supposed to do? I took the portfolio to the makeup room, Matt trailing behind me, to give the book to Stan who was sitting in a makeup chair surrounded by his Lifers in the middle of a discussion.

"What is it?" Stan asked as I entered the room.

"This was just dropped off," I said, and handed him the portfolio.

"Who is it from?" Stan asked.

"Derek Devoe." I answered.

"And he was wearing a purple pig mask." Matt chimed in.

At the sound of Derek's name, Stan sank into his chair a few centimeters and sighed. "Okay," he began, "here's an example of a very talented individual I would never hire because of their personality."

He went on to explain that the night before, as he was leaving, Stan was accosted by Derek who insisted that Stan look at his portfolio before he drove home. Derek's insistence and lack of respect for policy rubbed Stan the wrong way. Stan politely looked at his portfolio (flip, flip, flip, flip) and left Derek in the parking lot holding his book.

To my knowledge, even after I left Stan Winston's studio, Derek never worked there. Ah, the best laid plans of mice and men...

Instead, artists Lenny McDonald and Eric Fiedler (with whom I had worked on *House*) joined the crew.

John, Emilio and I worked on the Wolfman sculptures in the additional unit away from the main shop. Rosengrant had roughed out the head in green Roma oil clay on a fiberglass head that could be removed from a stand and attached perfectly onto the fiberglass body form. That way, John could be sure to keep the head to body proportions perfect. The body, which would eventually be completely covered in hair, was an exaggerated, sculpted musculature. I had the duty of sculpting the hands and feet, while Emilio worked on a sculpture of John Gries' back that would be used for a transformation effect. There had been a lot of talk on the set of *Amazing Stories*

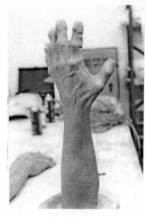

about the monsters, and one of Stan's ideas was to have two different actors playing the human victim of lycanthropy and the resulting wolfman. Stan, by the way, was quick to distinguish the difference between a Wolfman (who was a man, bitten by another Wolfman who would take on a wolf's characteristics) and a Werewolf (who was a human who could shape-shift into a wolf or a wolf-like creature). Make no mistake, we were producing a Wolf-MAN!

The final Wolfman arm sculpture I did in one day after my original arms were deemed too large.

This was 1986 and by then the public had seen two *very* effective transformations of man-into-wolf: Rick Baker's in *An American Werewolf in London* and Rob Bottin's work in *The Howling*. These transformations were done by a combination of air bladders hidden beneath prosthetics combined with successive puppet heads, complete with facial features altered by in-

The palm of the revised Wolfman hand. After sculpting the other hands for four days or so, these were done in a matter of hours!

ternal mechanisms, and this had become commonplace. Stan had even transformed actor Simon MacCorkindale, from man into black leopard weekly on the television series *Manimal*.

Stan, ever attempting to push the envelope, wanted to go one step further. He told us that this transformation was going to happen inside of a telephone booth (remember those?). The idea became that the camera would be mounted onto dolly tracks in a circle around the booth and that using the window frames as matte lines, we would utilize Gries in a series of makeups, segue into a puppet head and then finally into complete Wolfman after moving around the booth 360 degrees. With the camera constantly moving, it would be like a staged magic trick (you know, like a magician rotating a box on stage prior to an illusion) and the audience would not be able to discern how the effect happened without seeing film cuts.

In actuality, I had more than a pair of hands to sculpt. I also had the task of sculpting a transformation puppet

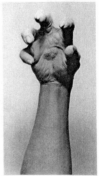

Sculpting the Wolfman's feet.

My sculpture of the Wolfman's mid-transformation puppet arm that never made it into the final film.

arm that would be in mid-transformation between man and wolf. Stan, in an attempt to outdo previous transformations, asked for an arm puppet that could grow hair and pointed nails all in one shot. As easy as it might sound, it was actually a monumental task.

After the arm was sculpted, molded, and run in foam

latex, Eric Fiedler stepped in and drilled holes all over the fiberglass core until it looked like it had been riddled by a miniature machine gun. These holes allowed Eric to punch hairs one at a time through the foam latex skin and the core only to be tied together in groups and attached to lines that fed out of the bottom of the arm. Pointed fingernails were mounted onto cables and run through cable housings to a controller that enabled them to

The Gillman suit as sculpted and painted by Matt Rose and Steve Wang. Eyes made by Lenny McDonald and worn by Tom Woodruff, Jr.

A Monster Squad rogues gallery. From L – R: An assembly of prosthetics on Tom Noonan's face cast by Tom Woodruff, Jr. that was utilized as a paint master, a Halloween-style Frankenstein mask sculpted by Steve Wang, a skull, and finally a skull-like mask made by Lenny McDonald that was worn by Duncan Regeher for a subliminal flash of horror during a lightning storm.

either be pushed outward or withdrawn inward.

The idea was that, when cued, the extended nails would be pulled inward, then all of the punched hair pulled in through the skin while the camera rolled. When the footage was reversed, it would look like hair was sprouting all over the arm while pointed fingernails grew from the fingertips.

Dave Kindlon mechanized a puppet head of John Gries in mid-Wolfman transformation so that the cheekbones and nose grew outward simultaneously to simulate the Wolfman's final features. To round out the transformation was the back that Emilio had designed and built. Three sections of sculpted vertebrae mounds were mounted on top of air bladders that when inflated looked like Gries' spine was undulating and changing. It all seemed fairly simple.

There were some things that I didn't understand: When Richard showed me the fingernails mounted onto the cables, there were *very* noticeable gaps between the nails and the finger tip area. When I pointed it out, his solution was to hand me a small pastry bag syringe he had made that contained brown-tinted petroleum jelly for me to

The Mummy puppet that was used for shots where Mummy performer, Michael McKay, was not emaciated-looking enough.

A casting of the first-stage "Dracula-Bat" sculpted and painted by Alec Gillis.

squeeze into the cracks. That seemed dubious; however, what really made no sense was that he had mounted the arm assembly on a heavy duty garage spring base. Just looking at it, I knew it wasn't right, but Richard was a Lifer and I was just a punk who hadn't gone to England and shared in the *Aliens* experience. So I kept quiet and, for some strange reason I'll never understand, no one else questioned Richard either.

The night we shot at the Culver Studios, I recall that the transformation effects were shot by a second unit camera department led by producer Peter Hyams. John Rosengrant got into the phone booth and puppeteered the head, while Dave Kindlon, Emilio and I operated the rest of the facial features. We shot several takes of it at different angles and speeds. Then it came time to puppeteer the hand.

The base was mounted on a grip C-stand. Eric Fiedler had lubricated the hair with silicone grease to decrease the friction as he pulled the hair through the foam latex skin. Hiding below the camera, he grabbed the cables and got ready for his cue. I explained to the cinematographer that there was only one shot at this effect; once the hair had been pulled through the skin, that was it.

We were directed to slam the hand against the side of the glass which didn't make sense since the hand was not in a fist or open palmed configuration, and trying to hold the arm by the spring base didn't help either. Needless to say, the camera rolled, the arm was pressed against the glass, Eric tugged at the hair cables, which pulled nicely until they hit the grease then all but vanished into the skin, while the fingernails withdrew into rolls of brown petroleum jelly. This all happened while the arm quavered on its spring.

When the cinematographer cut the camera, he said the effect was no good because he couldn't keep the arm in focus while it was shaking on the spring. Richard apologized to me on set and I told him not to worry about it, but I had learned an important lesson: Always go with your gut and don't accept anything if you instinctively know that it isn't right.

That night, I was able to observe Matt Rose and Steve Wang suit up Tom in their impressive Gillman suit. Matt and Steve had proven to be an impressive team. Matt had sculpted the head and hands, while Steve sculpted the body and feet. They had meticulously designed the suit closures to be hidden within patterns of scales so that there was no evidence of how the performer was able to get in and out of the suit. Their instincts about shaving the sculpting core down were correct as well. The snug suit didn't wrinkle but instead acted like a second skin. Tom had the ability to roll his abdomen muscles and it was kind of creepy to see it beneath the foam latex .

I wish I could say that this incredible feat secured Matt and Steve a position of permanence at the studio; however, weeks earlier, Stan had done something which had set those two young artists up for heartache.

He hadn't meant to hurt them – quite the opposite.

As was Matt and Steve's *modus operandi*, they never seemed to leave the shop as long as there was work that needed to get done. They worked tirelessly, first on the sculptures, then assisting Jackie Tischner with running the foam latex on the suit, then finally designing and painting everything. Matt painted the head while Steve painted the body.

One Monday morning we all returned after our weekend. In the annex shop where Rosengrant had led the Wolfman crew, there sat the first completed, painted Gillman suit. When Stan saw it, he did something unprecedented. He stopped the entire shop, had them gather in a circle around the finished Gillman and proclaimed that it was *the* best suit he had ever seen in his career and then led the shop in applause.

If there had been a spark of jealousy toward Matt and Steve by the Lifers, it was then fanned into a flame. By that time, Tom Woodruff had sets of painted Frankenstein appliances and at least one makeup test on Tom Noonan by Stan and long-time makeup associate Zoltan Elek had been executed. Shane's Mummy suit was nearly completed, John's Wolfman was all but finished and we were working on the ancillary effects, and Alec was leading a group of sculptors including Lindsay on a large bat-into-Dracula mid-transformation body.

Everyone was doing outstanding work; however, it was Matt and Steve who had been singled out to have praise heaped upon them. Stan might as well have put a target on both of their backs. Not that anyone, especially Tom, had anything negative to say about the suit. I know that Tom, especially, *loved* the suit. It was just Stan's reaction that had rubbed them the wrong way. However, all of us, I'll say it again, all of us still wanted to impress Stan with our work. Punishing Stan was not in the Lifer game book, but someone would have to suffer for it.

I couldn't be sure if it was this effort to impress Stan, or just being a bunch of willful young artists that pushed us to attempt new things on *Monster Squad*. For example, there was a scene where the Wolfman had a stick of dynamite shoved in his waistband and was pushed out of a window where he exploded in mid-air. Upon landing on the ground, in pieces, the parts dragged themselves back together (this was *years* before *Iron Giant*) and the Wolfman was re-assembled as if by magic. According to Dekker's script, the only way to kill a Wolfman was with a silver bullet , so blowing a lycanthrope up would not be fatal.

We ran parts out of the various Wolfman molds and added tattered rubber flesh to the dismembered body and limbs; however, we still had to figure out how we were going to motivate all of the parts back together. Stan wanted one of the dismembered arms to have mechanical wrist and finger movement.

Various incarnations of the Wolfman. From L-R: The blown-up Wolfman, the mid- transformation puppet head, and the final Wolfman suit.

I'm not sure who came up with the idea, but someone in the mechanical department, probably Dave Nelson, who was a radio-control car enthusiast, suggested that not only would the hand have the required movement operated by radio control, but it would also have wheels and would be able to drive itself back to the rest of the injured Wolfman. Who was I to disagree?

The assignment fell to Steve James who built the arm to drive on a diagonal rather than a straight in line with the arm and hand. After a number of trials, he added a couple of skid wires hidden beneath the fur, to prevent it from rolling when it hit an obstacle or when it turned. The final piece was impressive, and Steve took it for a trial spin around the parking lot, hopping it over speed bumps with the greatest of ease!

We were so proud of our arm that we couldn't wait to bring it to set. On the night we were scheduled to re-assemble the Wolfman, Rosengrant, Grant Arndt, Steve James and I set up the half-body of the blown apart Wolfman that John puppeteered directly. Stan appeared to supervise the positioning of the limbs when Steve drove the arm past. We thought he would be impressed, or even laugh, but instead he asked, "What is *that*?!"

Steve and I showed him that it was basically a modified R/C car and that it had the wrist and finger action. Steve put it back on the ground and drove it around again to demonstrate. Stan, with a tired, dead look in his eyes, watched the arm circle around the ground and asked, "How much did I pay for that?" It was hardly the reaction we were hoping for.

He then went on to say that for the effect, we could have just attached mono-filament fishing line to the piece and have dragged it which, coincidentally, was how we were going to drag the legs back to the body. Stan left Steve and me, like a couple of scolded children. When the cameras rolled, the arm drove in a straight line for about two feet before it was out of frame. It could have been dragged with a wire. Oops.

With the failure of the Wolfman transformation arm, and the excessive spending on the Wolfman dismem-bered arm, I was convinced that I was on the chopping block. Luckily for me, that was not the case.

Two events transpired that would forever change my world, and, as in any good story, if just one of the events had been a millimeter out of line, then my fate would have been different.

Because there had been so much work to accomplish on *Monster Squad,* much of the time the Lifers would be on set, while the crew remained in the shop continuing to build. *That's* how you make an R/C Wolfman hand without anyone noticing! On such an occasion, three people had visited the shop to meet with Stan: producers, Joel Silver and Beau Marks, and director John McTiernan.

They had wrapped their film *Predator* some months before having decided that the creature in the film that had been provided by BOSS Film effects was insufficient for their needs. Since it was a 20th Century Fox film, Silver and company had been recommended to Stan because of Stan's undeniable success with *Aliens* (which had opened that summer with blockbuster reaction). They had production art which they shared with Stan and then asked him if he would be interested in providing a new creature for the film.

At the same time, Stan was on the verge of attaining a life-long goal. During *Monster Squad,* writers Gary Gerani and Mark Carducci had approached Stan to attach him as a director to their film *Pumpkinhead.* The three of them had begun re-writing the script with Stan's input.

So, with *Monster Squad* still in production, *Pumpkinhead* in development, and *Predator* about to start, it looked like it would have taken more than just a couple of arms to get me thrown out of the studio. In fact, I was about to have much more responsibility laid upon my shoulders.

CHAPTER 28

Predator

The world breaks everyone, and afterward,
some are strong at the broken places.
"A Farewell to Arms", Ernest Hemingway

LOS ANGELES:

Aliens had been a phenomenon in the summer of 1986. We were invited to a cast and crew screening, and by this time I was used to directors and producers thanking everyone and saying that they were proud of the work done by everyone involved, only to sit through a lackluster film. Not so with *Aliens*. Producer Gail Anne Hurd thanked everyone, and director James Cameron advised the audience to get ready for a hell of a roller coaster. He wasn't kidding. The film became an international sensation.

At the center of it all was Stan Winston, the creator of the Queen Alien. In 1986, Stan Winston was the biggest makeup effects artist in the world. Stan could basically write his own ticket and the opportunity for a creature effects artist to direct a film was rare. Historically, there had been no directors who had come from makeup effects, although both James Cameron and Douglas Trumbull, the director of *Brainstorm*, had both directed films. John Beuchler, of MMI, had directed the low budget

Charlie Band movie *Troll,* however that didn't count in my book because...well, have you seen *Troll*?

It was certainly a crossroads for Stan and the studio. *Monster Squad* was still shooting, Stan had his *Pumpkinhead* script in-hand, ready to begin pre-production, and now here was *Predator* offering Stan the opportunity to act as savior/superhero while working with his good friend Arnold Schwarzenegger.

In typical Stan Winston style, he decided to cover all of the bases. Stan began doing preliminary drawings for *Predator* using a piece of artwork generated by production illustrator and VFX artist Alan Munro. It depicted an anthropomorphic figure holding a spear, sporting dreadlocks and wearing a helmet over his face. Stan's assignment was to draw the face UNDER the mask.

Stan had said that, when flying back to Los Angeles with James Cameron from the London screening of *Aliens,* they had discussed the Predator and had brainstormed ideas back and forth. Stan had at least two of his tracing paper illustrations that served as the departure point of the creature.

Even though Matt Rose and Steve Wang still had Gillman obligations on *Monster Squad,* Stan decided that based on the success of the suit, he would turn the lion's share of

Matt Rose sculpts the revised Predator helmet while Shane Mahan attempts to be entertaining.

the sculpture and painting over to them, leaving his Lifers to finish *Monster Squad* and then begin *Pumpkinhead.*

Enter actor Kevin Peter Hall. Production had interviewed and hired the 7' 2" actor, who had recently finished shooting *Harry and the Hendersons.* Upon meeting Kevin, I liked him immediately. It was nearly impossible to have any other reaction to him. I could pile up a list of adjectives to describe him such as sensitive, jovial, warm, funny, etc., and still not paint an accurate description of him.

The suit performer who had been in the failed Boss Films *Predator* suit had been famed kick-boxing actor Jean-Claude Van Damme. Where the Boss Films suit, built under the direction of Rick Baker protege, Steve Johnson, resembled a giant insect, production had changed their idea of what *Predator* should be. With the success of the Schwarzenegger film, *Commando,* they now wanted the ultimate adversary for the biggest, most famous action star in Hollywood. A 7'2" actor was a good start.

Kevin stripped down to his boxer shorts and socks (he complained that his feet were cold) and cooperated while Stan had him pose in a variety of action poses for reference photos. We then took him back into the main shop to do a body cast on him, which became our first challenge.

Body casts were traditionally made using straight plaster bandage without the use of soft alginate since the shape and proportions were more important than skin details needed on a face cast. However, Kevin was so tall that we couldn't just do our typical back and front casts. If we had attempted it, the material would have warped and twisted because of his height.

Instead, we had to cast from his feet to his hips in two pieces, then do his torso and arms in two pieces. When the casts were done we attached the four pieces and ran the rigid urethane foam in them just like we had for the Gillman. We then cast his head, hands, and feet in alginate backed with plaster bandage.

Stan had hired a rather odd sculptor named Wayne Sturm to come in to sculpt the Predator maquette. I describe Wayne as odd because of the photos he had shown me in his portfolio. There, amongst his paid, professional work, were photos of sculpture portraits he had done of late-night personality Johnny Carson, and actress Bo Derek, that he had sculpted in styrene plastic. Styrene plastic? I asked him how he did it and he said that he melted down the lids of take-away beverages and used the plastic to build up forms. And by the way, the portraits were amazing.

Wayne was hired to sculpt a portrait of Kevin Peter Hall first, and then sculpt the maquette of the Predator on top of this portrait. As was Stan's philosophy, there would be no "cheating" in the design. If it worked on the maquette, it would work full size, and while the rest of us prepared the casts out of the body molds, Wayne began his sculpt...in clay rather than styrene.

When Matt Rose and Steve Wang returned from set, Steve began doing sketches of the Predator, focusing on the armor and costume he would be wearing while Matt started working on the finger extensions that would transform Kevin's already large hands into spidery claws.

After Wayne had finished the Kevin maquette, it was photographed, and then he mixed silver powder into five-minute clear epoxy and coated the entire maquette until it resembled a silver statue. That way, Wayne would know the limitations of the Predator maquette; if he hit silver, the sculpture was too thin. He began fleshing out the maquette, taking direction from Stan, Matt, and Steve.

The weary Lifers returned from the *Monster Squad* set and didn't appear to be too excited to just jump back in and get to work. Alec and I helped Steve Wang build up water clay onto the body form, John began roughing out feet, and Tom began sculpting the wrist weapons; however, within a week or two, they were called into a meeting with Stan to begin design work on *Pumpkinhead*, leaving the sculpting work up to Matt and Steve.

Steve, feeling the pressure of the deadlines, expressed his concerns to Stan about the quality of the body sculpture. Stan told Steve, "This creature is all about the paint job, and I know you'll come up with a great design." This didn't reassure Steve too much at the time, but what else could be done?

Before jumping into *Pumpkinhead* design duties, the Lifers had decided that they had earned a well-deserved break and they left the studio for a few weeks. It was then that Stan pulled me into the parking lot and had that life-changing conversation.

He told me that I was going to be put in charge of *Predator* with the following stipulation: Matt and Steve were *artistically* in charge, where I would be responsible for all of the logistics. "If this project fails," Stan said, "it's *your* ass!" With that, he got into his car and drove away. When I told Matt and Steve what had just transpired they seemed relieved. We were a team now. I began facilitating wherever I could, from helping rough out and finish the dreadlock sculptures to assisting Matt in pouring the enormous silicone rubber head mold. However, where I think I did the most amount of good was in the foam rubber department.

Jackie Tischner had run most of the foam for *Monster Squad*, and there had been complaints. It wasn't bad enough that John had sculpted the Wolfman in a permanent scowl, but the foam was so dense that Dave Kindlon's servo-motor mechanics had to strain against the rubber. I decided to step in and personally supervise Jackie, now that I had the authority to see what the problem was.

Because of the amount of foam latex that had to be run on *Monster Squad*, Stan had purchased industrial, restaurant-sized mixers for the task. There were two sizes, small, which could accommodate twelve quarts of liquid, and a large size that held twenty quarts. Jackie was weighing out so much raw foam material in the smaller mixer that it was impossible to increase the volume of the foam (in order to make it softer)

A pair of Predator feet waiting for Kevin Peter Hall's feet.

without it spilling over the top of the bowl. That is why the foam was dense.

I reformulated the mix to half of what she had normally been running, and was able to get that foam to the top of the bowl which resulted in foam that was so soft, that mechanic Richard Landon was afraid that it was *too* soft!

With no other supervision in the shop, and with a very ambitious deadline hanging over our heads, we focused less on keeping the shop tidy, as was the Stan Winston way, and focused more on all of the work that had to be accomplished. The result was that the shop was a mess, but bear in mind that Matt Rose was twenty-one years old, Steve Wang was twenty years old and I, the supervisor, was twenty-four years old. We were emotionally and mentally ill-equipped to understand and balance the work duties with shop maintenance. In fact, one evening, I was so frustrated with some aspect of the project that I punched the door to the makeup room and put a hole in it!

Hey, someone has to seam all of the Predator's dreadlocks! Steve Wang offers encouragement to Eddie Yang, charged with the task!

Once again, the cold eels of panic began to tumble in my belly! How the hell was I going to explain *this*? Tired from their non-stop hours of working, Matt and Steve looked at the damage I had just done. With little reaction, they began to repair the door. Matt mixed some automotive body filling putty, and repaired the door, sculpting the wood-grain texture that matched the surrounding grain perfectly. Then, Steve stepped in and painted it. Again, the color match was perfect, and within a few minutes the door looked like nothing had happened to it. To my knowledge, Stan never learned about the incident, and I believe that it was then that Matt, Steve, and I became "brothers."

That November of 1986 was important to me, because it was that month that Tracy and I decided to get mar-

ried after living together for
nearly two years. Because of
the distance and immediacy
of this decision, we did not
have a "wedding" but instead,
got our license and had a civil
ceremony the Wednesday pri-
or to Thanksgiving Day. Our

Matt Rose's revised Predator helmet.

thinking was that a.) we had been stung with a huge IRS
bill in April because we were filing as two separate entities rather than joint-filing and this way we could joint
file in 1987 and b.) Thanksgiving Day weekend would be
the only guaranteed days off during the *Predator* schedule.

Stan had asked if Tracy and I wanted to house-sit for
the Winstons while they enjoyed a Thanksgiving vaca-
tion and we agreed. We drove to the Winston house in
Encino, and he and Karen gave us a tour, introduced us to
their dogs, Bo, a bulldog, and Petey, a boxer. He showed
us to the master bedroom, sat on the bed, and told Tracy
and me that this is where "He gave it to Karen," and that
we, too, were supposed to have sex. We giggled nervously but didn't know how to respond to that information.
Again, that was Stan –shameless. I think that Tracy and
I have the distinction of being the only non-Winstons to
have had sex on that bed. It was our honeymoon weekend so what did you expect?

On a less explicit note, when Tracy and I arrived at
their house, we found a beautiful chocolate torte surrounded by holiday cookies on a kitchen counter. On
the breakfast table we found a congratulations card from
the Winstons with a check inside for $900! However,

the torte began to confuse us. It was so beautiful that it couldn't have been for us, could it? We didn't touch it; however, I was (am) a self-confessed "cookie monster," and I began sneaking the cookies off of the tray until I had eaten them all.

The following week, when the Winstons returned, Stan called to find out if everything had gone well. During our conversation, I asked about the torte, to which he said, "*Yeah*?!" I went on to explain that we didn't know if we were meant to eat it, to which he replied, "Of course you were meant to eat it. You ate all of the cookies! We came home to find a dusty torte on our counter and we couldn't understand why you didn't eat it!" Lesson learned. If you ever find yourself house-sitting and there is an extravagant dessert on a counter or table, just eat it.

The seamed, foam latex Predator suit waiting for Steve Wang's painting magic! The paint job he and Matt Rose created would become iconic.

In December, Steve was working out the details of the paint job that Stan was so sure was going to save the Predator suit. Initially, Steve designed a paint scheme for the armor that was a metallic magenta highlighted with gold trim. For the skin of the Predator, he showed me a photograph of a particular cricket and told me that this was going to be the colors of the suit. My youthful ignorance and inexperience prevented me from understanding the over-all plan, but Stan had said that Steve was artistically in charge, so I trusted him and did what I could do to facilitate his plans.

There were other aspects to the Predator that went beyond just making the creature suit. We had to create the character's weapons and helmet for one thing. With no official design from production, Matt Rose sculpted a beautifully designed mask that had interesting facial features that complimented the creature's face beneath it. Steve sculpted the gun, the back pack, the wrist-blades, and a sword. A mechanic named Wayne Storm designed and assembled the pneumatic pistons that drove the blades in and out of the wrist pack, while Dave Kindlon designed and built the servo-motor-driven shoulder gun mechanics.

January 1987 brought with it our first test fitting of Kevin Peter Hall in what was completed of the Predator suit for John McTiernan and Joel Silver's approval. Wearing a suit painted by Steve and the hero head (sans dreadlocks) painted by Matt Rose, Kevin stood nearly eight feet tall. Kevin had brought his friend, Chris Gillman to the fitting. Chris ran a specialty prop and wardrobe manufacturing company called Diligent Dwarf; one of their specialties was a "cool" suit that would not become the industry standard until a couple of years later.

A cool suit consists of a capillary vest (which is made of mesh material with vinyl tubing snaking through it, and an ice cooler that had a pump and a cooling coil in it. The idea was that you put the vest on, filled the cooler with ice and then the pump moved cold water through tubes that connected to the vest, cooling the performer's physical core and therefore keeping him or her comfortable. Chris' system pumped not water, but Propylene Glycol (which lowers the freezing point of water, thereby allowing the system to work at lower temperatures).

Kevin had worn a cool suit on *Harry and the Hendersons*, and pretty much insisted that we provide him with one to wear in the hot jungles of Mexico where we would be shooting. Steve, Matt, and I understood that this was going to be a very necessary piece of equipment on set; however none of us was too excited about the necessity of moving the twenty pound cooling unit around the jungle. The three of us thought about it for a minute, then Matt Rose suggested that we take Brian Simpson with us to set.

This would be unprecedented. Brian's job was to drive around Los Angeles and pick up materials for us and he had proven himself to be the best runner I had ever worked with in my career to that point. He was fast, efficient and very patient; we could send him to the same hardware store 7 times in a day and he'd never complain. He was the younger brother to *Invaders from Mars* Drone performer Doug Simpson, and was similarly possessed of a quiet confidence and honesty. However, it was generally true that just artists and mechanics were taken to filming locations. Runners, if they were needed, were hired locally, because of their knowledge of surrounding resources. But Brian was strong, certainly strong enough to move Chris Gillman's cool suit unit around the jungle. We presented the idea to Stan, and he agreed. Brian was in.

Chris Gillman not only provided Kevin's cool suit, but was also working with Kevin to develop a "culture" for the Predator and the two of them discussed several behavioral possibilities that would affect the character's physicality. I recall that they had discussed a "tribal dance" the Predator would do after he removed his weapons in order to face Dutch Schultz, played by Schwarzenegger.

While Kevin and Chris discussed dance moves, the rest of us were getting notes from McTiernan and Silver. They didn't like Matt Rose's helmet. Although they thought it looked good, they believed that it telegraphed the visage beneath, and asked for a featureless alternative. We also had to lose the sword that fit into a slot in the backpack. When Kevin turned his head, the mandibles would hit the hilt of the sword so away it went! Neither production nor Kevin liked the long fingers which McTiernan and Silver thought made the Predator look more creepy than powerful; Kevin felt it limited his dexterity.

Kevin donned the mechanical Hero Predator mask, and Richard demonstrated the movement for everyone. The brows were capable of a range of emotion from worry to fury, the corners of the eyes could squint and, of course the mandibles opened and closed. "Can he raise one of his upper mandibles?" McTiernan asked. Richard explained that in order for one operator to be able to puppeteer the mandibles he had to have the uppers and lowers tied together on two separate channels. McTiernan answered that he wanted the Predator to be able to raise one mandible for a specific shot he had in mind. Stan stepped in and assured McTiernan that it would be able to do that once we got to location. Never say no.

Stan also told Richard that he wanted the bottom mandibles to not just open, but spread out wide to stretch the mouth bigger. Richard told Stan that the head already housed 9 servo motors but he would figure something out. A couple of days later, Richard brought the hero head to us with two new cables trailing out of the back of it attached to a fist-sized servo motor. "You have to find a place to hide this." he said to Steve, Matt and me. Luckily, the Predator's armor was so thick, we were able to take a razor blade and cut out a space that would accommodate the big servo. Problem solved.

With our February deadline rocketing toward us, we had a lot of work to accomplish in a very short amount of time. Matt went immediately to work on the new helmet, Steve knocked out quick glove alternatives, and we subcontracted the construction of a medical pack to a prop maker friend of Alec Gillis' named Brent Scrivener. However, there was still more work that needed attention!

Also at the fitting was the visual effects supervisor, Joel Hynek. Hynek worked out of New York for Robert Abel and Associates, and had been instrumental in the development of the Predator's invisibility effect. In order to produce the effect, Hynek required a "red suit" that was as close to an exact replica of the Predator completely in red. He showed us some videotape of the shots that they had done during the Puerto Vallarta shoot and we could see Van Damme dressed in a red creature suit, running through the jungle or pulling a victim away from camera. He needed the red because the surrounding foliage was green (the reverse of how most video artists use green screens for making composites today).

He provided me with yards of red spandex and cans of matching red spray paint and left the rest for us to figure out. With so little time there was one thing that we knew for sure: there was no way that we were going to get the dreadlocks figured out in time. We ran latex and soft urethane pieces out of the molds and I contacted my friend, Leslie Neumann, to see if she would be interested in doing the job.

Leslie was married to my CalArts friend Drew Neumann, a music composer and animator. She was a seamstress and fabricator who had worked at a place called Shafton's, which made walk-around characters for amusement parks and big-headed mascot-type specialty costumes. She had "retired" from studio work, but still had a small workshop in her home. She drove out to the studio to meet me and learn what the job entailed. After seeing the pieces and fabric, she assured me it would be no problem and we loaded everything into the back of her car and off she went.

With just a couple of weeks until the truck arrived to transport all of the suits and equipment to location, I went into coordinator-mode. This meant that I'd have conversations with the local production coordinator (I wish I could recall her name; I must have called her ten

times a day), relay them to Matt and Steve, who would then ask me questions that I'd have to call the production office back to have answered. However what I gleaned was this: we were to be in Palenque, Mexico, this time, as opposed to Puerto Vallarta, where they had shot before. It was going to be dense, wild jungle. We were scheduled to be there for two weeks of shooting and it was sug-

The Los Angeles Predator crew: From L-R (standing) Screaming Mad George, Brian Simpson, Shannon Shea, Emilio Gonzales, Kevin Peter Hall, Richard Landon, Brent Schrivener, Eddie Yang, Grant Arndt. Jackie Tischner, Jackie Lancette (in the middle) Seated in front: Shane Mahan, Matt Rose holding his original Predator helmet, Stan Winston, Steve Wang.

gested that we dress appropriately.

Rip-stop camouflage pants were recommended as well as military boots to protect us from the "two step snakes." *Snakes*?! Apparently, the jungle was home to asps so venomous that if they bit, the victim dropped dead in two steps. Wonderful. Sonny Burman, try though he might, had certainly not cured me of my fear of snakes and now we were going into snake country. It was suggested that we not wear the canvas-style boots, but leather boots that extended past the ankle.

Then the production coordinator asked how soon she could get everyone's passports so she could begin getting Mexican work permits. Huh? I asked around and no one on the crew save for Richard Landon and Shane Mahan, who would be joining us, had passports. With a sigh, she told me that she would call me back with information.

I don't know how she managed to do it, but Matt, Steve, Brian, and I had to get four passport photos taken each, grab our birth certificates, and drive down to the Federal Building in West Los Angeles to have expedited passports issued. Again, now this is a fairly simple process, but then it was madness. We arrived at the Federal building and were met by a worker who had us fill out forms, then took our documentation, two of the photos, and told us to wait. Within an hour, each of us had passports in our hands. We then had to provide the extra two photos and the passports to production, who had us fill out the necessary paperwork for the Mexican work permits.

During these last weeks, the Lifers had returned to the studio, and they didn't seem very pleased. Although we had done our best to restore the studio to some semblance of normalcy, we still had pieces under construction, suits and masks cluttering the tables, piles of support materials and tools ready to be packed and loaded. John Rosengrant pulled me aside and, with quavering voice, told me that he expected the entire studio to be cleaned once the location truck left.

Stan had been absent during those last few weeks working with the *Pumpkinhead* writers on their script. However, it was understood that he, too, would be going to Mexico for our two-week shoot. One of the last items that we received were hard contact lenses for Kevin Peter Hall to wear. Steve had designed the paint job, and Professional Vision Care had produced the lenses. This meant that one of us would have to put the lenses into Kevin's eyes. It seems crazy to me now that in those days, it was acceptable to have anyone push a piece of hard plastic into an actor's eyes without having a "lens tech" on set. In contrast, today, even with the use of soft, comfortable lenses, a bonded lens tech *has* to be on set whenever special effects lenses are in use.

A truck arrived at the rear bay door, and Matt, Steve, Richard, Brian, and I began to load everything into the back of the truck while Shane and the rest of the Lifers were in the art room doing drawings for *Pumpkinhead.* I could tell that Shane really didn't want to be separated from the rest of the group for the next couple of weeks. He and John did have to step in the last day to finish the Predator body sculpt because Steve had worked himself to exhaustion and got sick, but I guessed that he didn't feel a strong connection with the creature at that point. It really was Matt and Steve's baby. However, since Shane had been with Stan longer than the rest of the Lifers, he was also one of the most trusted, and Stan insisted that he come along.

The truck drove away and Rosengrant appeared in the back with us and began pointing to what he wanted cleaned before we left the shop. He took me on a tour of what he interpreted was negligence on our part and since I was the coordinator, I was solely responsible in his eyes. Of course, Brian, Matt and Steve had no problem helping right the studio, and after the brooms were neatly stacked, we all agreed to meet at the airport the next morning.

Tracy and I had been married only two months and a few weeks, the morning Tracy drove me to the airport early. There would be no cell phones. No text messages. No computers. I would have to call long distance when I arrived at the hotel. I hugged her, kissed her, and told her that I'd see her in two weeks.

I found Steve, Matt and Brian outside of the airport and we went to check in together. Richard and Shane met us at the gate. We were told that we were going to meet a production contact named Harry in Mexico City, our first leg of travel. He would have our work permits and get us through all of the necessary lines so that we could get on our plane from Mexico City to Villa Hermosa, our second leg of travel. From Villa Hermosa, we were to meet a driver who would drive us the rest of the way to Palenque.

Matt Rose, afraid of flying, had gone to the airport bar and had a beer or two with Brian Simpson in an effort to calm his nerves. Kevin Peter Hall appeared (how could you miss him?) and sat with us and waited for the plane. Since he was working on a SAG contract, he was flying first class while the rest of us were in coach.

MEXICO:

Aside from Matt being petrified to fly, our flight from Los Angeles to Mexico city went without a hitch. We arrived at the gate and were greeted by a man who looked like a Mexican version of Marin Scorcese. This was "Airport" Harry. Harry shook our hands, took our passports, had our Mexican work permits and began herding us past long lines of passengers disembarking and going through passport control. He would approach armed guards wearing khaki uniforms and begin speaking rapidly in Spanish. The result was always the same: The guard would open a gate or a chain and let us through instantly. In mere minutes we had passed through all of the annoying government agency stops and in no time were all sitting outside an airport cafe drinking beer with Harry.

Harry advised us about the rest of our trip and assured us that he would be waiting for us there upon our return flight, because getting out of Mexico was more difficult than getting us into Mexico. We thanked him, got on our next plane, which was smaller and more frightening to Matt, and flew to Villa Hermosa.

It was getting close to sunset when we arrived in Villa Hermosa. We were greeted by two drivers in Volkswagen vans. Again, I wish I could remember our driver's name – he

The Mexico Predator crew: Matt Rose, Brian Simpson, Shane Mahan, Stan Winston, Kevin Peter Hall, Steve Wang, Shannon Shea, Richard Landon.

was so good to us. Our luggage was loaded into one van, Matt Rose had packed a foot locker FULL of food and water, no kidding, and we all piled into another van.

Once we got outside of Villa Hermosa, the road to Palenque was barely paved, bumpy and had no street lights. As the sun went down, the only light came from the vans or the other cars driving the opposite way down the small road. I was shocked at how clear the night sky was; I could see so many stars I was unused to seeing in the Los Angeles sky. About an hour and a half later, we drove through downtown Palenque on cobblestone streets, past shops closed with metal garage-type doors, and out to our hotel which was about a quarter of a mile away. Clouds of small insects buzzed around the few street lights between the town and our hotel, and as we pulled into the circular drive, we were instructed to wait while our driver made the necessary arrangements with the hotel.

Stan appeared in the lobby of the hotel and told us that we were going to leave our luggage with the porters and drive out to Mishol Ha, the location, to meet John Mc-Tiernan. Our luggage was stacked on carts, and we all piled back into the Volkwagen van and drove out back into the night.

It was so dark that I couldn't see where we were going except that I had the sense that we were moving uphill until we arrived in a lit clearing that revealed a semi-circle of trucks. This was our base camp and would be our "home" on set for the next two weeks.

As we pulled to a stop, the first thought I had was that I wasn't wearing my leather boots or rip-stop camouflage pants and I was in snake country. Shit. Well, there was nothing I could do about it now. We got out of the van and were met by a production assistant, who took us down a path toward a section of jungle illuminated by movie lights. Walking toward the set, we were passed by makeup artist Jeff Dawn and Arnold Schwarzenegger, who was completely covered in mud and leaves. He stopped to exchange pleasantries with Stan (actually, it was more like good-natured ribbing) and promised to see him back at the hotel later.

We climbed down the side of a hill to where production was wrapping up for the night. John McTiernan, wearing a pink polo shirt, khaki pants and tennis shoes, was nursing what appeared to be a tumbler of scotch over some ice. He stood up from his director's chair when he saw us approaching.

"Stan!" John said, "I'm glad you're here! I want to show you where the final fight is going to take place." Stan shook John's hand and then reintroduced us all; then we followed McTiernan away from the workers, who were covering equipment with tarpaulins and carrying heavy equipment back up the hill.

John hopped from log to rock to path like it was his backyard all the time describing how the final fight between Dutch Schultz and the Predator was going to be staged. "We'll start here," McTiernan said, indicating a shallow pool of water surrounded on two sides by large boulders. He continued, "Arnold will get pinned to that log with the Predator's wrist blades like gigging a frog." *Huh*? I thought. The wrist blades were about three inches wide and I knew for certain that Arnold's neck was at least three times the size of that. I whispered my concerns into Shane's ear, and was silenced with the wave of his hand.

McTiernan went on describing where the Predator would take his helmet off, which rock the Predator's hand would strike, causing sparks, where the shot of the Predator flexing his *one* mandible after being kicked by Schultz would occur, when suddenly, the lights went out! We could hear the winding down of the generator as the sounds of the jungle increased in contrast.

This didn't faze John. He just went right on leading us deeper into the dark jungle. And that, folks, is when the bats began whizzing by our heads!

At first I thought they were birds or bugs until it dawned on me exactly what it was. Stan figured it out much more quickly; I heard him exclaim, "Bats!" as he began waving his hands over his head. Taking no notice of the flying rodents, McTiernan continued showing us locations where we would be shooting the various scenes featuring the Predator, only to be interrupted by Stan barking the word, "Bats!" over and over again to make sure that we all knew what was flying past us.

I don't know whether John finally figured out that Stan was too distracted by the bats to be paying attention any more, or if he finally was paying attention to Stan's pleas to leave the area, or if the bats were finally getting to him as well, but John agreed that we should make our way back to base camp.

As we climbed up the hill, I could still hear Stan exclaiming, "Fucking bats!" In the dim light I could make out Stan still waving his hands over his head defensively, while unknown to him, Shane had a leafy branch that he was swishing past Stan's head.

We checked out our gear at the truck for the next day and then returned to the hotel.

I was unpacking my suitcases when Kevin knocked on my door. "What did you tell them about me?" he asked. "Who?" I replied. "The hotel! Have you seen my room?" Kevin asked. He went from door to door, knocked on the other guys' rooms and had us follow him to his room. When we arrived he opened his door to reveal most of his room was taken up by an enormous bed! "You told them I was a giant, didn't you?" he asked me. I denied using the word "giant," but I had told production how tall Kevin was and they had taken it upon themselves to make sure his comfort was accommodated. He confessed to me later that it was the first time as an adult that he slept in a bed that actually fit him.

We left Kevin's room and went down to the lobby of the hotel. Just behind the wall of the front lobby was a restaurant bar which was almost exclusively populated with the cast and crew of *Predator*. At the main table, holding court was Arnold Schwarzenegger, surrounded by Joel Silver, John McTiernan, producer and first assistant director, Beau Marks, second unit director Craig Baxley, Jeff Dawn and Stan Winston. We sat at an adjoining table with actors Shane Black and Richard Chavez. Amid beers being served and cigars being smoked at the Schwarzenegger table, we all spoke about the previous shoot and the rumors we had heard and other small talk until Steve Wang pointed past us all to the window. "Look at the size of that frog!" he said. We all looked and couldn't believe our eyes.

Now, being from Louisiana I've seen my share of frogs and toads. As a child I had accompanied my father to

Hannibal, Missouri for the shooting of the film *Tom Saw-yer* and had participated in a frog jumping contest and those were big frogs! But what was hopping outside the window was one of the biggest frogs I had ever seen in my life. As it sat, legs folded beneath it, I would have to say that it was at least the size of a large grapefruit. At least. It was smaller than a bowling ball, but bigger than a baseball for sure! I am a bit fuzzy about what happened next.

Someone, probably Shane, at our table thought it would be funny to put some of these frogs in Stan's room. There was about a two second pause, then everybody shot up from the table, except Shane Black, and ran out of the restaurant. Grabbing wastepaper baskets, we grabbed as many frogs as we could; it was difficult to count with all of the activity, but I know that it was at least fifteen of these grapefruit-sized frogs.

Richard Chavez, who spoke Spanish, convinced a ho-tel worker to give us the key to Stan's room. We crept in and began depositing frogs all over the bedroom and bathroom, then we quietly retreated back to the restau-rant after making sure all of Stan's room lights were out.

We weren't scheduled to shoot the next day, but we were to suit Kevin up in the morning to present to pro-duction. The party in the restaurant broke up, and we all began heading back to our rooms when Stan stopped me. "You brought Lysol spray, right?" he asked me. I told him that I had, and he asked if he could borrow it and followed me to my room. I handed the can to him and he said that he'd bring it right back.

I kept my door open until I heard Stan yell, "Get them out of here! Get them out of here *now!*" All of us ran to

Stan's room where he was standing outside of his door. He was half-way laughing and half-way pissed. My guess was that he had been startled pretty badly and was in the midst of recovering. He accused us of putting the frogs in his room, which we all denied vehemently. However, we agreed to go into his room and help him remove the frogs. We walked in, grabbed a few of the frogs and set them loose in the grass. We all said goodnight and left Stan again. I hadn't reached my door when he began to yell again. Apparently he had discovered the frogs in his luggage and bathroom.

We went back in and again he accused us of putting the frogs in his room and again we all denied it. Suddenly a look of realization played across Stan's face as he hissed, "Schwarzenegger! Schwarzenegger did this!" He pointed to the frogs hopping around his room and trying to get out of his luggage. "Pick them all up for me!" he said.

We brought in our wastepaper baskets and collected the frogs and gave them to Stan. To my knowledge, none of us followed him to Schwarzenegger's room, where Stan deposited all of the frogs.

The next morning, in the restaurant, Stan found Arnold eating his breakfast. Stan dropped into a chair opposite Arnold and smiled. "How did you sleep last night?" Stan asked Arnold. "Fine," Arnold replied. Stan got confused. "Really?" Stan pressed. "What's gotten into you?" Arnold asked Stan. The more Stan hinted around that there should have been a reason for Arnold to have been disturbed the night before, the more confused Arnold got from Stan's behavior, until Arnold was told that his ride to set had arrived. Arnold left a very confused Stan. "I wonder if I put them in the wrong room?" Stan asked rhetorically.

Years later, while I was on the crew for *Child's Play II*, I bumped into Arnold shooting pickup shots for *Total Recall*. I asked him about the incident, and he said that after the party had broken up, he had to meet his newly wed wife, Maria Schriver, and bring her back to the hotel. She found the frogs and began screaming. Instantly he knew it was Stan who had put the frogs in his room, but denied ever having experienced it. And, he told me, that to that date, he had never given Stan the satisfaction of having pulled off the practical joke. It was the ultimate revenge!

The next morning, the sun shone amber on low mist that blanketed the surrounding jungle. We piled into the Volkswagen vans and began the trek through the hills to base camp. We arrived and began to prepare to put Kevin into the suit for his debut to production. The Predator suit inventory included two hero suits, completely finished with netting that we purchased from Spencer's gift store in the local Northridge, California, mall. We had one "helmet head" which was a latex and soft polyfoam head that had the face details cut off to allow Kevin to see and breathe more easily when the Predator was wearing his helmet. The "hero head" was the servo-motor driven head for use when the Predator took his mask off and the "stunt head" was an exact duplicate, with positionable mandibles for quick shots when any face movement would be hidden or imperceptible. We had two sets of hero feet and four sets of hero hands and then there was the "red suit," which had multiple gloves and boots. All had arrived safely, so we readied ourselves for Kevin's arrival.

Kevin wore a baby blue spandex body suit under his

clothes that he would wear under the foam latex Predator suit. Not only would it absorb SOME of the sweat, but it also prevented his skin from chafing next to the foam rubber. He stepped into the suit and we tried to pull it over his hips when we realized that the suit had shrunk, as foam latex normally does. Ordinarily we would use baby powder to reduce the friction between suit and skin, but Kevin, fearing the amount of sweating he was about to do, insisted we use K-Y lubricating jelly instead. With his assistance, we lubed his legs, arms shoulders and torso so that the suit slid easily over Kevin's body.

We zipped the back of the suit up to discover that the foam had shrunk so much that there was a two inch gap that exposed most of the length of the zipper! None of us recalled that during the fitting in Los Angeles, but there was a gap now and it had to be fixed immediately. I made the sugges-

Kevin Peter Hall suited up for the first time to be seen by production in Mexico. He is wearing Matt Rose's original helmet that was decided transmitted the face beneath too much.

tion of taking more of the insulation foam that we had used to make the metallic hoses and create more pipes and hoses within the backpack and armor. Brian and Richard Landon pushed up on the shoulders of the suit trying to help close the gap, when Steve Wang jumped into action. He grabbed a human spine that was going to be used for a spine-ripping effect, took a length of leather cord and strung the vertebrae together. He knotted the cord, threw it over Kevin's head and one of his arms and then pushed it into the gap. It fit perfectly. Problem solved. So many of the little bits of the suit would arise out of necessity over the course of the shoot. There was just no time to go into lengthy repair, so when there was an issue, it was generally dealt with by the use of on-the-spot costuming.

Richard attached the hero backpack which housed the servo-driven gun, Matt helped Kevin on with the helmet head and then we all took one last look to make sure that we hadn't overlooked anything. Outside of our trailer, we could hear Stan selling to John McTiernan and Joel Silver, and almost exactly on cue we opened the door of the trailer and the Predator stepped out.

There was no applause, no big gasp, but instead conversations began breaking out amongst the crew that had gathered there. The Australian director of photography, Don McAlpine, asked questions and discussed how the Predator was to be lit and featured; the stunt team, led by Craig Baxley wanted to know how easily it would be to put one of the stunt team into a suit when necessary, et cetera. Kevin, standing nearly eight feet tall over production, was an impressive sight, no matter what.

Because we were young and stubborn, we tried once again to sell the first helmet that Matt Rose had sculpted. We removed the plain mask and put the more ornate mask on. There was no doubt that the superior quality of Matt's sculpture confounded them, but after much consideration and input from the department heads, the plain mask was chosen and Matt's mask went back into the truck to be hung on the wall like a decoration over the unused sword Steve had made.

Matt brought out the hero head so that everyone could

see the face beneath the mask, but the servos were not hooked to the batteries and puppeteered; that would have to wait until later. However, Richard fired up the backpack and the gun lifted up and pointed at the crowd. Under Stan's careful guidance, Richard attempted to sync the movement of the gun to the movement of Kevin's head. When they synced up, it was very effective.

Beau Marks finally asked if there were any more questions and then led everyone back down the path and into the jungle to continue working. I recall hearing Joel Silver and John McTiernan both thank Stan. He had saved their asses for sure.

We were instructed to get Kevin out of the suit and to be prepared for our first shot the next evening. We wouldn't

Kevin fully suited up, wearing the revised helmet and the radio-controlled shoulder cannon.

need the hero head or backpack, we had a "stunt" backpack that was made of soft urethane foam, complete with a gun permanently pointing down in its holstered position. However, we needed to address the "frog gigging" effect.

Since the hero wrist blades on the Predator's right arm were driven by air, that meant that whenever they were used, we'd have to hide lengths of tubing that could be attached to a compressed air source. Having to have that option with every shot would have been a logistical nightmare, so we made a "dummy" wrist blade pack that could be opened and different sets of soft or hard blades could be attached. Most of the time, the blades would be retracted so we had little 2.5 inch soft blade tips Kevin could wear without fear of hurting himself. However, no matter what blades we would use the 3" distance between them would be a constant.

Richard and I worked together to solve the gigging effect. He took a set of the hard blades and using brass, made an armature that spread the blades apart wider, while keeping the parallel. Shane had gone to Schwarzenegger's trailer to measure his neck, since they already knew each other from *The Terminator*. Using plastic drinking straws, I camouflaged the brass assembly making it look like a series of metal pneumatic pistons. Whew! Another problem solved.

We were instructed to head back to the hotel that afternoon because there would be a special screening of a cut of the film for us to see that had storyboards (illustrations) inserted into it indicating the shots we needed to get in order to complete the movie. During the down time, Shane and I took the opportunity to explore the location. He had brought the shop video camera with him and we took turns shooting on set. Being in the jungle struck Shane's imagination, and being a huge fan of David Attenborough's television series *Life on Earth*, he took the opportunity to have me film him imitating the famous British naturalist/journalist.

As we made our way to the large, natural waterfall and pool at Misol Ha, we saw a crew of people adding vines to trees. It turned out to be John Reinhardt, the art director from *House*. I have to admit, he recognized me first. I'm good with situational memory, but horrible with names! He showed Shane and me the grotto they had been dressing for the beginning of showdown between Arnold and the Predator. The log bridge was fabricated, but you would never know it. There was a huge pile of branches made to look like a deadfall; beneath that would be the giant bonfire Arnold would light to attract the Predator. It was amazing! It all looked absolutely real. One of Shane's favorite pieces was a sideways tree. Made for a red-suit shot, it would be filmed sideways to give the illusion of an upright tree,

Standing on the log-bridge build by the Art Department.

but the Predator could crawl down the length of it without the use of wires to make it look like he was climbing down the tree.

Of course, Shane had me film him on the tree to try out the effect.

Having run around the set, and confident that we were ready for the next day of shooting, we were transported back to the hotel for the screening.

Above the bar/restaurant in the hotel was a big banquet room that production had converted into a gymnasium for Arnold. A screen, projector, and folding chairs had been set up in the room to make it a makeshift theater. We were joined by Joel Hynek and a couple of other people, although I have no memory of Stan being there. My guess is that he was in his room, working on *Pumpkinhead*. Since what we were looking at was a rough assembly of the movie, not only were the Predator shots missing, but all of the post-production visual effects shots were missing.

That meant that the film we saw began not with the Predator's ship approaching earth, but with helicopters landing at the Central American military post. Alan Silvestri's music score had not been composed, so appropriate music from other sources was used, which included many cuts from the *Aliens* score. As the film continued, we heard two people enter the room. They were Arnold and his wife Maria Shriver. They took seats directly behind us, and suddenly we had a running commentary as Arnold attempted to explain what was happening on screen to his wife.

What we saw then was pretty much what was released in theaters with the exception of a couple of sequences that had been cut down: The flight into the hot zone in the black helicopters seemed longer, as did the scene just after Jessie Ventura is killed and the surviving soldiers blast the hell out of the surrounding jungle.

Just about the time in the film that Arnold threw a knife into an enemy soldier's chest and said "Stick around," we could hear Maria say, "Arnold, this is a stupid movie!" He went into full sales mode, "No you don't understand," he said, "there is an alien hunting us and this is the scene where..." She didn't seem impressed or to care that much. She stuck by her opinion of the film and suggested that they leave. They got up and and left us to finish watching the film.

There must have been some sort of psychic-wife connection because by the point Arnold and the commandos were setting traps for the elusive Predator, I was told that there was a phone call for me at the lobby phone. It was Tracy. I told her about what had just happened and that it had taken the wind out of all of our sails. She reminded me that it was only a couple of weeks and I'd be home before I knew it.

Little did she know; little did *we* know.

We stayed up late that night because we had a late call the next afternoon; our first shot of the Predator would be a night shot. Stan, wanting to buy cigars so he could smoke with Arnold, encouraged us all to walk to the neighboring town to try to find dinner...and cigars. We found a little restaurant, and I'll never forget Stan, attempting to speak broken Spanish, ordering items not on the menu. The joke was on me, because he ended up with a plate of sauteed shrimp, garlic, and oil that smelled incredible. But then the joke was on him because the only cigars he could find were local hand-rolled affairs that looked more like big dark brown joints than like fine Cuban cigars. Arnold saw them and just called them "cat turds."

The next night we suited Kevin up for his first shot as the Predator. It was a complicated shot where Arnold appeared to be hanging beneath a fallen log while the Predator walked across the top of it. Kevin got into position and then said, "I can't see anything." It turned out that the combination of the dark, and the reflective Mylar lenses in the helmet made it impossible for him to see where he was walking, especially across a log eight feet in the air. Had he fallen, he wouldn't necessarily have died, but he would definitely have been injured.

Stan looked through the lens and saw that during most of Kevin's walk across the log, the camera actually moved to feature Arnold hanging on for dear life beneath it, when in actuality Arnold had a wire hooked to his belt holding him in position. Based on Stan's suggestion, the camera started on Kevin, standing from a squatting position as if he had just jumped down from the trees. As the camera moved, Stan ran across the log, grabbed Kevin by both hands and walked him carefully across the log, and when the camera moved up to reveal the Predator's back, Stan ducked behind a tree. Problem solved!

With that shot, the "machine" clicked into gear. Matt, Steve, Richard, Brian, Shane, and I began working like a coordinated team. We knew the best way to get Kevin in and out of the suit; Matt Rose protected the heads (whichever one we were using), and we were prepared for whatever combination of extras production asked for. They began to learn our vernacular: "We need Kevin in the stunt mask, with the hero back pack and the dummy short blades."

Kevin and Matt clown around prior to driving to location. Many mornings were foggy but would burn off to humid heat for the rest of the day.

After a day or two, we broke out the red suit for stunt man Tony Brubaker to put on for a shot of the Predator escaping gunfire, wounding his leg. We had entered Joel Hynek territory and did he let us know! Since the suit was being used to generate a visual effects matte, less of the Stan Winston crew needed to be on set, while Joel would whine about every speck of dirt or leaf that attached itself to the red suit. He would insist between takes that I run in with the red spray paint and try to eliminate any stain or piece of dirt, no matter how small. Seriously, it could have been the size of a pencil point and Joel would walk up to me and, indicating the stain, would say, "Can you go spray that area? I can see dirt." It also didn't help that the noxious smell of the spray paint annoyed Tony.

It was bad enough that before we arrived in Mexico Joel had been on me to provide "glowing Predator blood." Try as I might, the only color I could get from the manufacturer of the famous Cyalume sticks was green. He explained that they had already established that the Predator's blood was orange during the Puerto Vallarta shoot. I told him that all I could get was green. He then asked if I had attempted to try to change the color from green to orange. I wanted to cooperate, but my back was against the wall at Stan Winston's just to get the Predator suits completed. Orange blood? Green blood? I just didn't see how it was my problem. Eventually, Joel had to acquiesce and rotoscope all of the orange blood to match our Cyalume green blood.

Not that it is an excuse, but remember I was only twenty-four years old. I had been put in charge of my first show and the stress was monumental. I asked Joel if I could borrow his Swiss Army knife; I promised I would return it just as soon as I was finished using it. I then walked up the hill to the path and kicked the knife from set to base camp and back again. I'm not proud of it, but I did return the battered knife to a confused Joel. "What happened to my knife?!" I apologized and told him that I had slipped and the knife fell down the stone stairs that led to the pond and waterfall. I was lucky that I hadn't broken my neck. He was thunderstruck, and I walked away like nothing had happened. Yes, I was really a jerk, but I would receive my comeuppance soon.

It became a sort of a ritual that every day, no matter where we were, no matter what we were shooting, around four o'clock the second assistant director, Tom Archuletta, would stop us and the entire film crew would dash down to the pond to shoot the scene where the Predator rose from the water only to discover that he could no longer see his human prey because Arnold ("Schultz") was covered head to toe in mud. Shooting this scene during the two hour window referred to as "magic hour" resulted in the scene having been beautifully lit by nature.

Matt paints Kevin's eyes black prior to putting on the Predator mask.

In addition, I learned one of the most important lessons in film-making which is enforced on nearly every movie set to this day: *Get the expensive assets off of the set as soon as possible.*

To be clear, it means that in order to stretch a budget, shoot with your expensive actors, like Schwarzenegger *first*, wrap them, and then shoot everything else. By the end of the first week, we had shot some shots with Kevin, but mainly the cameras had focused primarily on Arnold.

That first weekend in Palenque, we took a visit out to see the Aztec pyramids. Shane beat on about it being "the spirit of adventure." But I thought that if there was going to be any opportunity to step on a big snake, then this was going to be it.

"Youth is wasted on the young." is the old cliché, and our

Brian Simpson makes a last minute adjustment.

visit to the pyramids couldn't have been more proof of that. Yes, I thought they were beautiful. Yes, I appreciated their age versus their complex design and construction. It was just that I truly would rather have been home with my wife than running up and down stone stairs. Shane then decided we were going to shoot a movie there. Using the shop video camera and my casette-tape-walkman and external speakers, I played baroque music holding the speakers on either side of the camera's microphone while Shane shot. The result was kind of a strange music video of the Aztec sights set to a Bach piece.

As if we hadn't had enough time in the jungle, Shane decided that we were going to leave the clearing and head into the wilderness. "Spirit of adventure," he kept repeating. What was I supposed to do? Run in the opposite direction? I followed Shane into the jungle, where we climbed

over treacherous boulders and pushed our way through thickets. The entire time I was complaining and Shane kept repeating his mantra, "Spirit of adventure!" After I watched him attempt to swing on a vine and accidentally pull down a branch from a tree, we found a path that led us back to the pyramids.

Just before we emerged from the jungle, we noticed

Shane Mahan ready to indulge in the "Spirit of Adventure."

signs facing away from us. When we reached them, there had been a hand-painted message in red. We flagged someone down who could translate the sign for us. They told us that it was a warning to stay out of the jungle because a puma had recently attacked people in the area. This just made Shane's day! In the jungle with a dangerous mountain lion! That truly was the spirit of adventure, to which I answered, "Fuck adventure."

Even though we hadn't seen any wildlife during our jungle escapades, there were animals in pens at the hotel. There were two monkeys and a lemur that seemed to be there for tourists to enjoy. John McTiernan spent hours trying to devise a way that the larger of the two monkeys could safely enjoy more freedom than being stuck in a pen, and constructed wires and

The Mexico crew poses deep inside of an Aztec temple.

such so that the monkey could be tethered yet move freely about the tree it was next to. I truly believe that he, like the rest of us, just wanted to set it free, and by the time we left Mexico, the monkey was long gone. I like to think that John had helped it to escape.

By the end of the second week of shooting, working with Kevin in the suit had become something of a routine. We would prep the suit just prior to his arrival, which sometimes meant fetching it from where it hung beneath the fan of the huge generator that acted like a blow drier to dry the suit. Kevin would show up and we'd dress him in the suit and feet but leave everything else off until the last minute. Then, when they were closer to needing him on set, we'd grab the heads, weapons, etc., and drag it all out to where they were shooting and finish dressing him on set.

When we were shooting the final fight scene between Dutch and the Predator in that shallow pond McTiernan showed us on the first day, Kevin attempted to incorporate some of the moves that he and Chris Gillman had rehearsed back in Los Angeles. McTiernan watched nonplussed and then asked, "Can't you just walk over to him and face him?" Kevin, ever the professional, performed as he was directed, but between scene set ups complained quietly to us. "I don't get it." he said, "John's not letting me do anything." If that wasn't enough, Arnold never greeted Kevin by name. For whatever reason, any time he would see Kevin, Arnold would say, "Hello monster."

Kevin's spirits began to dip.

For the scene where Dutch is crawling away from the Predator at the top of a hill, McTiernan watched as Kevin appeared through the trees creeping forward and yelled "Cut!" Again he said to Kevin, "Can't you just walk after him?" Kevin was confused and John tried to explain, "You are confident. You're a hunter. Think of yourself as Dirty Harry from space." That helped Kevin a bit, but after the disastrous screening and having received that kind of direction from McTiernan, Kevin began to have doubts about being the Predator.

He told us contrasting stories about his experiences on *Harry and the Hendersons* and how he had been encouraged to act against co-stars John Lithgow and Melinda Dillon. He felt that the only thing that he was bringing to *Predator* was his size.

At the end of the second week of shooting, the high-end assets of production: Arnold Schwarzenegger, his entourage, Joel Silver, and Stan Winston all left. We didn't however. At the end of the second week, we were told that there was still more to shoot. Just before he left, Stan had a conversation with me that changed my experience on the rest of the shoot.

He said, "You are in charge, but as my representative, you need to do whatever they ask of you. You need to take whatever they throw at you. Understand?" I agreed but didn't understand just what he was implying until the next week of shooting.

With Arnold gone, all we had left to shoot was the Predator and stunt men filling in for Arnold and the rest of the commandos. This meant that now, Kevin was the most expensive asset on the film and they were attempting to film him and wrap him. We still would have to run down to the pond to continue shooting the Predator coming out of the water at magic hour and firing his gun.

We managed to get Kevin submerged under water in the suit, but by the time they were satisfied with the shot of him rising out of the water, the sun was going down.

We barely got the shot representing Dutch Schultz's point of view (POV) of the Predator walking ashore before we had to call it quits and go back to shooting in the jungle. We needed to continue the sequence the next day, so we delivered the shoulder cannon to Chovi, who was the Mexican physical effects coordinator, who was going to rig black powder and ignition charges into the three brass tubes that made up the barrel of the gun.

In my effort to get a cool shot of the Predator firing his shoulder cannon, I shot this series of photos that ended in an accident where the gun exploded instead. Luckily Kevin was completely unhurt.

The next day, at sunset, I was perched on a rock with my Pentax 5000 35mm film camera with my zoom lens ready to get the picture of a lifetime: The Predator firing his gun! Chovi hooked up the ignition wires to a battery and a nail board that served as a trigger. The cameras rolled, McTiernan yelled "Action!" and I tensed up as I heard the countdown: 3...2...1... *click/**POW**!*

Through the viewfinder of my camera, I saw an explosion! I threw my camera into the case and ran down the stone steps to join everyone at the shore of the pond. Kevin Peter Hall stood confused. He had heard a loud "pop" noise but just thought that was the gun firing when, in fact, the gun was *missing*! Matt removed Kevin's helmet and mask while Richard searched for the missing body of the gun. The rest of us removed the hero back pack from Kevin; luckily, we had the stunt backpack standing by to continue shooting.

Beau Marks approached me to ask what had happened. I had no idea. I could see by the look on his face that he was angry. Tom Archuleta, the second assistant director approached and told Beau that Chovi had left the gun out, loaded with gunpowder over-night, and it had accidentally compacted, turning it into a bomb rather than a sparkling charge. Beau asked how long it would take to remove Kevin from the suit and put it on stuntman Henri Kingi before we lost the magic hour light entirely. I told him we could begin immediately.

Kevin, his head protected by latex, fiberglass and one inch of soft urethane foam, was completely unaware of what had happened. It wouldn't be until we were re-united in Los Angeles that I would show him the photo I snapped. I didn't get my cool photo of the Predator firing his gun, but I did get a cool photo of the gun exploding in a fireball that obscured Kevin's head! "You guys nearly *killed* me!" he said, as he looked at the photo. I reassured him by reminding him that the photo had been taken weeks earlier and he was still standing, unharmed. However, the photo is rather frightening.

As a confused Kevin Peter Hall was taken from the shore of the pond to recuperate for safety reasons, the rest of us put 6'2" stuntman Henri Kingi into the suit. You can see Henri in the film as the long-haired rebel who jumps into the pickup truck at the beginning of the commando raid just before the truck explodes. Both he and Tony Brubaker were very nice, fun-loving, but supportive professionals. We zipped up the suit and it looked like a child was wearing its father's clothes. The thigh armor hung down over his knees, and the proportions were appalling. No one in production seemed to care.

Cameras rolled and Henri ran, jumping from rock to rock along the shore of the pond away from camera in a long shot.

We began scratching needed shots and sequences off of our list that required Kevin to perform them, including the scene where the wounded Predator repairs a laceration in his leg. We had run a foam latex and soft urethane foam leg out of the suit mold and finished it with paint and netting. Steve cut the leg and we dressed to make it look like a wound. Trying not to fumble with his gloves, Kevin was able to use the tools in Brent Scrivener's medical pack with little difficulty which was in stark contrast to our attempt at the Predator ripping the spine out of a human victim.

When we arrived at our truck in Mexico, prop master Tommy Tomlinson had delivered a full, latex and polyfoam male dummy to our truck that had been a left-over from the Puerto Vallarta shoot. Stan had instructed me to put together the spine ripping effect, which had to be somewhat self-contained. There couldn't be an existing hole in the back for Kevin to reach into; rather they wanted him to pierce the skin with the Predator's fingernails, reach in, grab the spine and rip it out.

I had taken plastic vertebrae and using thick, black, latex hose, had strung the length of the spine from neck to base. I created a blood-filled chamber for the spine to rest in and then sealed the surface of the skin. With the camera rolling, Kevin did his best to attempt to pierce the skin with his nails. When that didn't work I jumped in with a razor and cut a slit. He was able to reach into the slit and grab the spine, but when he pulled it, the tension

The Mexico crew flanked by Sven Ole Thorson and Arnold Schwarzenegger.

on the spine was greater than the strength of the rubber hose and the spine stretched, creating unrealistic gaps between the vertebrae. The effect was unusable and Beau Marks asked me to meet him in his office after the shoot.

And so began a new almost-daily ritual.

Toward the end of the third week, Shane left as well. He told me that he had told his contractor that he would only be gone two weeks, but had to return because the construction of his condominium was going to be stalled if he didn't go. Just before he left he handed me one of the six-inch long, glass tubed laser units (exactly like the ones mounted in the Predator's helmet). He had taken chromed plastic motorcycle model kit parts and glued them to the glass tube, and told me that it was "the magic tool."

I vaguely understood what he was talking about. McTiernan wanted a shot where the Predator, using his "magic tool" would clean the blood and gore from a human spine and skull, transforming them into a trophy for the alien hunter. He had been working on an effect where he had two identical spine/skull assemblies that mounted onto a piece of wood via pegs. In Shane's mind they would shoot a shot of Kevin, moving the "magic tool" from camera left to right, while Joel and his VFX crew would do a visual reveal of the clean spine. In theory, it would have worked fine. However, there were too many variables that hadn't been discussed with anyone on production, the first one being the aesthetics of the "magic tool" itself.

With Shane gone, Beau called me to set with the "magic tool." Ignorant of anything beyond what Shane told me, I took the laser set to show Beau. When he saw it, his face turned red. "What the hell is *this*?" he asked me. I explained what Shane had told me, to which Beau said that I had better get my ass back down to the truck, and put together a proper "magic tool." I went back to the truck and told them what had transpired. Richard took the laser and completely transformed it into a cool, futuristic soldering iron. I brought it back to set to show Beau.

"That isn't the magic tool," was all he said to me. I returned back to the trailer and a new panicked scramble began. We borrowed a rubber gun from Tommy Tomlinson, cut the handle off of it and then transformed the laser tube from soldering iron to a cool ray gun. I brought it back to set, showed Beau and all he said was, "Meet me in my office at the end of the day."

As was the pattern of our after-work meetings, it began with Beau sitting across from me at his desk screaming at me for being incompetent. He told me that Stan had charged him $10,000 for a magic tool and nothing we showed him on set reflected the cost he had been charged. He belittled me, threatened me, then dismissed me.

It goes without saying that I would communicate what had transpired in our meetings to the rest of the Stan Winston crew. Saying that it wasn't our fault was accurate but it didn't fix anything. Stan, focused on our getting the suits finished, must have felt that all of the ancillary effects he had charged them for in his initial breakdown would have just distracted us and prevented us from finishing the suit. He might have been correct, but we were paying for it on location.

With every on-set delay caused by our department (and 99.9% of the time the delay was no longer than ten minutes) Beau would call me aside and start yelling at me on set. As his anger grew, he started poking me in my chest, with his index finger punctuating his caustic remarks. This behavior had an adverse affect on the creature crew. One evening, Brian Simpson and Steve Wang offered to jump Beau in the dark jungle and beat the shit out of him. They meant it, and were both 100% capable of doing it. However, I had my orders from Stan. I was instructed to "take it."

The end of the third week we wrapped Kevin Peter Hall. We all shared his happiness, especially after that grueling third week. Kevin was barely able to tolerate being on the fallen log bridge for the scene where the Predator's invisibility device was damaged. He was walked into place and a safety cable had been hooked to his ankle. Kevin was able to do the action, but we hadn't any footage of him walking out on the log.

In fact, the more we thought about it, there were a lot of shots that seemed to be missing. When we shot the final fight scene when Arnold was still on set, most of the shots featured him. Now, with Arnold gone, most of the shots were filmed over stunt double Joel Kramer's shoulder. (Another Joel!) Even though Kevin's gloves had been rigged to spark when he swiped at a rock and Richard Landon finally disconnected one of the upper mandibles to get McTiernan's dream shot of the Predator reacting to being kicked in the face, it just didn't seem like we had enough fight footage.

It didn't matter to Kevin Peter Hall. He felt that he had given above and beyond to the *Predator* production and no one would have ever said otherwise. Kevin had worked his behind off in the suit, endured such discomfort and had been so enthusiastic and professional; he was the Predator – no doubt. After a joyous wrap, we all met for dinner, had a few beers and even made a short film that starred Kevin (although it was mainly just his hands). The next day Kevin got on an airplane and left for Los Angeles.

The rest of us stayed.

Kevin didn't know that, upon his dismissal, he was being replaced by a 6'10" amateur basketball player/actor named Darrell. I forget his last name and the poor guy wasn't credited at all. By the beginning of our fourth week, the remainder of the Stan Winston crew were veterans of the Palenque jungles. Darrell arrived having little idea of what was in store for him. Without much orientation or ceremony, we just started putting Darrell into the suit and, the poor guy had to clean up all of the shots that Kevin was unable to do. Darrell walked out onto the fallen log (actually, Tony Brubaker started the walk in the red suit), Darrell was put in the tree that exploded, Darrell's arm was filmed extending and retracting the blades, etc.

I was getting antsy. It was now twice as long as we were told we'd be on location. I kept having to call Tracy long distance to let her know we had been extended yet another week. Between the pressure being exerted upon me by Beau Marx and the additional weeks, I began to lose it. The window shades in my hotel room looked like astronomy maps because I had sharpened toy arrows and had strung a toy bow with a taut bungie cord, and fired at my windows out of frustration.

One of the last shots we did on location was the sequence where the Predator, his invisibility device damaged, stood on the fallen log and began wildly firing his gun into the surrounding jungle. Chovi and his team spent most of the afternoon rigging trees with explosives. We dressed Henri Kingi back into the suit, and the stunt team secured him to the log with a harness and safety cables. By this time it was dark and the entire company moved to the opposite side of the pond at Mishol Ha.

Cameras rolled, John called action and Beau cued Chovi. Boom! Boom! BOOM! Explosion after explosion ripped through the trees sending sparks cascading down through the jungle. It was an impressive sight.

As days progressed, more and more crew members were wrapped from set. During week three, Brian Simpson had donned the red suit for a couple of acrobatic shots. Darrell had been dismissed and so Brian filled in for the remaining few Predator shots. By all counts five different people had played the Predator in one guise or another, and that doesn't include the one shot in the film that remains of Jean-Claude Van Damme.

When we were finally wrapped, five weeks had passed. The wrap party, if you can call it that, was held in a small local restaurant that looked like a bombed out cinder block building. Inside, there was a folding table set up with fresh tortillas; beneath it was a cooler full of beer.

Few of the American crew showed up that night; so we shared a few beers with the Mexican crew, then returned to our hotel. I warned Richard Landon (who had been habitually late every day) not to be late the next morning, otherwise we'd leave him in Palenque. He assured me he'd be on time.

The next morning, with the rest of us packed and ready to go, I pounded on Richard's door, as I had most days, and helped him drag his luggage to the waiting van.

As we drove to the airport, all of us began feeling anxious. We all were in possession of our passports, as well as work permits that had expired three weeks earlier.

The flight from Via Hermosa to Mexico City was no problem because we weren't flying internationally. Thank God "Airport Harry" met us at the gate in Mexico City. He led us to immigration control and asked each of us for the equivalent of fifty dollars. As we reached the queue, Harry moved past the line to an armed guard. After some hushed words, the guard lowered the rope and Harry shook each of our hands as we rushed to meet our plane out of Mexico.

BACK IN LOS ANGELES:

Oh, the tale does not stop here. We hadn't finished *Predator* by the time we left location.

Beau called me into his office on the last day on location to tell me that we had to have everything repaired and ready a week after our return to Los Angeles. If there was anything that I didn't want to hear at that point, it was that I was going to have to continue working with Beau Marks back in Los Angeles.

It goes without saying that Tracy was happy to see me. I had a few days off to recuperate before I returned to Stan Winston's studio. To my knowledge, they were all deep into *Pumpkinhead*.

Richard, Brian, and I were all that were left of the crew to unload the truck from Mexico. The shop had been meticulously cleaned (by Rosengrant, I was sure) and I had been warned not to trash it again. I moved most of the boxes of supplies and the few personal things the crew packed to the annex shop.

Alec and Tom had been busy while we were gone. They had built sets and been shooting a short film, *The Demon with Three Tails*, while Stan was preparing to direct *Pumpkinhead*. Since the annex was cluttered anyway, adding a few more boxes wasn't going to help or hurt anything. However, one thing was made very clear to me: Neither Matt nor Steve were welcome back at the shop any time in the near future. I couldn't understand it.

Eventually, Stan had me call Matt Rose in for a few days to repair the Predator stunt head that had rolled through the bonfire and into the pond after a log was dropped onto it. We had put a makeshift dummy together on location for the log-dropping effect, and the stunt head had been damaged.

Matt came in for three days, worked in the sculpture annex repairing the head, and was released.

Howard Berger, my old friend, was working on *Pumpkinhead* and Stan told me that I could use him to help with the Los Angeles re-shoots.

We were sent to a studio in Culver City to pick up additional shots of Brian, wearing the red suit, or pieces of the Predator suit, as well as re-shooting the effect where actor Bill Duke is killed. A gelatin head of the actor had been shipped to us on location, but Chovi's squib explosives were not strong enough to blast a hole in the back of the head.

Effects technician Marty Beslin was hired for the pickup shots and lined a fresh head with primer cord explosives. When the head detonated, there was nothing left but a smoking stump, and atomized gelatin speckled the entire studio, including the ceiling, which was at least sixty feet high! It was *too* much. McTiernan (and Beau) were both pissed but I thought that it must have looked amazing. I had the nerve to call Joel Silver and tell him that he should at least look at the footage before we scrapped it.

Touching up the Predator back in Los Angeles during re-shoots. Howard Berger looks on.

The next day Joel arrived, and we reviewed the footage on a small, editor's Moviola screen. The head had been shot in slow motion and looked *amazing* as it blew apart, throwing fake blood and brains into the air. Joel loved it, watched it at least three times, and then said that it was perfect, but it didn't cut into the continuity and we'd have to shoot it again.

A few days into the filming, Kevin Peter Hall and Arnold returned for what they thought was just promotional photographs. A jungle set was put together and lit, then Arnold and Kevin both got into makeup and wardrobe. After the photos were taken, Joel and John McTiernan asked if they wouldn't mind just doing a couple more shots to help fill in the missing fight shots. Kevin grudgingly agreed, and was filmed punching through sapling trees and punching Arnold, who spit fake blood on cue.

We finally got around to shooting the "magic tool" on stage. What was it by then? It was a Paache "H" airbrush that had the two chromed plastic motorcycle model kit mufflers glued to either side of it, with the round bottom of a wax cup glued just beneath the nozzle. On action, a pile of iridescent powder was blown at the camera, obscuring a skull that had been dressed with fake blood and toilet paper.

Beau Marks was not amused. He made some comment to me about "never working in this town again," to which I responded that I didn't care and that I was an employee of Stan Winston's and Stan would hire me again. This seemed to amuse Beau.

"Let me guess what you make a week....$800?" He had hit the nail completely on the head and he wasn't paying me directly; I was on Stan Winston's payroll. "Do you have any idea how much he charges *me* for your services?" Beau asked me. I told him that it was none of my business; he ignored me and continued, "Stan charges me $2500 a *week* for you to be here on this set and he's paying you less than a third of that! Where do you think the rest of that money is going?" Again, I told him it was none of my business. Beau leaned in to emphasize his point, "The rest of the money is going into Stan's pocket, so think about that next time you align your loyalties." My face flushed red with an emotion that was somewhere between anger and shame.

A couple of days later, I was sitting in Stan Winston's office. He had taken a break from his *Pumpkinhead* pre-production duties to speak with me about what had happened on *Predator* in his absence. I saw no reason to withhold anything from him, so I began to explain what had transpired between me and the crew and Beau Marks. I ended my conversation by recounting what Beau had told me about my pay. It was then Stan's opportunity to turn red, but whether there was any shame involved I'll never know. He was; however, extremely angry.

He picked up the phone and called Beau Marks and then the yelling began, but this time it was Stan yelling at Beau. " You have no right to discuss how I run my business with one of my employees!" he began and at that moment he leaned down and took something out of a drawer and slid it across the desk. It was healthcare paperwork. Stan was still yelling at Beau but for some reason it wasn't making me feel better.

I understood what the healthcare paperwork meant. It meant that I had just earned my "Lifer" status. I had found a home, permanent employment, and that was very rare for the industry at that time. From the moment I had walked into that studio, I had wanted to be a Stan Winston Lifer. I had arrived. But as the sage says, "Be careful what you wish for."

I was about to discover what it meant to be a Lifer at Stan Winston's.

ACKNOWLEDGEMENTS

This book could not have been written without the encouragement and support of my wife Tracy, and my daughter Molly, both of whom will always tell me the truth, especially when I need to hear it. I have to thank Michael Spatola for coaching me through much of the publishing and advance marketing process; his advice was gold. It was through the generosity of Robert Kurtzman that I met my publisher, Mike Aloisi, and their belief in my story and as a writer has brought this book to legitimacy. I have to thank my family, friends, fans and students, who have carried me upon their collective wings. You all are the voice in my head that says "get back up" when I want to throw in the towel. Finally, thank you Mom – I wouldn't be anywhere without you.

CPSIA information can be obtained at www.ICGtesting.com
Printed in the USA
BVOW01s0946060816

457814BV00002B/37/P